HARRY FIG'S CARTOON BOSTON

20TH ANNIVERSARY COLLECTION

BY PETER WALLACE

LET'ER RIP!

published by The Boston Globe

The Boston Globe

This book is available in quantity at special discounts for your group or organization.
For further information, contact:

The Boston Globe Store
PO Box 55819
Boston, MA 02205-5819
Phone: (888) 665-2667
Fax: (617) 929-7636
www.BostonGlobeStore.com

Printed in U.S.A.
ISBN: 978-0-9790137-6-8

EDITOR Janice Page
COPY EDITOR Ron Driscoll

With special thanks to: Nancy Callahan, MacDonald & Evans.

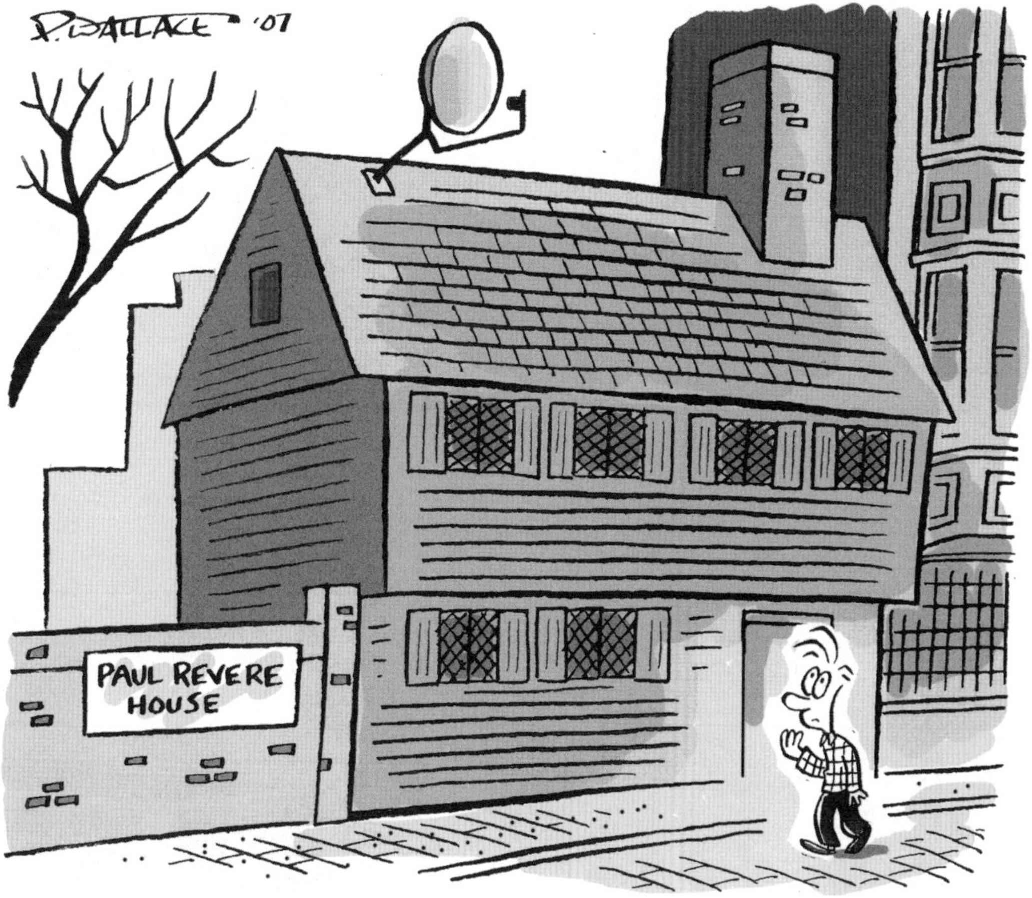
P. WALLACE '07
PAUL REVERE
HOUSE

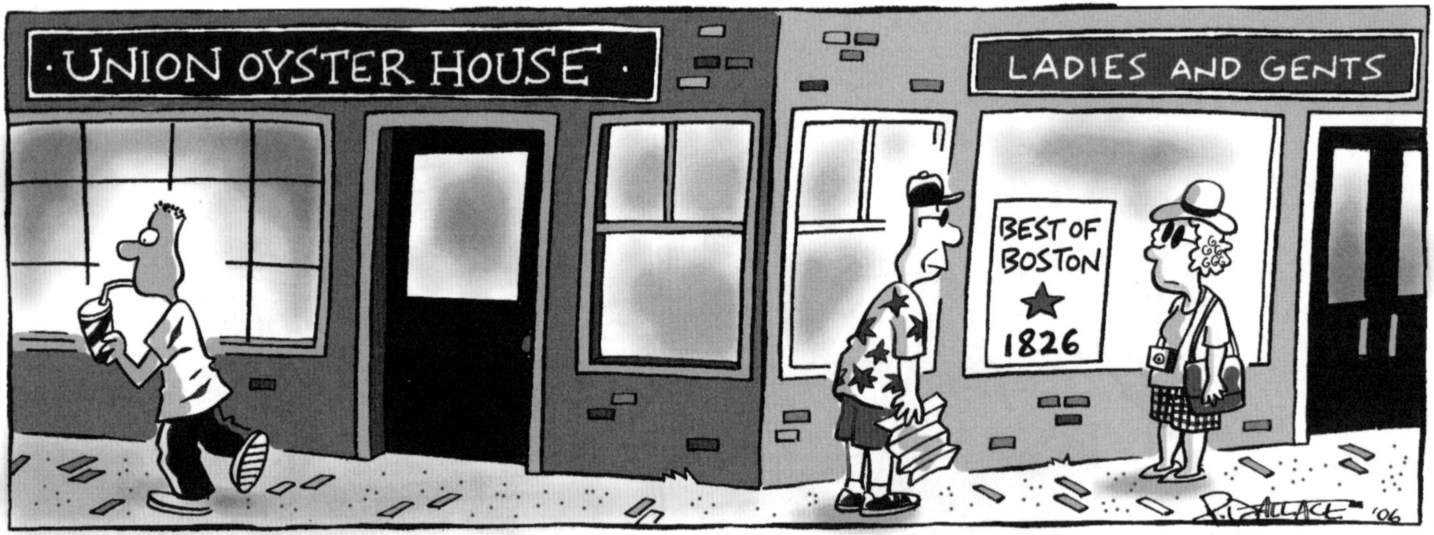

·UNION OYSTER HOUSE·
LADIES AND GENTS
BEST OF BOSTON ★ 1826
P. WALLACE '06

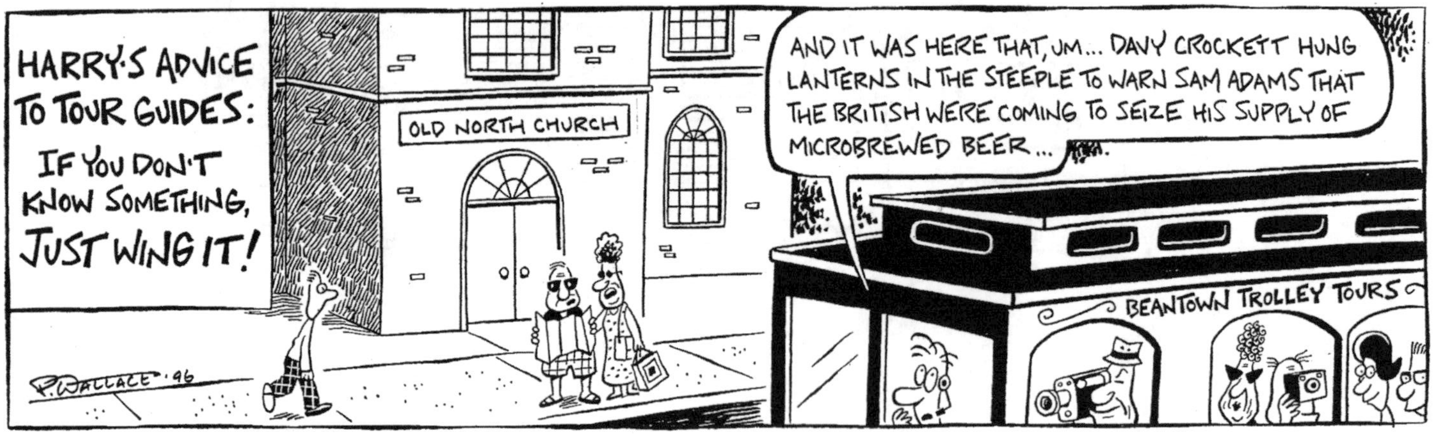

HARRY'S ADVICE TO TOUR GUIDES:
IF YOU DON'T KNOW SOMETHING, JUST WING IT!
OLD NORTH CHURCH
AND IT WAS HERE THAT, UM... DAVY CROCKETT HUNG LANTERNS IN THE STEEPLE TO WARN SAM ADAMS THAT THE BRITISH WERE COMING TO SEIZE HIS SUPPLY OF MICROBREWED BEER...
BEANTOWN TROLLEY TOURS
P. WALLACE '96

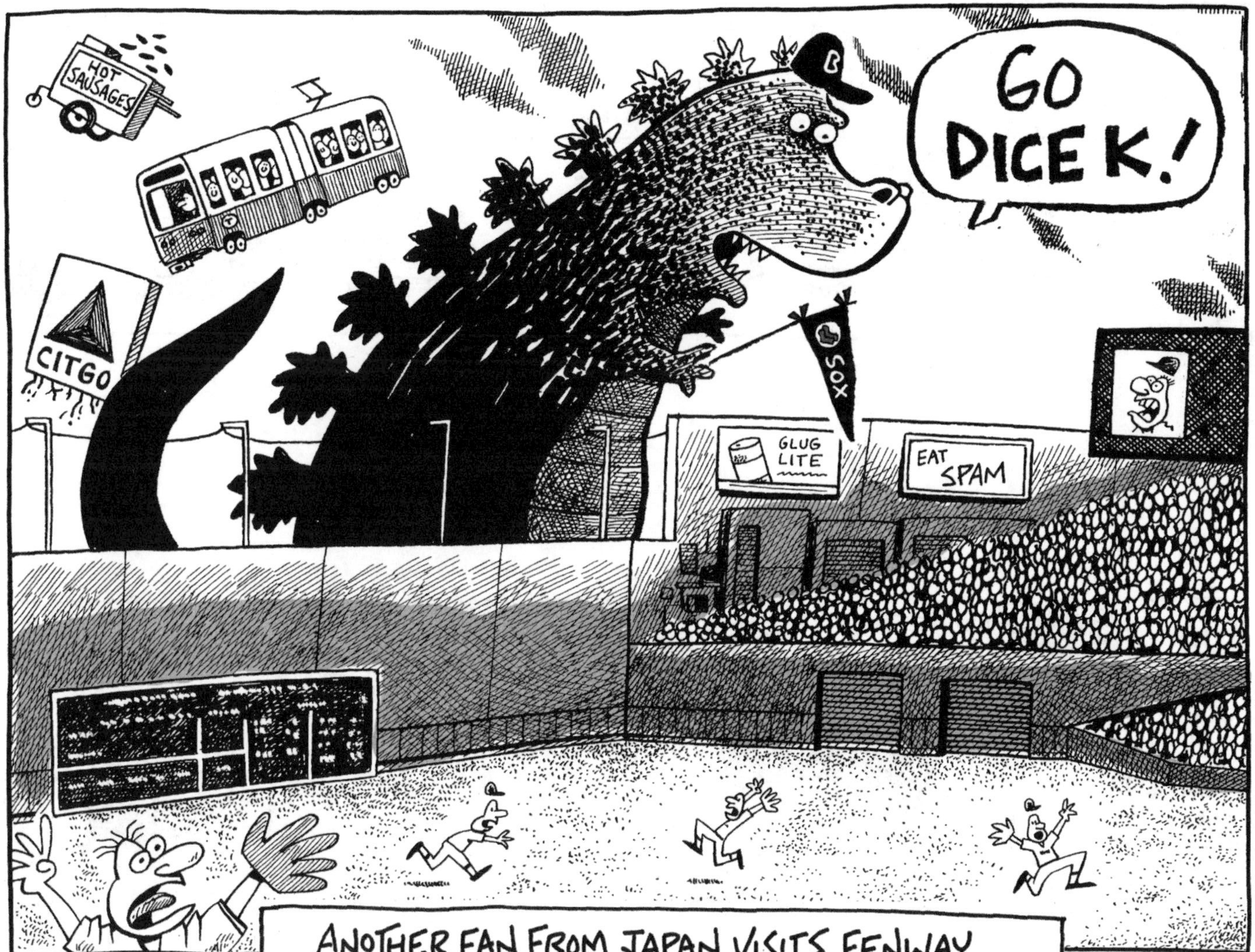
GO DICE K!
HOT SAUSAGES
CITGO
SOX
GLUG LITE
EAT SPAM
ANOTHER FAN FROM JAPAN VISITS FENWAY

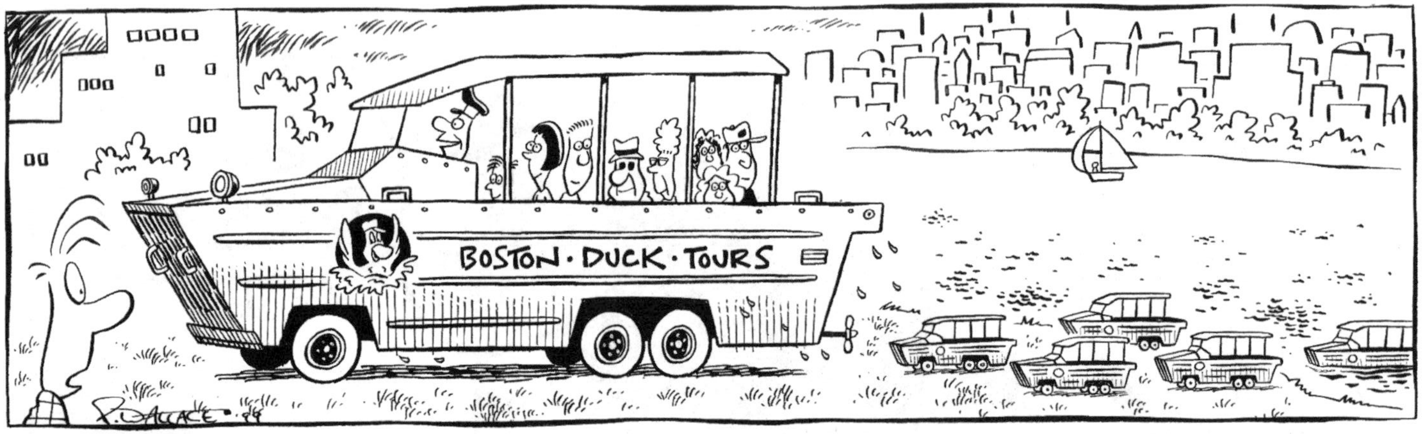
BOSTON · DUCK · TOURS
P. WALLACE

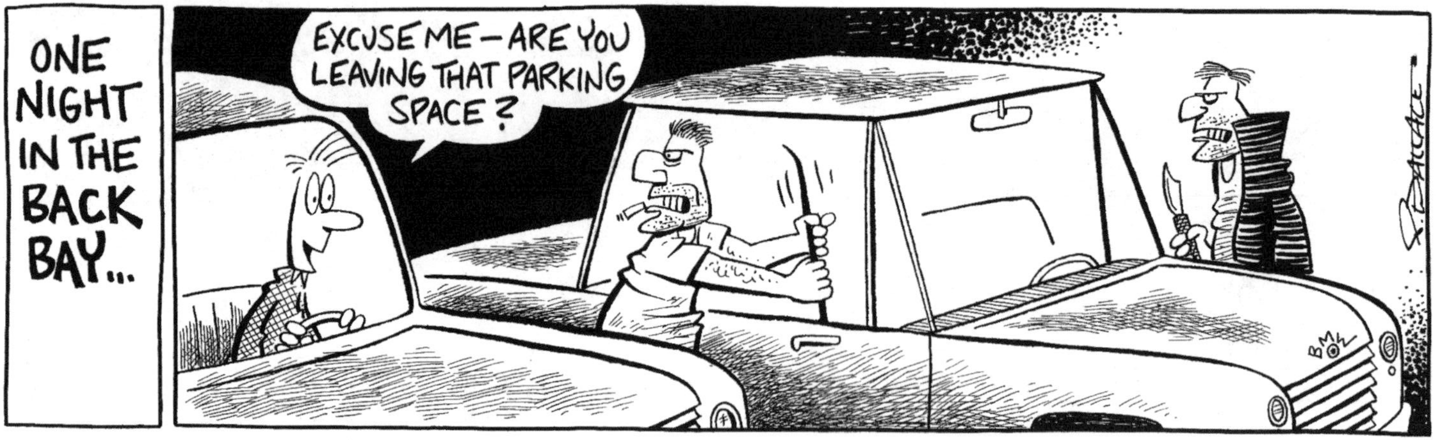
ONE NIGHT IN THE BACK BAY...
EXCUSE ME — ARE YOU LEAVING THAT PARKING SPACE?
P. WALLACE

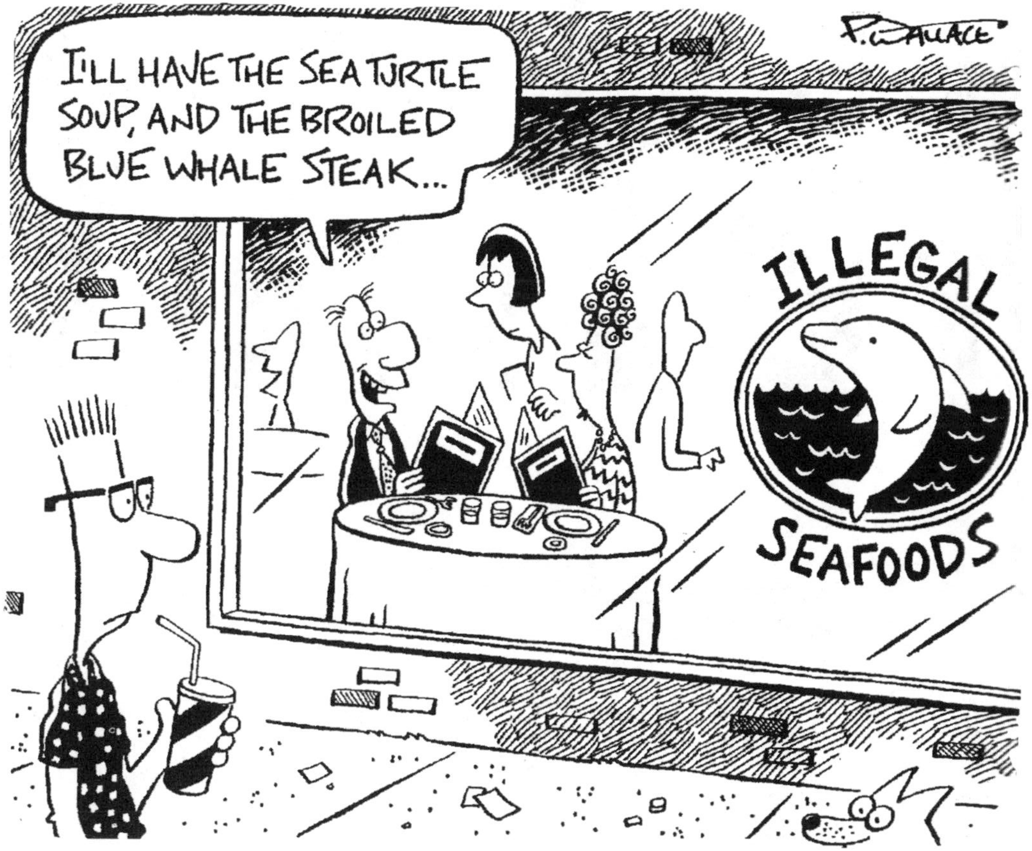
I'LL HAVE THE SEA TURTLE SOUP, AND THE BROILED BLUE WHALE STEAK...
ILLEGAL SEAFOODS
P. WALLACE

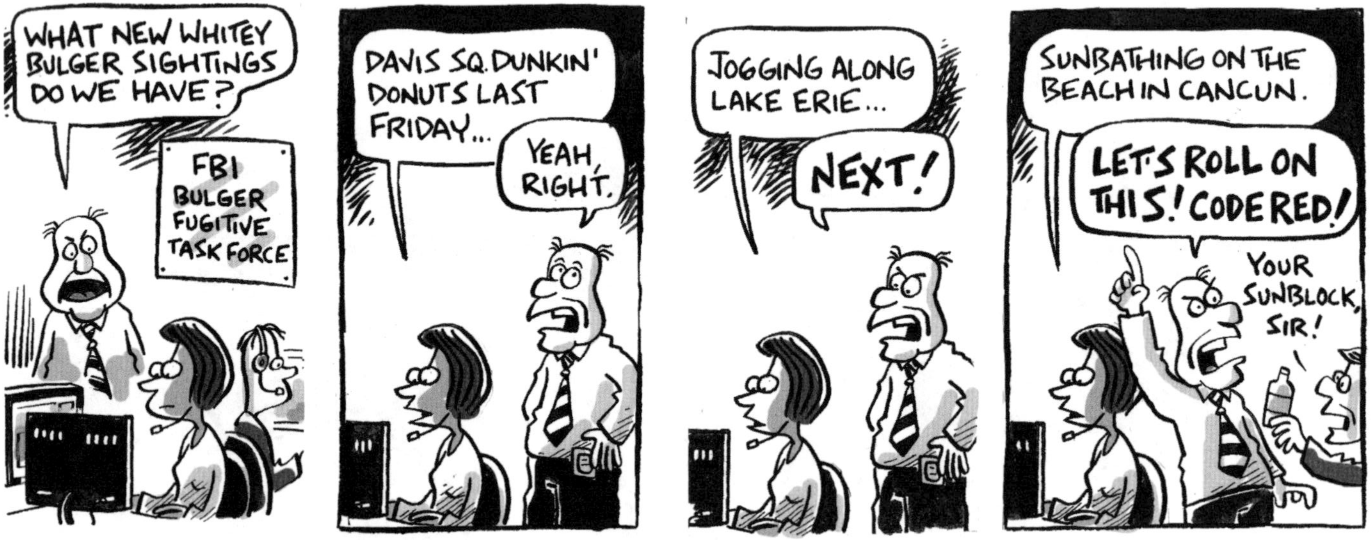
WHAT NEW WHITEY BULGER SIGHTINGS DO WE HAVE?
FBI BULGER FUGITIVE TASK FORCE
DAVIS SQ. DUNKIN' DONUTS LAST FRIDAY...
YEAH, RIGHT.
JOGGING ALONG LAKE ERIE...
NEXT!
SUNBATHING ON THE BEACH IN CANCUN.
LET'S ROLL ON THIS! CODE RED!
YOUR SUNBLOCK, SIR!

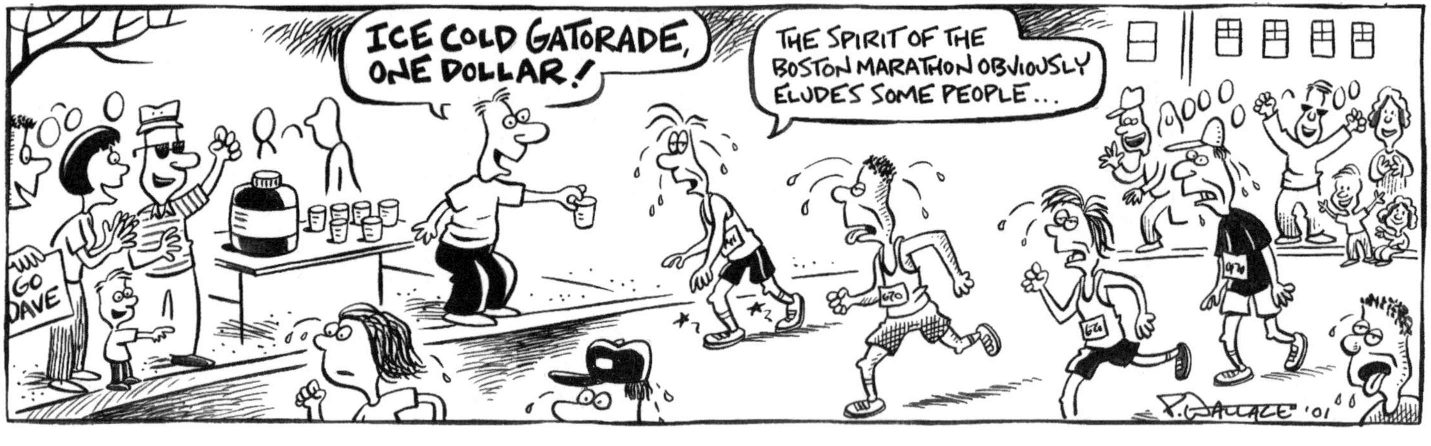
ICE COLD GATORADE, ONE DOLLAR!
THE SPIRIT OF THE BOSTON MARATHON OBVIOUSLY ELUDES SOME PEOPLE...
GO DAVE
P. WALLACE '01

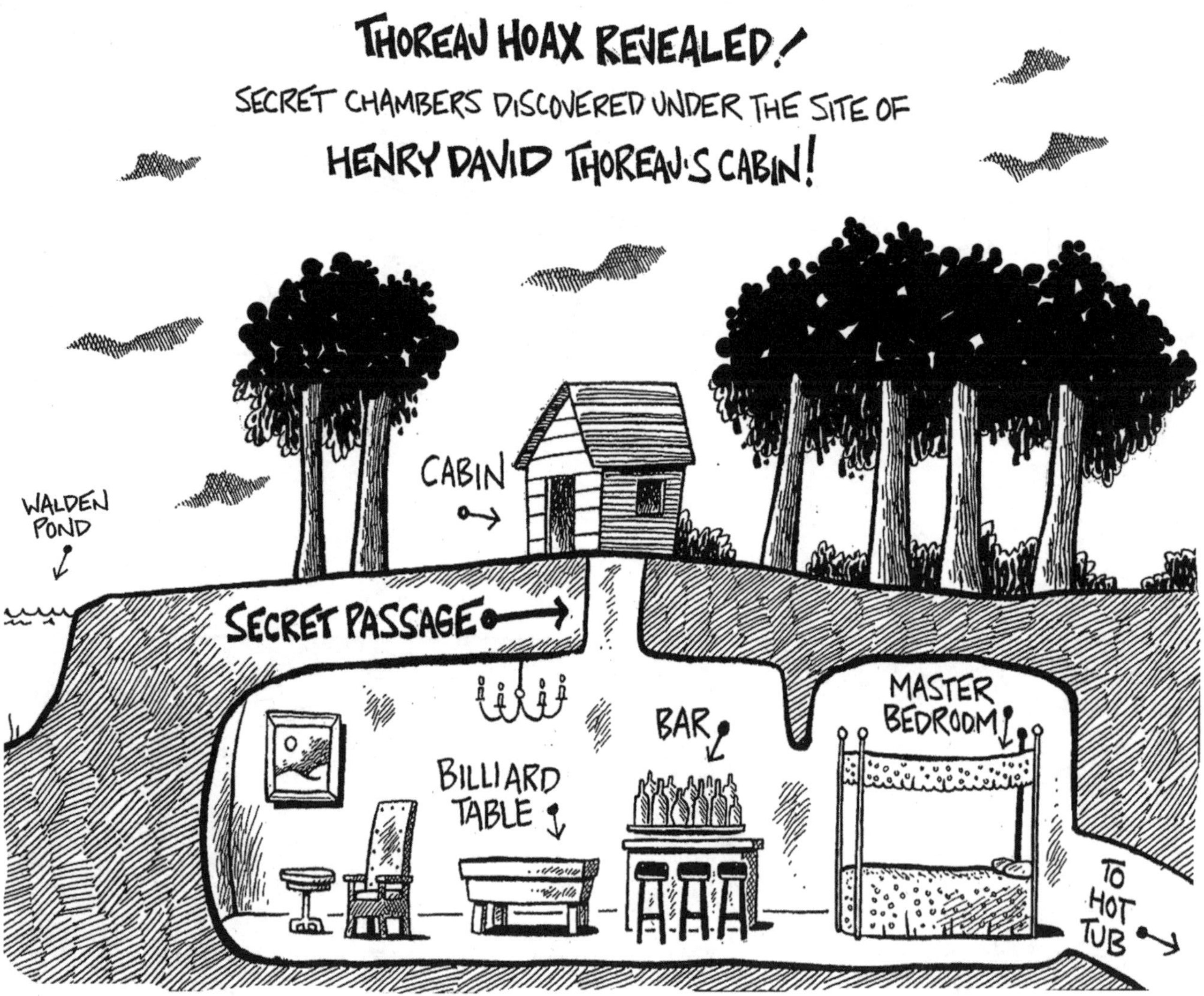
THOREAU HOAX REVEALED!
SECRET CHAMBERS DISCOVERED UNDER THE SITE OF
HENRY DAVID THOREAU'S CABIN!
WALDEN POND
CABIN
SECRET PASSAGE
BAR
MASTER BEDROOM
BILLIARD TABLE
TO HOT TUB

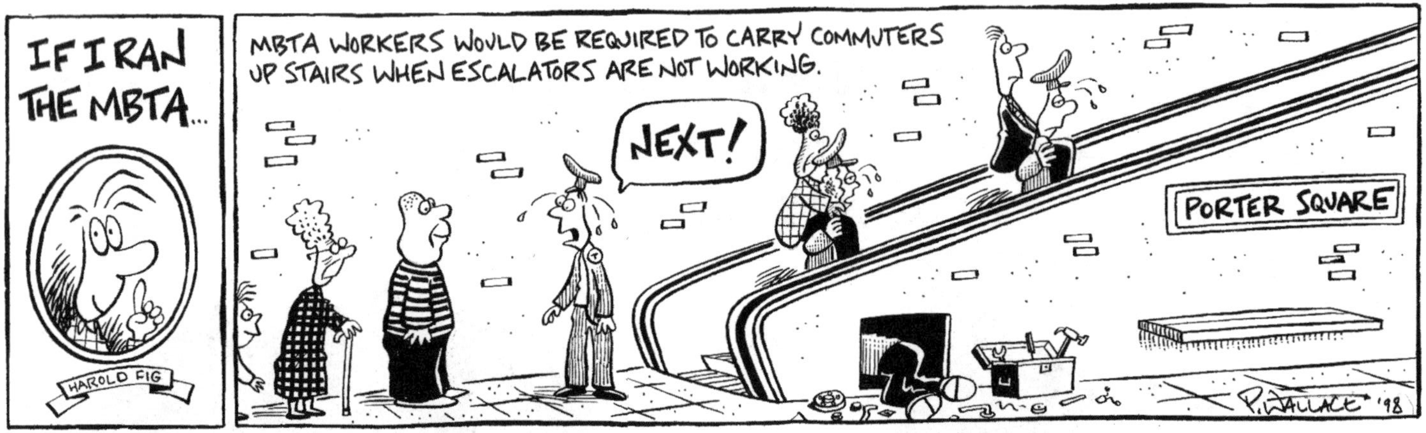
IF I RAN THE MBTA...
HAROLD FIG
MBTA WORKERS WOULD BE REQUIRED TO CARRY COMMUTERS UP STAIRS WHEN ESCALATORS ARE NOT WORKING.
NEXT!
PORTER SQUARE
P. WALLACE '98

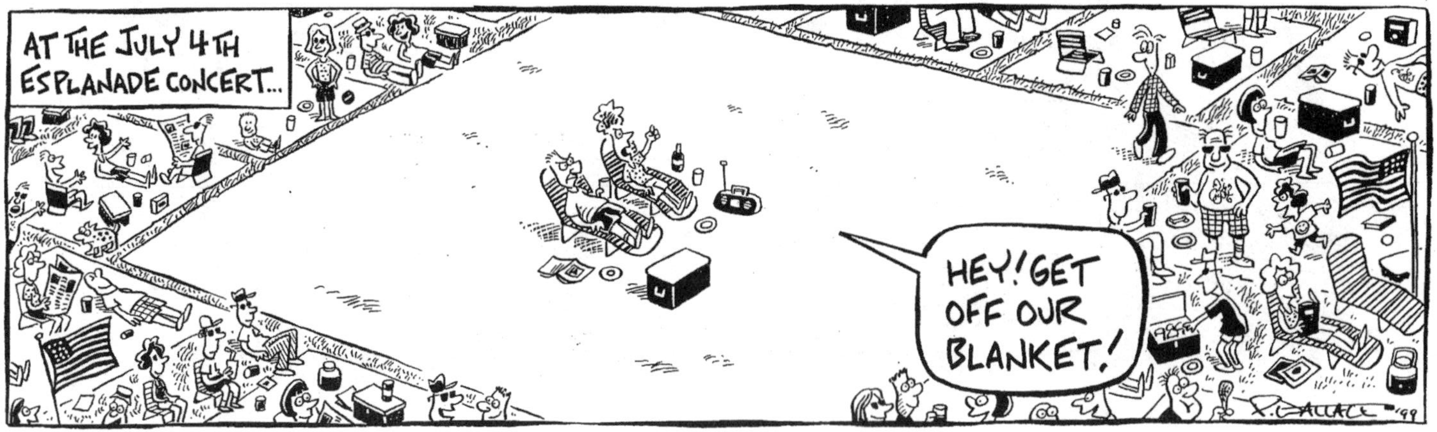
AT THE JULY 4TH ESPLANADE CONCERT...
HEY! GET OFF OUR BLANKET!
P. WALLACE '99

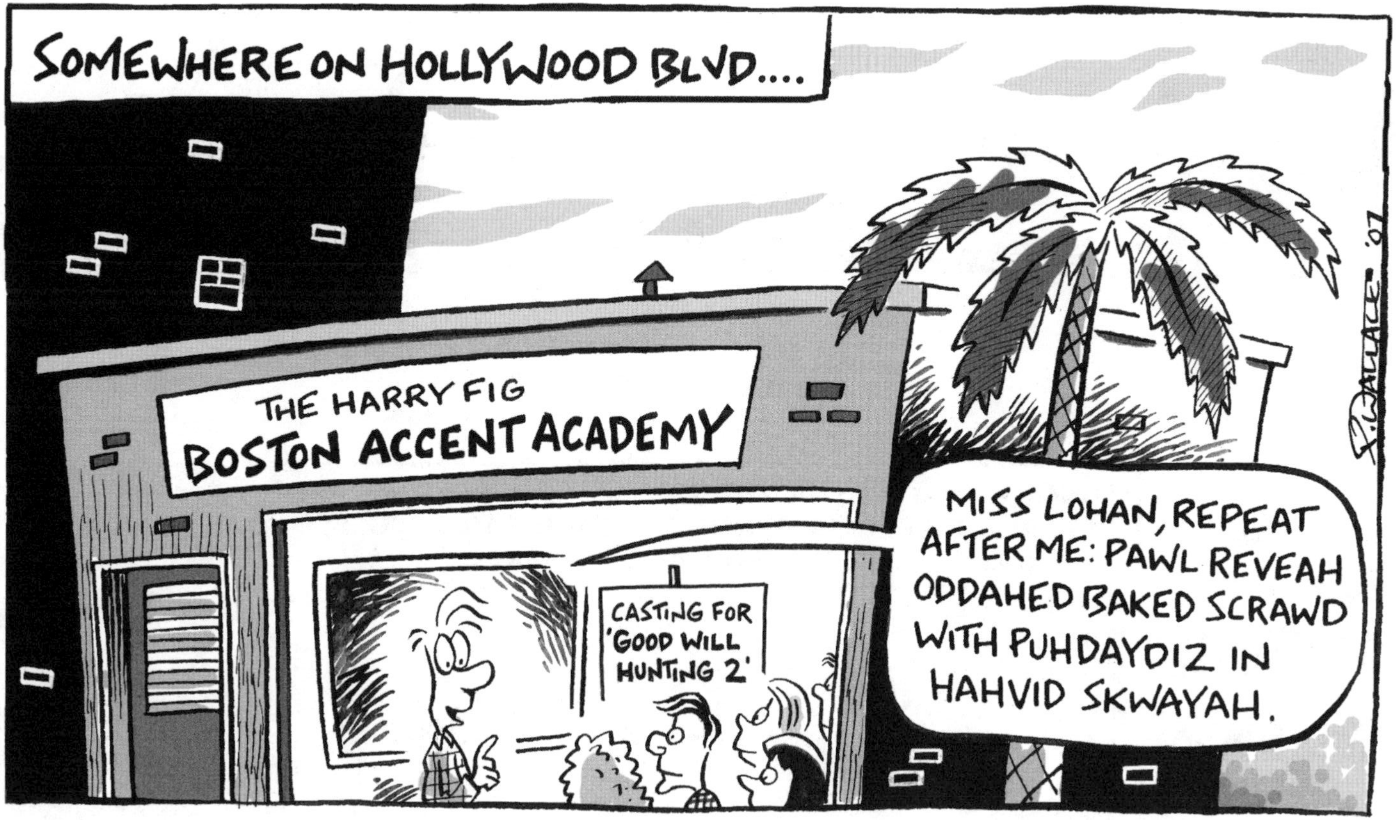
SOMEWHERE ON HOLLYWOOD BLVD....
THE HARRY FIG BOSTON ACCENT ACADEMY
CASTING FOR 'GOOD WILL HUNTING 2'
MISS LOHAN, REPEAT AFTER ME: PAWL REVEAH ODDAHED BAKED SCRAWD WITH PUHDAYDIZ IN HAHVID SKWAYAH.

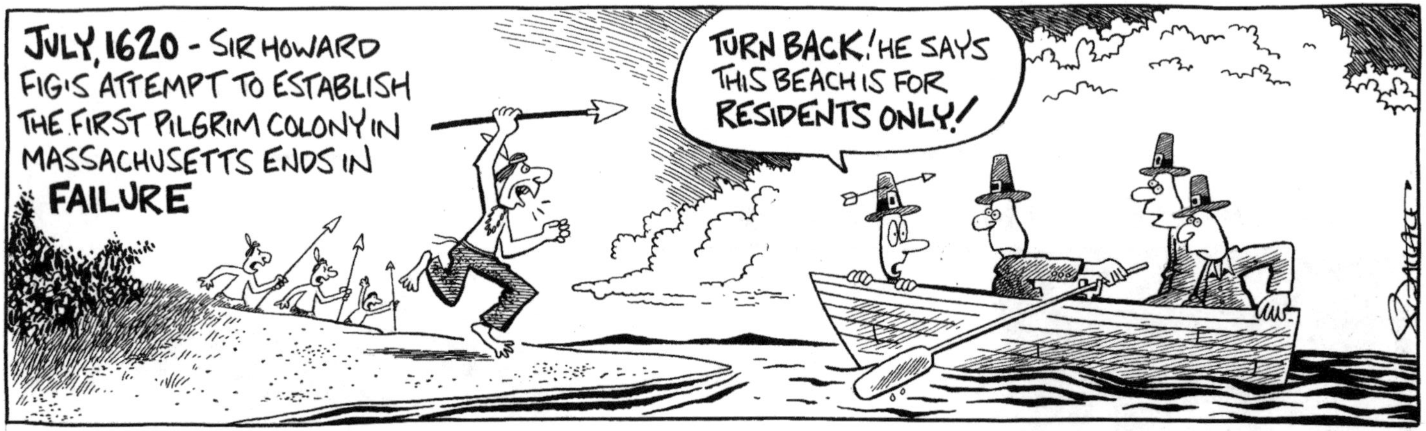
JULY, 1620 - SIR HOWARD FIG'S ATTEMPT TO ESTABLISH THE FIRST PILGRIM COLONY IN MASSACHUSETTS ENDS IN FAILURE
TURN BACK! HE SAYS THIS BEACH IS FOR RESIDENTS ONLY!

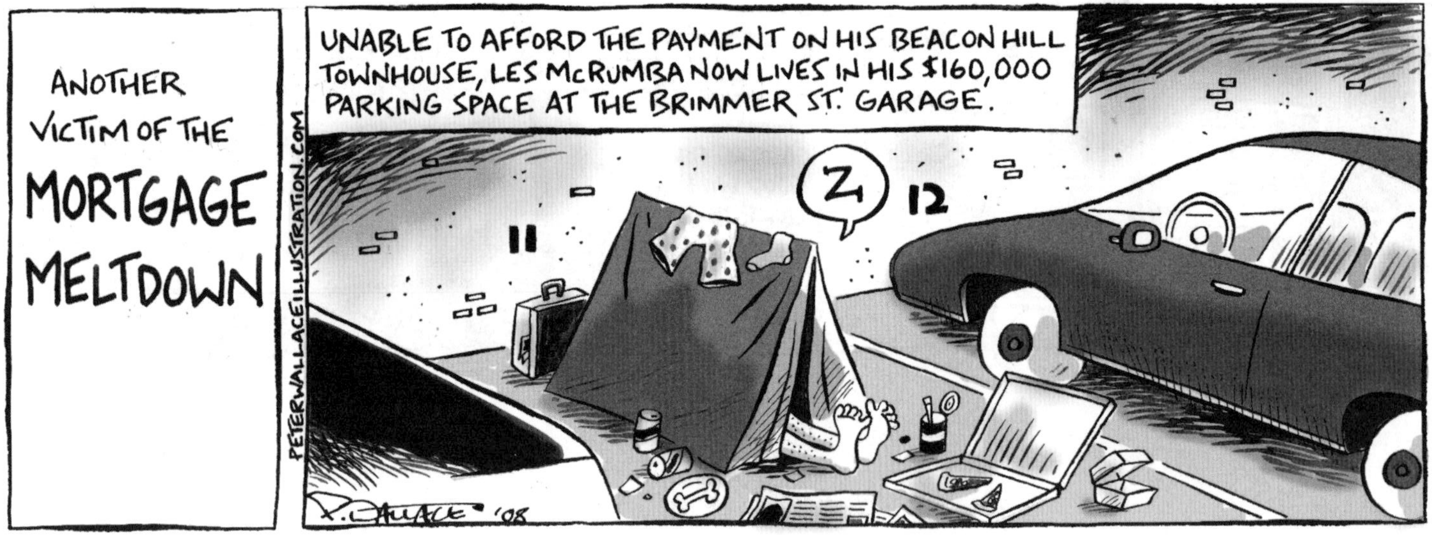
ANOTHER VICTIM OF THE MORTGAGE MELTDOWN
UNABLE TO AFFORD THE PAYMENT ON HIS BEACON HILL TOWNHOUSE, LES McRUMBA NOW LIVES IN HIS $160,000 PARKING SPACE AT THE BRIMMER ST. GARAGE.
Z
11
12
PETERWALLACEILLUSTRATION.COM

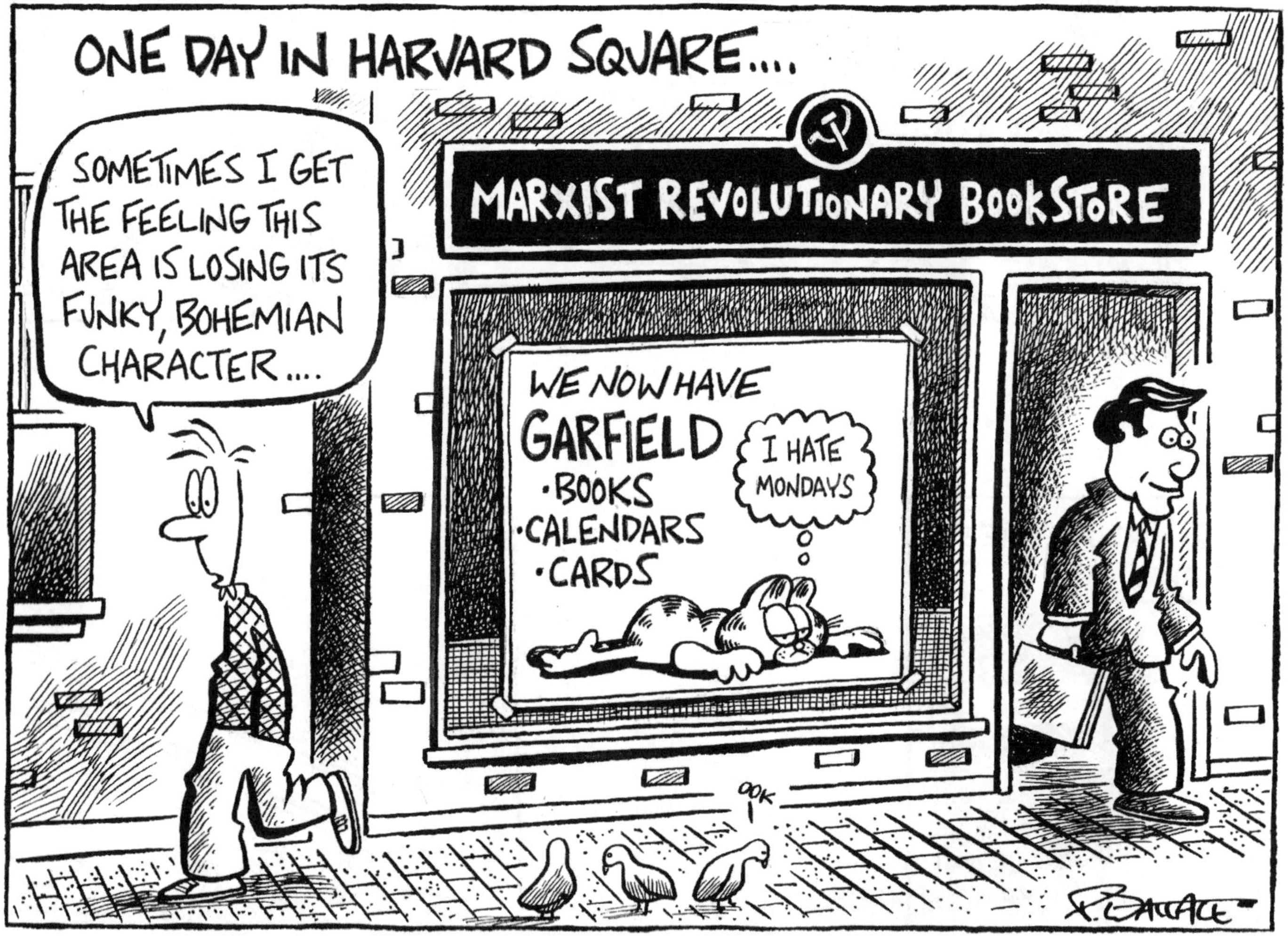
ONE DAY IN HARVARD SQUARE....
SOMETIMES I GET THE FEELING THIS AREA IS LOSING ITS FUNKY, BOHEMIAN CHARACTER....
MARXIST REVOLUTIONARY BOOKSTORE
WE NOW HAVE GARFIELD
·BOOKS
·CALENDARS
·CARDS
I HATE MONDAYS
OOK

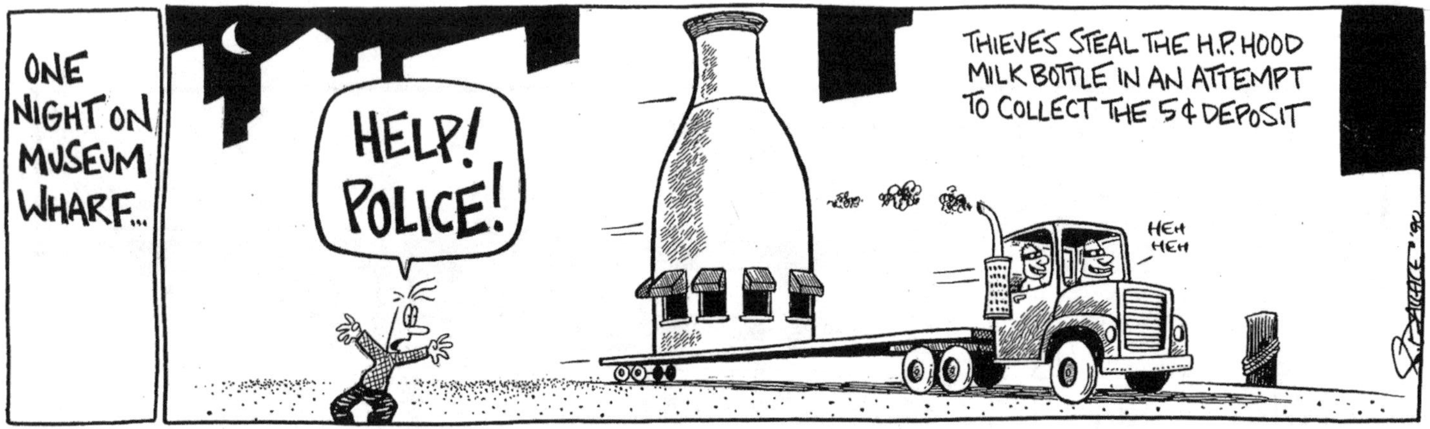
ONE NIGHT ON MUSEUM WHARF...
HELP! POLICE!
THIEVES STEAL THE H.P. HOOD MILK BOTTLE IN AN ATTEMPT TO COLLECT THE 5¢ DEPOSIT
HEH HEH

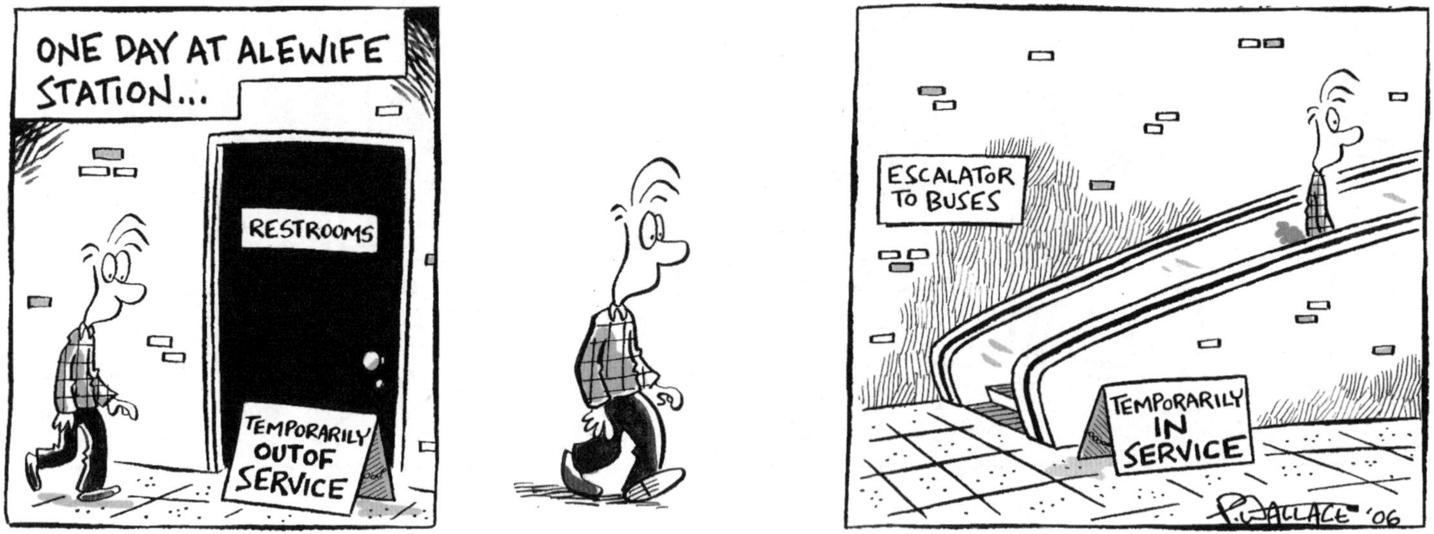
ONE DAY AT ALEWIFE STATION...
RESTROOMS
TEMPORARILY OUT OF SERVICE
ESCALATOR TO BUSES
TEMPORARILY IN SERVICE
P. WALLACE '06

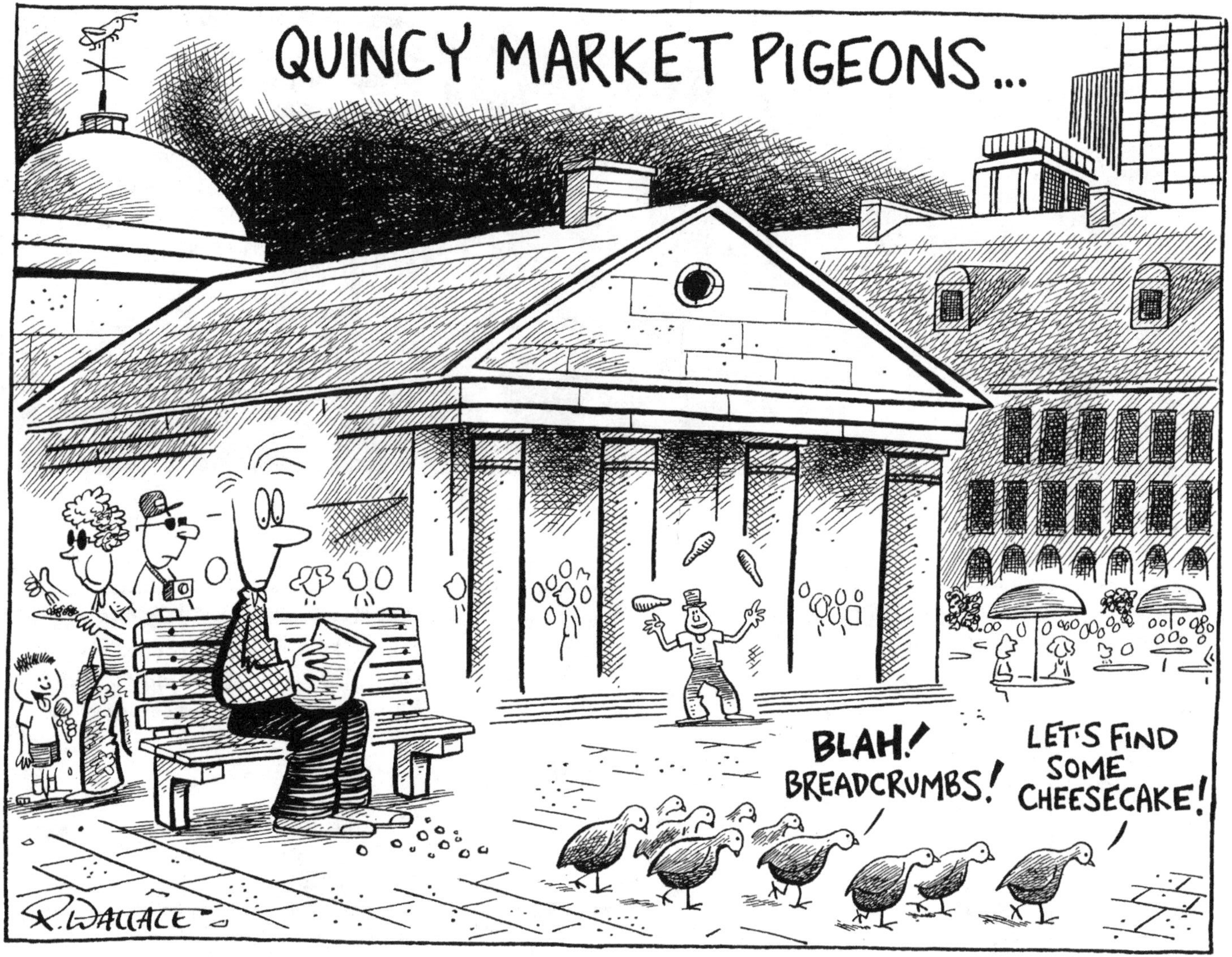
QUINCY MARKET PIGEONS...
BLAH! BREADCRUMBS!
LET'S FIND SOME CHEESECAKE!
R. WALLACE

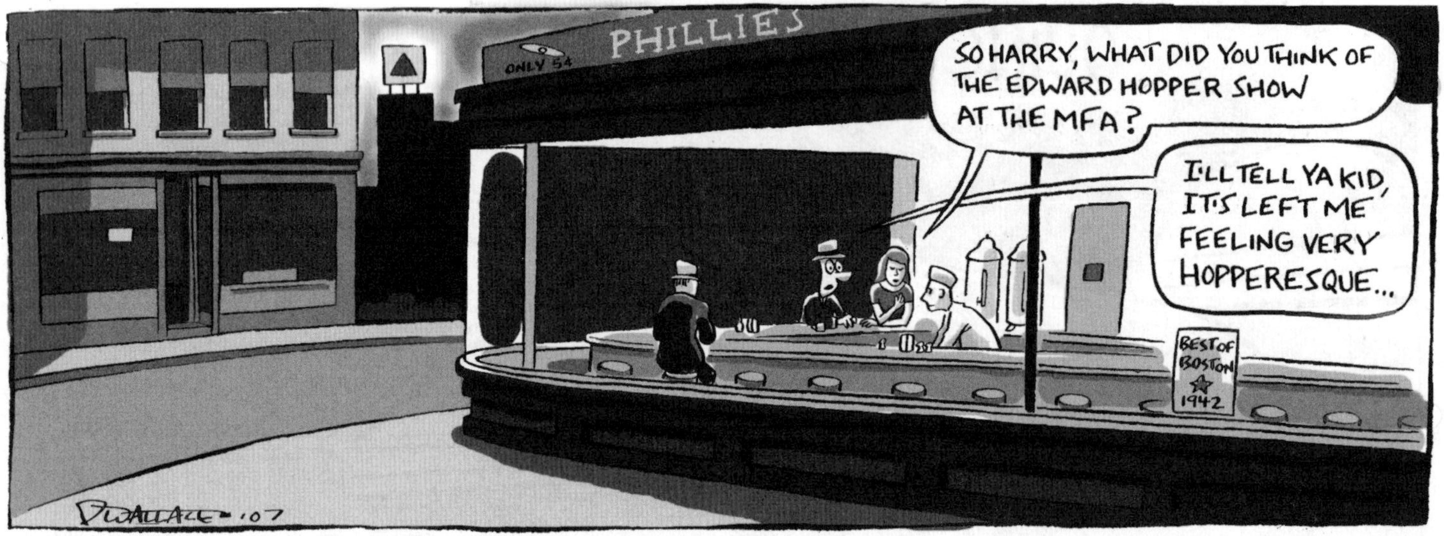
PHILLIES
ONLY 5¢
SO HARRY, WHAT DID YOU THINK OF THE EDWARD HOPPER SHOW AT THE MFA?
I'LL TELL YA KID, IT'S LEFT ME FEELING VERY HOPPERESQUE...
BEST OF BOSTON 1942
D. WALLACE '07

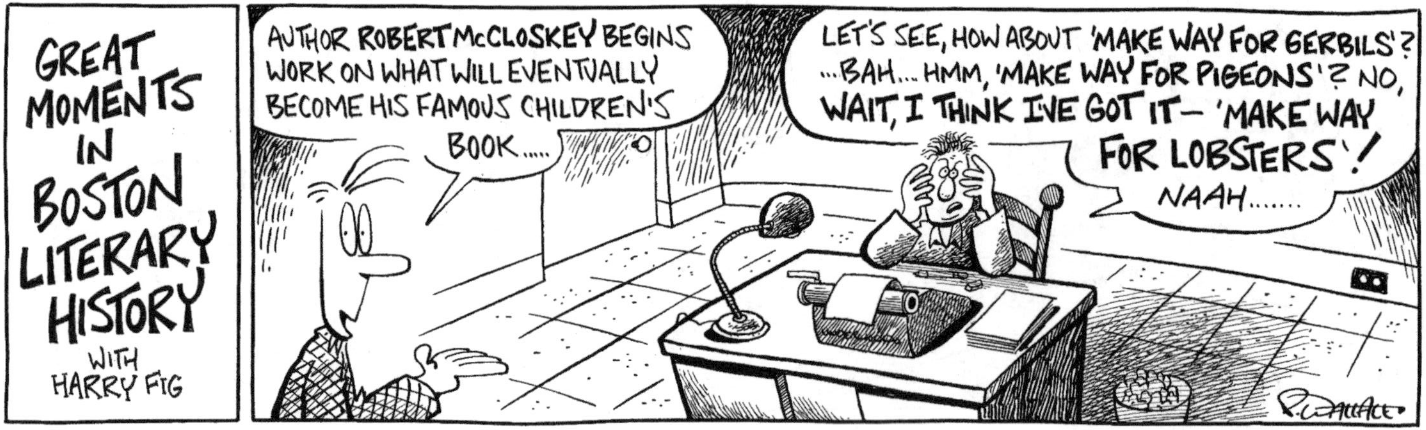
GREAT MOMENTS IN BOSTON LITERARY HISTORY
WITH HARRY FIG
AUTHOR ROBERT McCLOSKEY BEGINS WORK ON WHAT WILL EVENTUALLY BECOME HIS FAMOUS CHILDREN'S BOOK.....
LET'S SEE, HOW ABOUT 'MAKE WAY FOR GERBILS'? ...BAH... HMM, 'MAKE WAY FOR PIGEONS'? NO, WAIT, I THINK I'VE GOT IT— 'MAKE WAY FOR LOBSTERS'!
NAAH.......
D. WALLACE

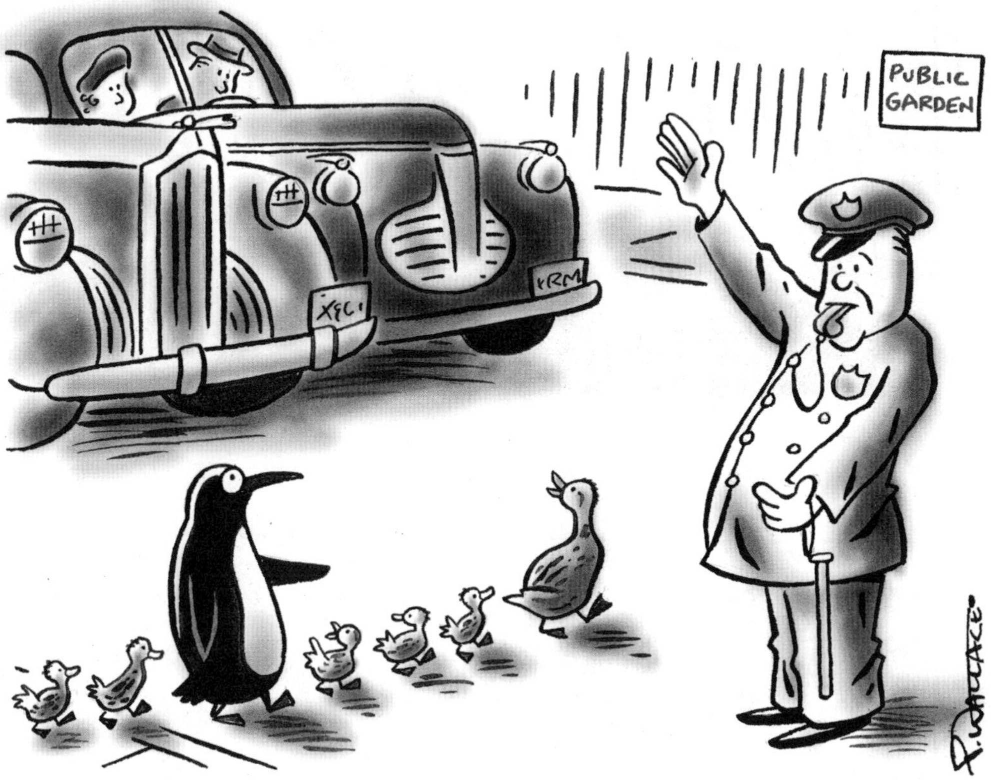
PUBLIC GARDEN

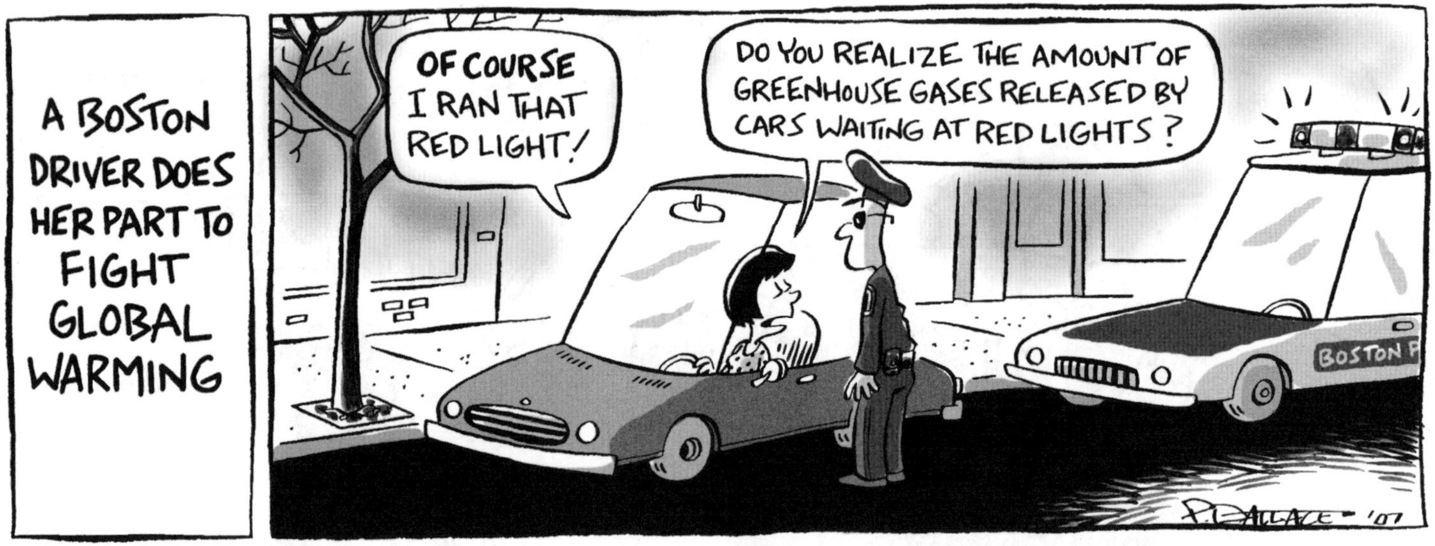
A BOSTON DRIVER DOES HER PART TO FIGHT GLOBAL WARMING
OF COURSE I RAN THAT RED LIGHT!
DO YOU REALIZE THE AMOUNT OF GREENHOUSE GASES RELEASED BY CARS WAITING AT RED LIGHTS?
BOSTON
P. WALLACE '07

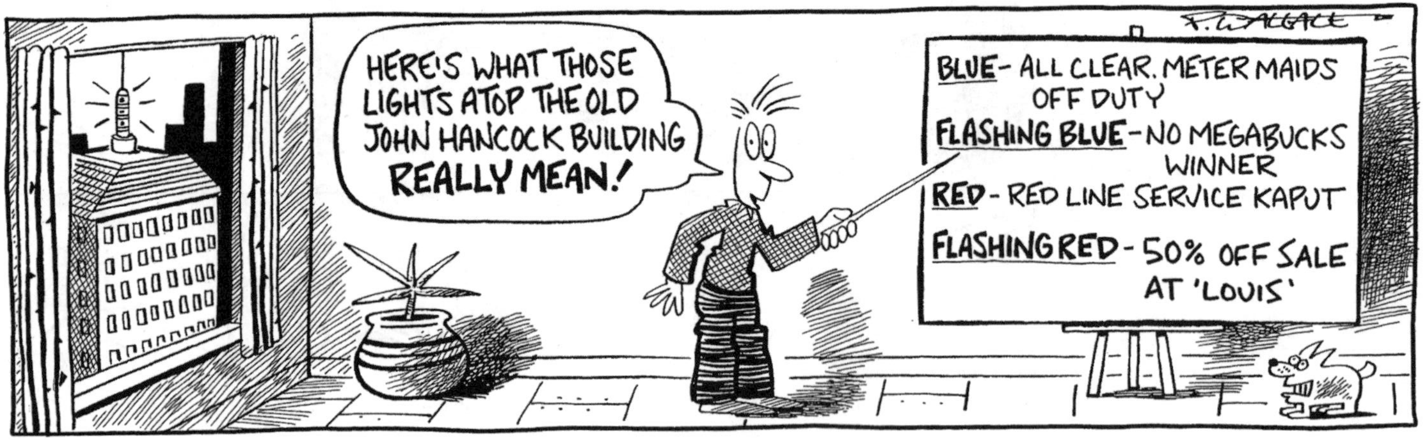
HERE'S WHAT THOSE LIGHTS ATOP THE OLD JOHN HANCOCK BUILDING REALLY MEAN!
BLUE - ALL CLEAR. METER MAIDS OFF DUTY
FLASHING BLUE - NO MEGABUCKS WINNER
RED - RED LINE SERVICE KAPUT
FLASHING RED - 50% OFF SALE AT 'LOUIS'
P. WALLACE

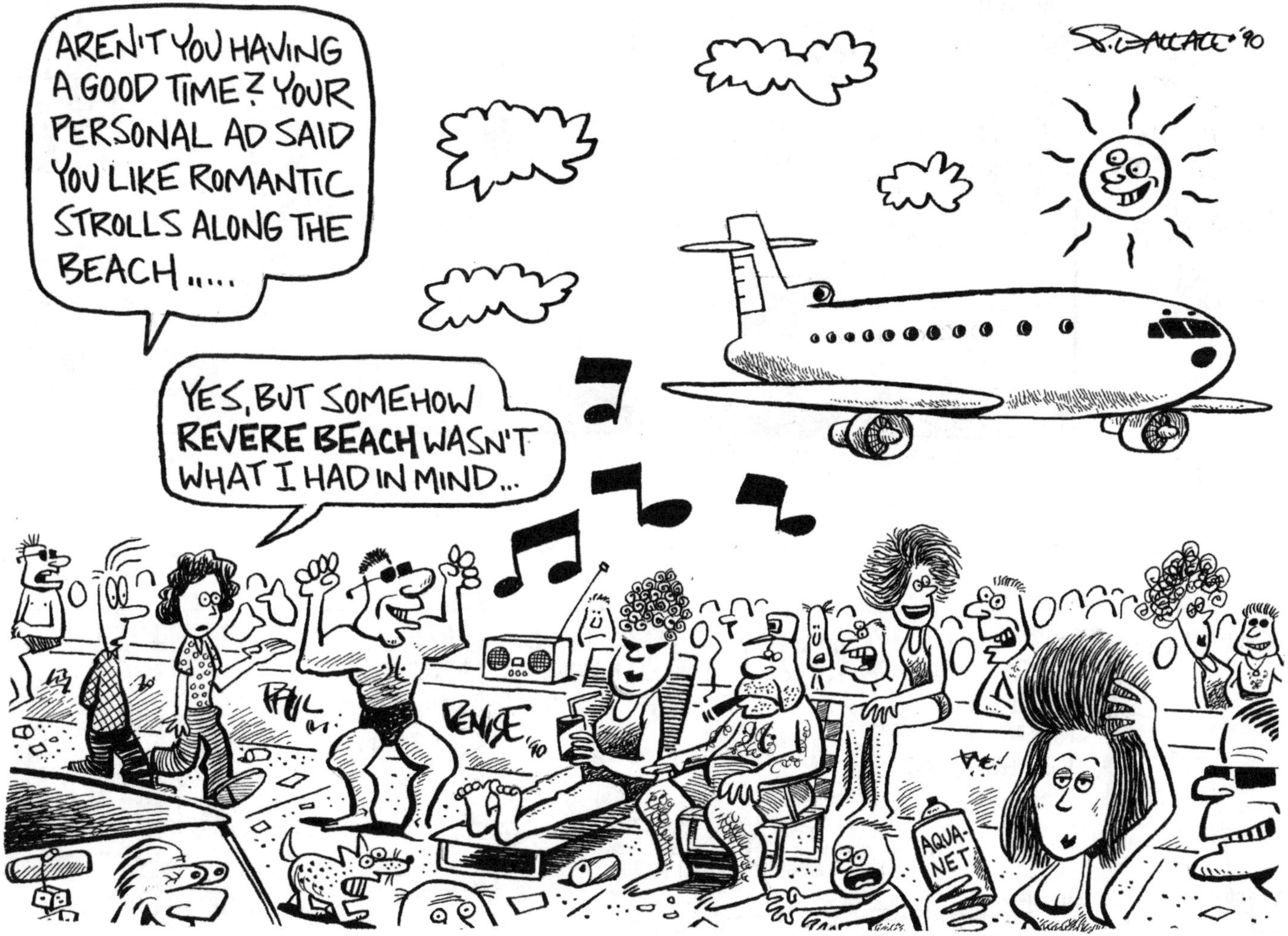
AREN'T YOU HAVING A GOOD TIME? YOUR PERSONAL AD SAID YOU LIKE ROMANTIC STROLLS ALONG THE BEACH.....
YES, BUT SOMEHOW **REVERE BEACH** WASN'T WHAT I HAD IN MIND...
PAUL
DENISE '90
AQUA-NET
R. WALLACE '90

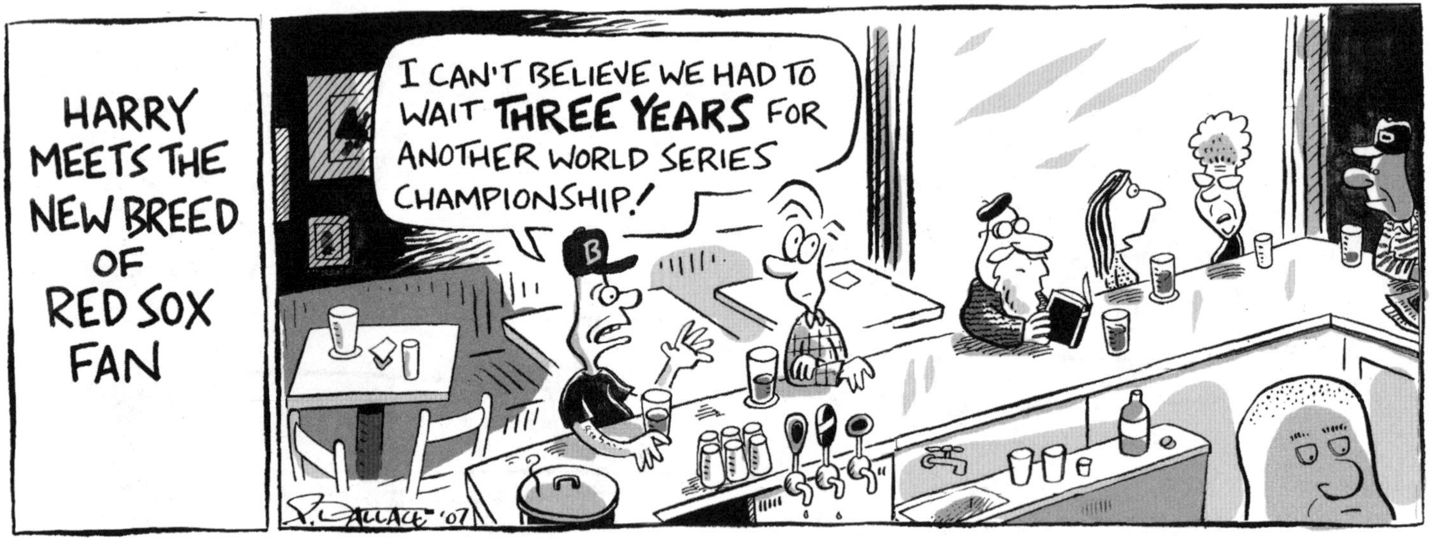
HARRY MEETS THE NEW BREED OF RED SOX FAN
I CAN'T BELIEVE WE HAD TO WAIT THREE YEARS FOR ANOTHER WORLD SERIES CHAMPIONSHIP!
P. WALLACE '07

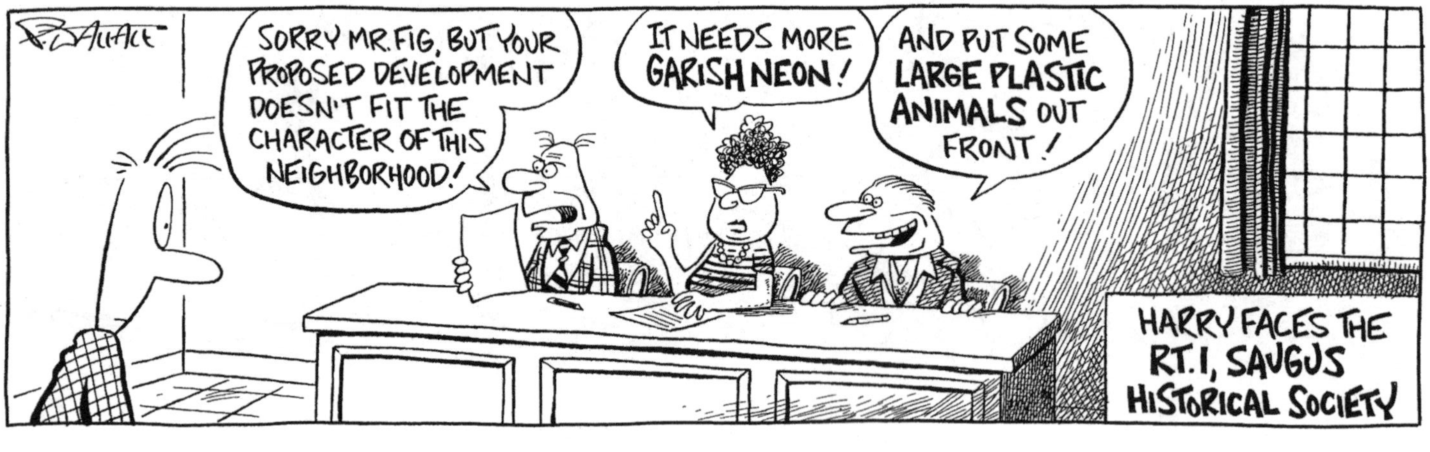
P. WALLACE
SORRY MR. FIG, BUT YOUR PROPOSED DEVELOPMENT DOESN'T FIT THE CHARACTER OF THIS NEIGHBORHOOD!
IT NEEDS MORE GARISH NEON!
AND PUT SOME LARGE PLASTIC ANIMALS OUT FRONT!
HARRY FACES THE RT. 1, SAUGUS HISTORICAL SOCIETY

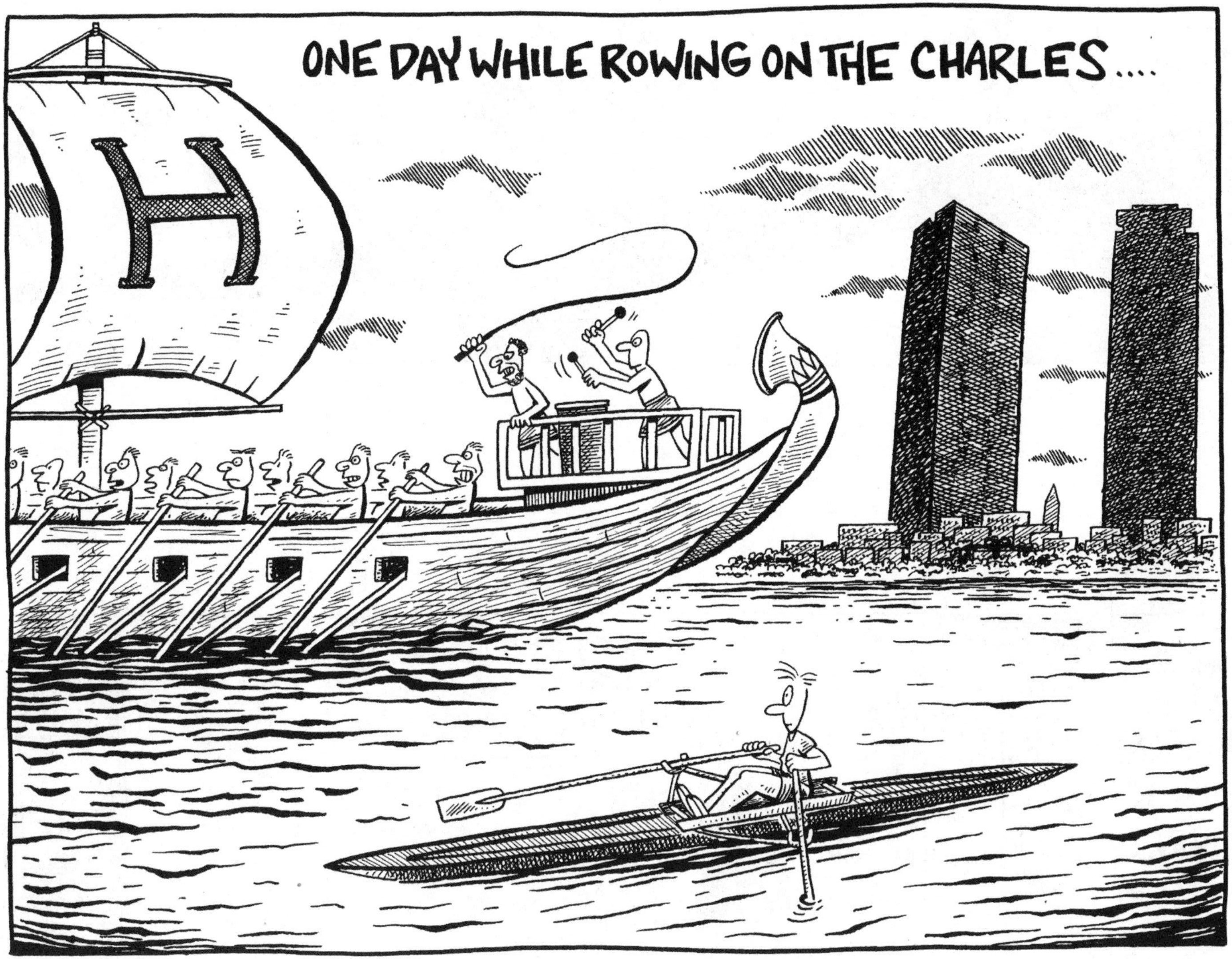
ONE DAY WHILE ROWING ON THE CHARLES....
H

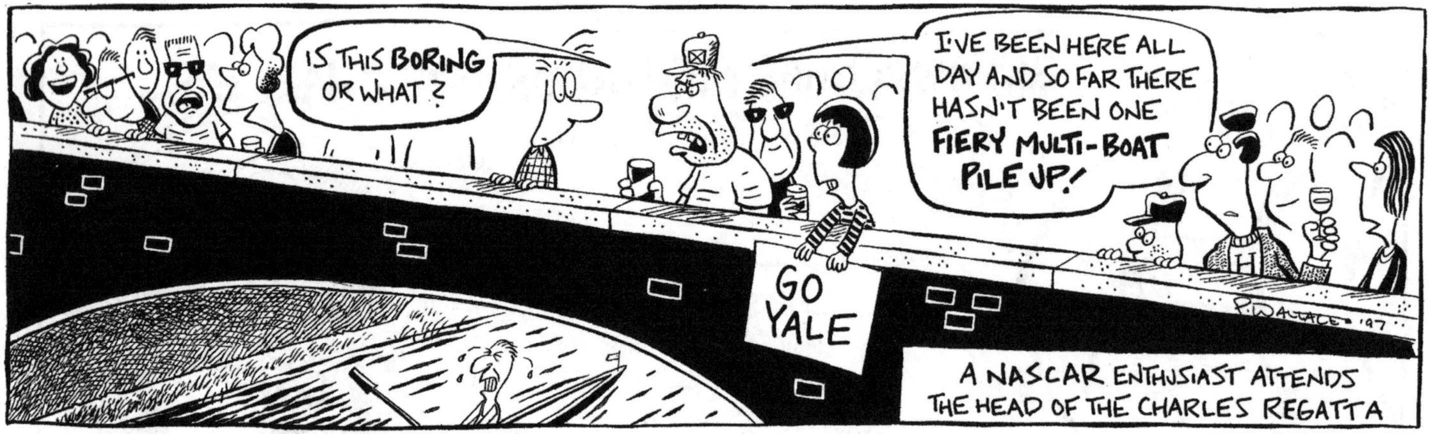
IS THIS BORING OR WHAT?
I'VE BEEN HERE ALL DAY AND SO FAR THERE HASN'T BEEN ONE FIERY MULTI-BOAT PILE UP!
GO YALE
R. WALLACE '97
A NASCAR ENTHUSIAST ATTENDS THE HEAD OF THE CHARLES REGATTA

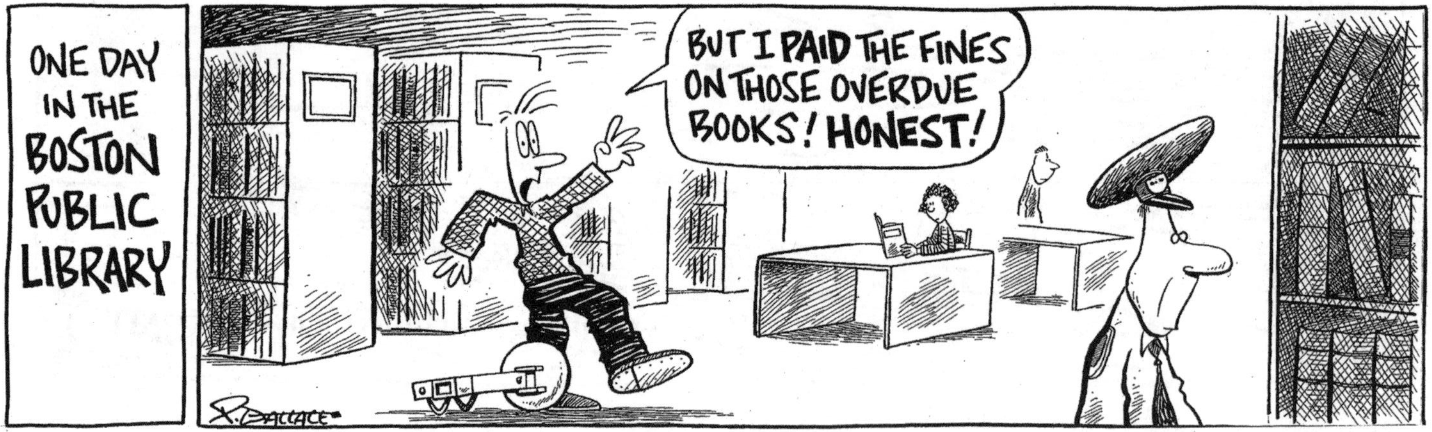
ONE DAY IN THE BOSTON PUBLIC LIBRARY
BUT I PAID THE FINES ON THOSE OVERDUE BOOKS! HONEST!
R. WALLACE

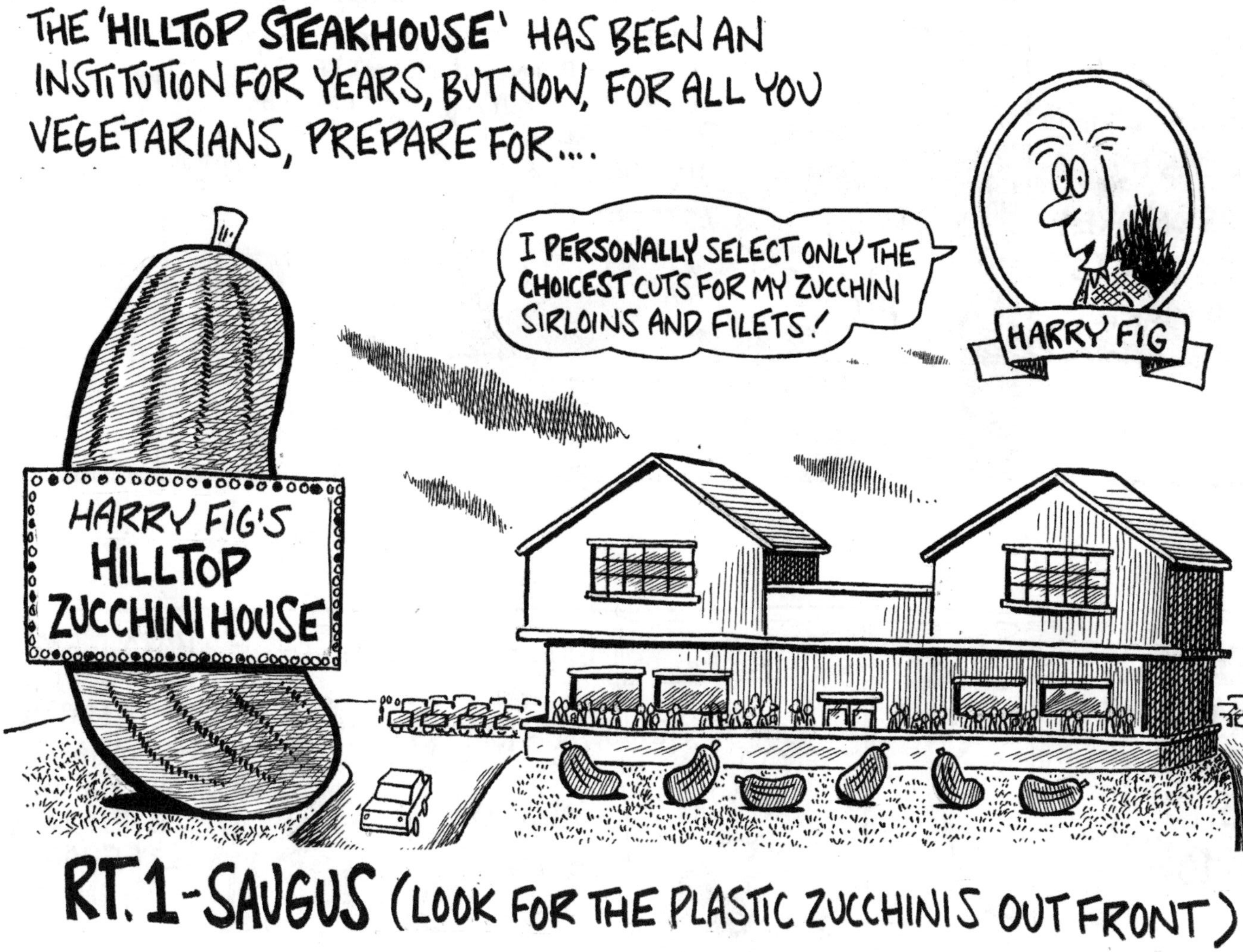
THE 'HILLTOP STEAKHOUSE' HAS BEEN AN INSTITUTION FOR YEARS, BUT NOW, FOR ALL YOU VEGETARIANS, PREPARE FOR....
I PERSONALLY SELECT ONLY THE CHOICEST CUTS FOR MY ZUCCHINI SIRLOINS AND FILETS!
HARRY FIG
HARRY FIG'S HILLTOP ZUCCHINI HOUSE
RT. 1 - SAUGUS (LOOK FOR THE PLASTIC ZUCCHINIS OUT FRONT)

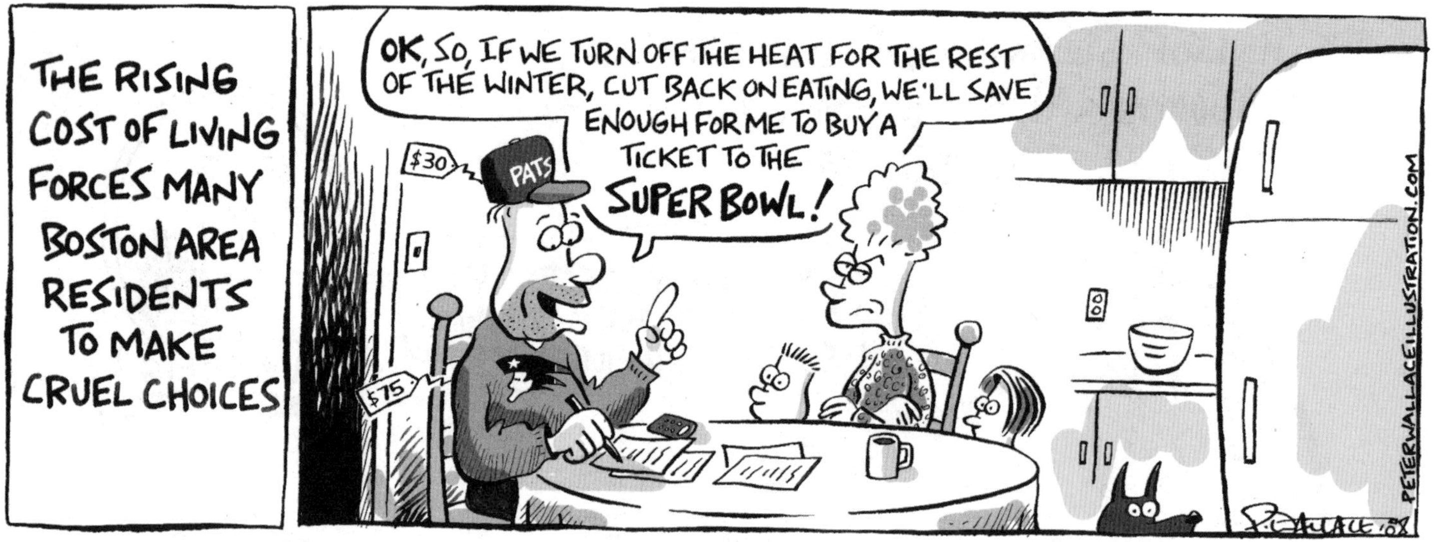
THE RISING COST OF LIVING FORCES MANY BOSTON AREA RESIDENTS TO MAKE CRUEL CHOICES
OK, SO, IF WE TURN OFF THE HEAT FOR THE REST OF THE WINTER, CUT BACK ON EATING, WE'LL SAVE ENOUGH FOR ME TO BUY A TICKET TO THE SUPER BOWL!
$30
$75
PATS
PETERWALLACEILLUSTRATION.COM

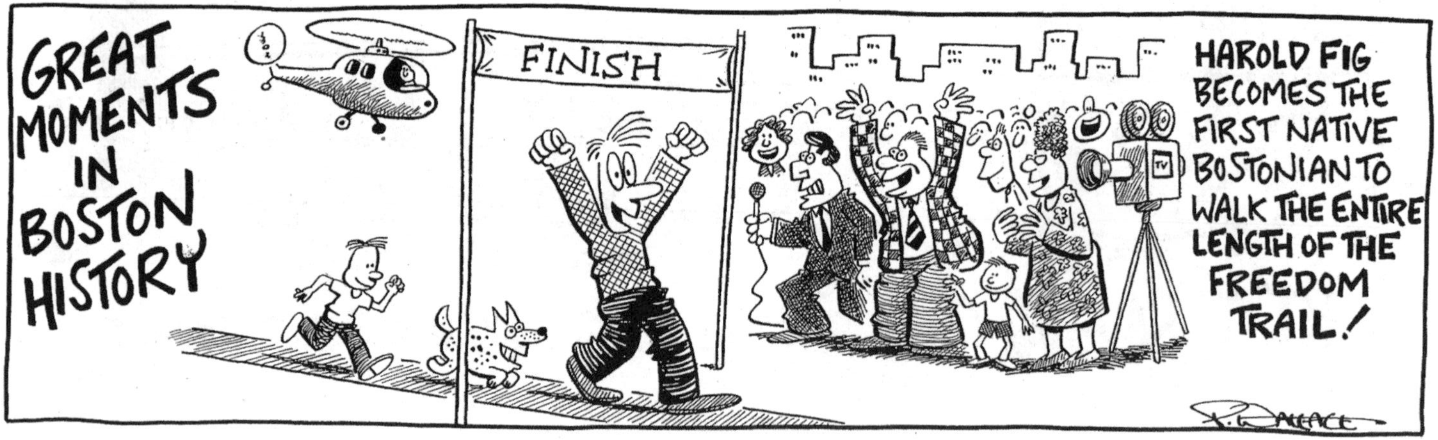
GREAT MOMENTS IN BOSTON HISTORY
FINISH
HAROLD FIG BECOMES THE FIRST NATIVE BOSTONIAN TO WALK THE ENTIRE LENGTH OF THE FREEDOM TRAIL!
TV

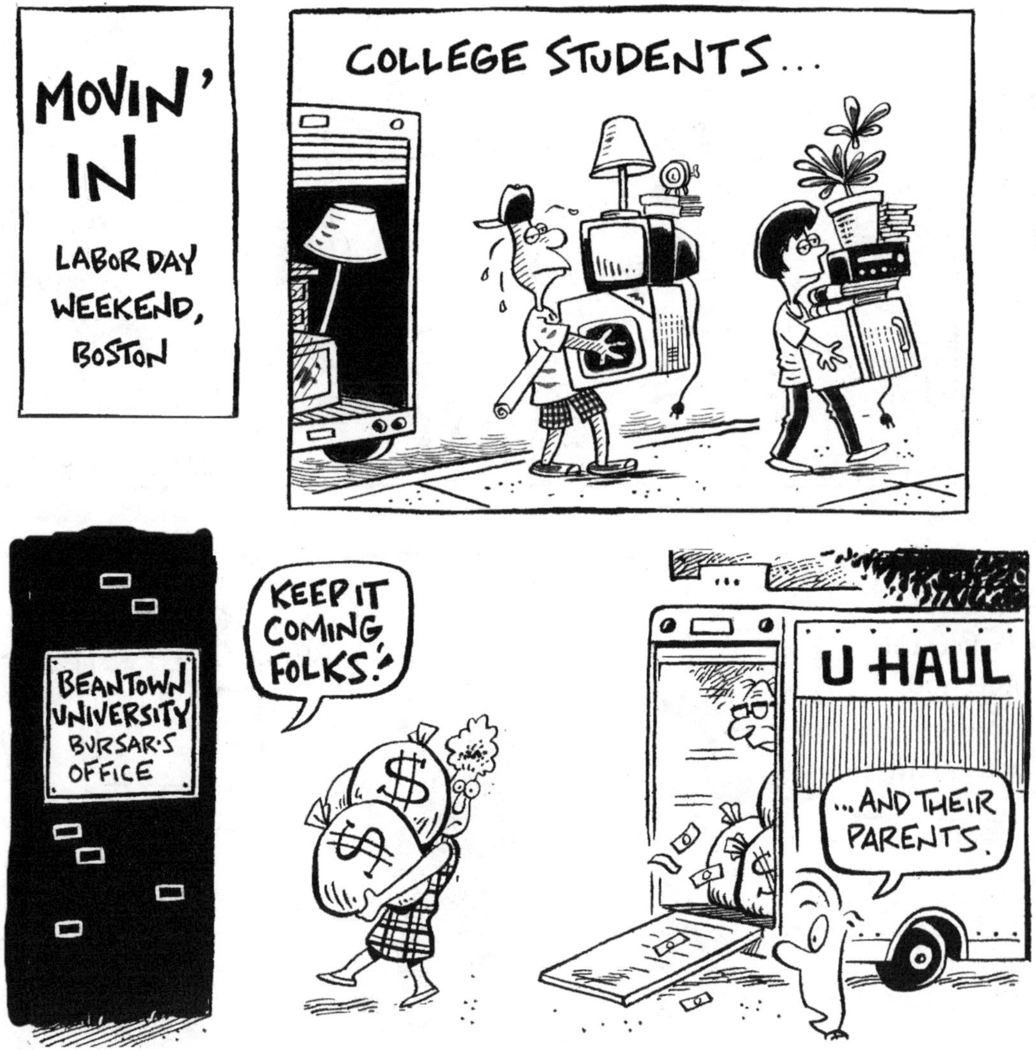
MOVIN' IN
LABOR DAY WEEKEND, BOSTON
COLLEGE STUDENTS...
BEANTOWN UNIVERSITY BURSAR'S OFFICE
KEEP IT COMING, FOLKS!
U HAUL
...AND THEIR PARENTS.

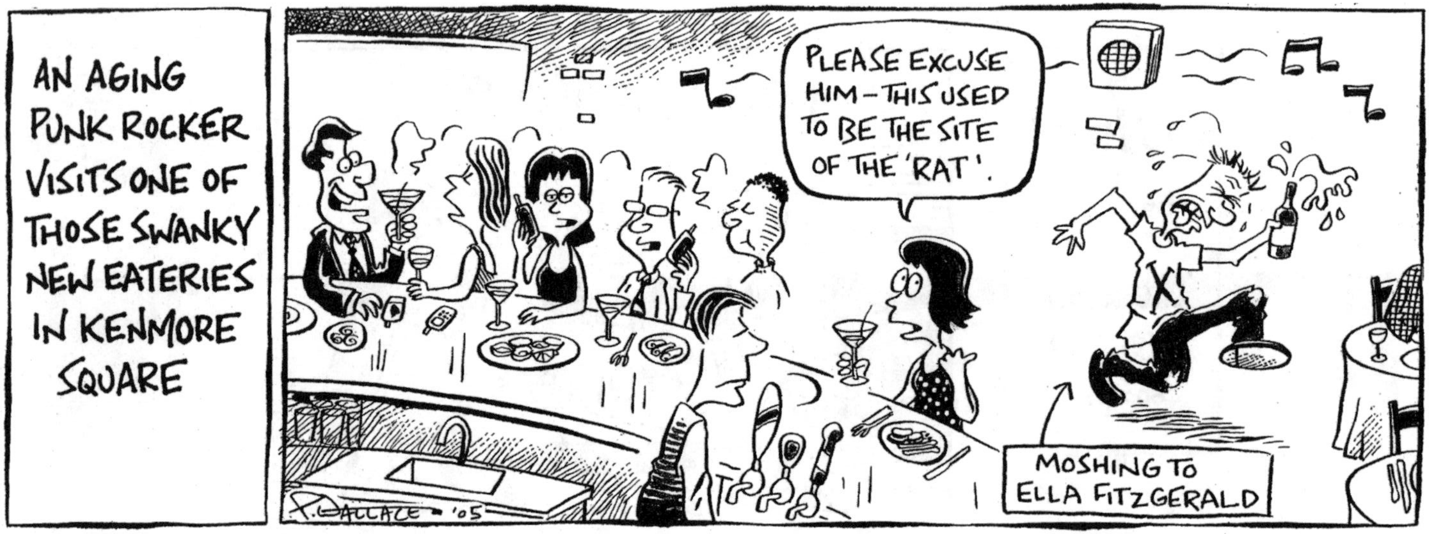
AN AGING PUNK ROCKER VISITS ONE OF THOSE SWANKY NEW EATERIES IN KENMORE SQUARE
PLEASE EXCUSE HIM – THIS USED TO BE THE SITE OF THE 'RAT'.
MOSHING TO ELLA FITZGERALD
P. WALLACE '05

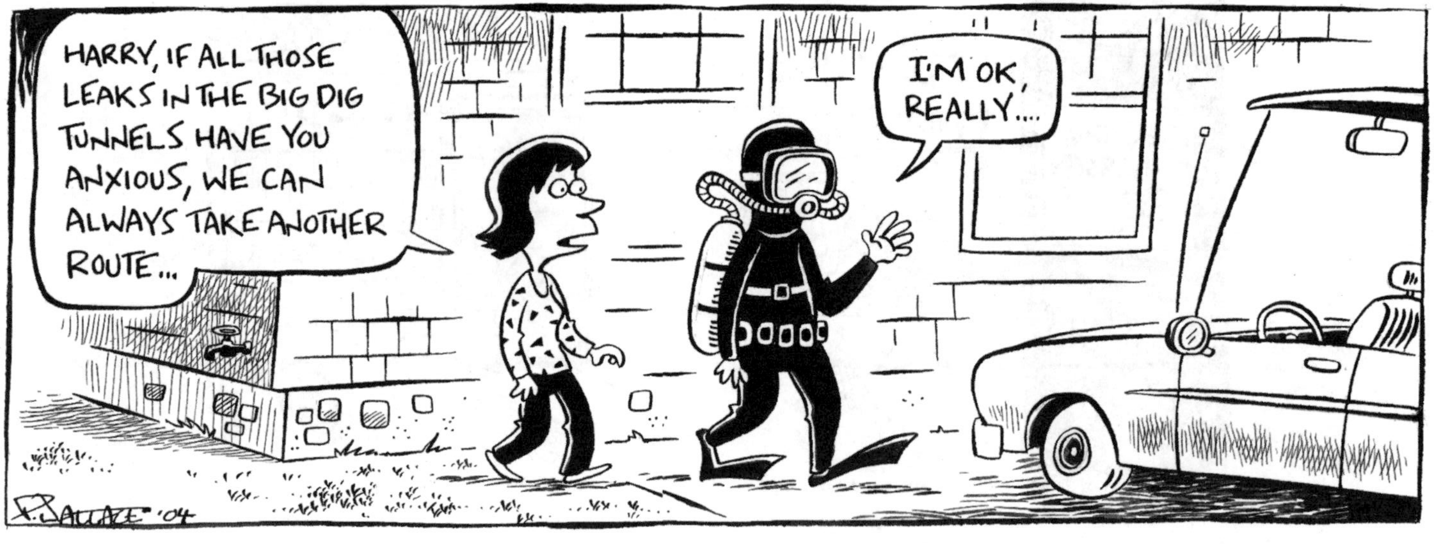
HARRY, IF ALL THOSE LEAKS IN THE BIG DIG TUNNELS HAVE YOU ANXIOUS, WE CAN ALWAYS TAKE ANOTHER ROUTE...
I'M OK, REALLY....
P. WALLACE '04

THE HUB'S LATEST TOURIST ATTRACTION

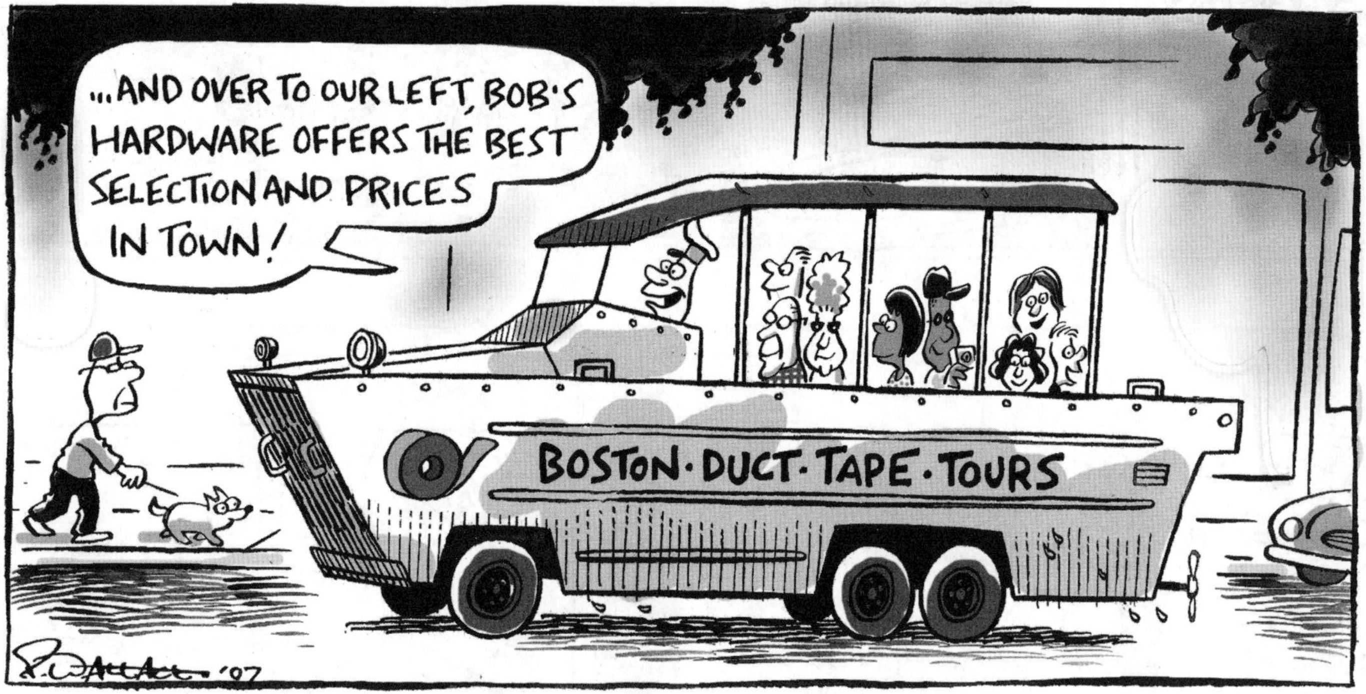
...AND OVER TO OUR LEFT, BOB'S HARDWARE OFFERS THE BEST SELECTION AND PRICES IN TOWN!
BOSTON · DUCT · TAPE · TOURS

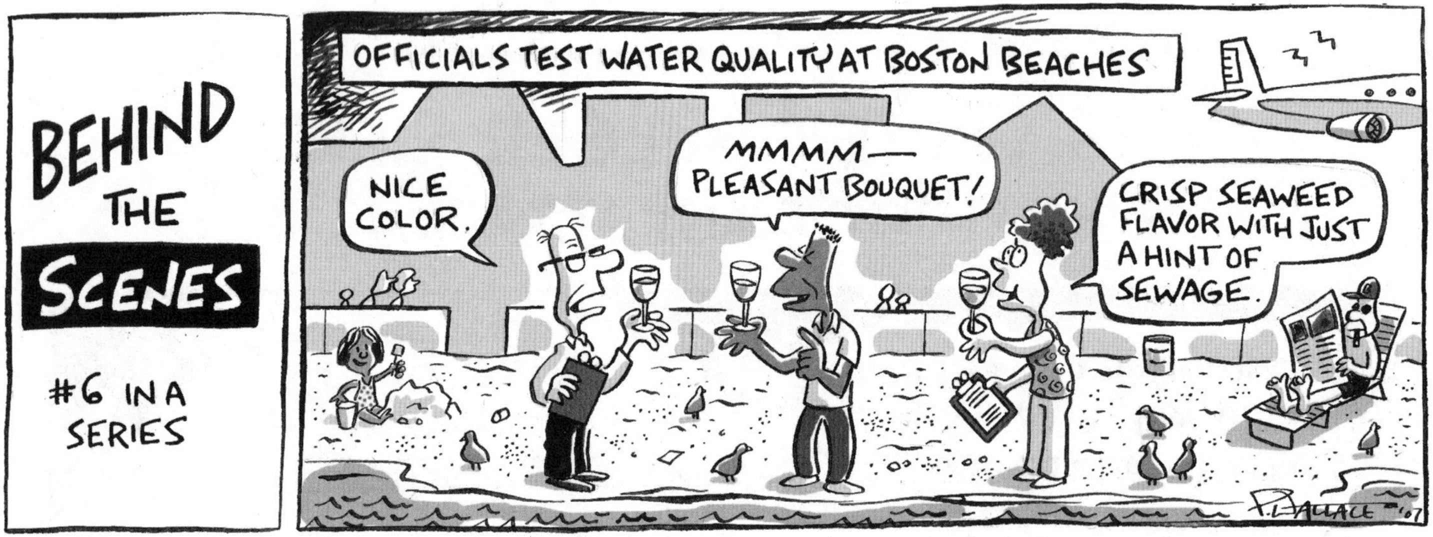
BEHIND THE SCENES
#6 IN A SERIES
OFFICIALS TEST WATER QUALITY AT BOSTON BEACHES
NICE COLOR.
MMMM— PLEASANT BOUQUET!
CRISP SEAWEED FLAVOR WITH JUST A HINT OF SEWAGE.

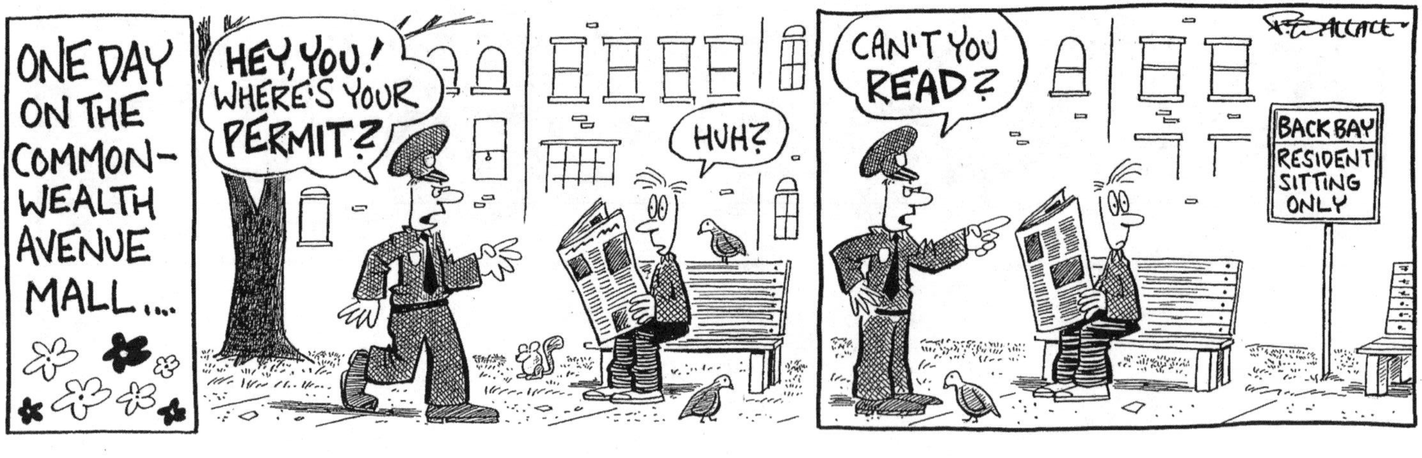
ONE DAY ON THE COMMON-WEALTH AVENUE MALL....
HEY, YOU! WHERE'S YOUR PERMIT?
HUH?
CAN'T YOU READ?
BACK BAY
RESIDENT SITTING ONLY

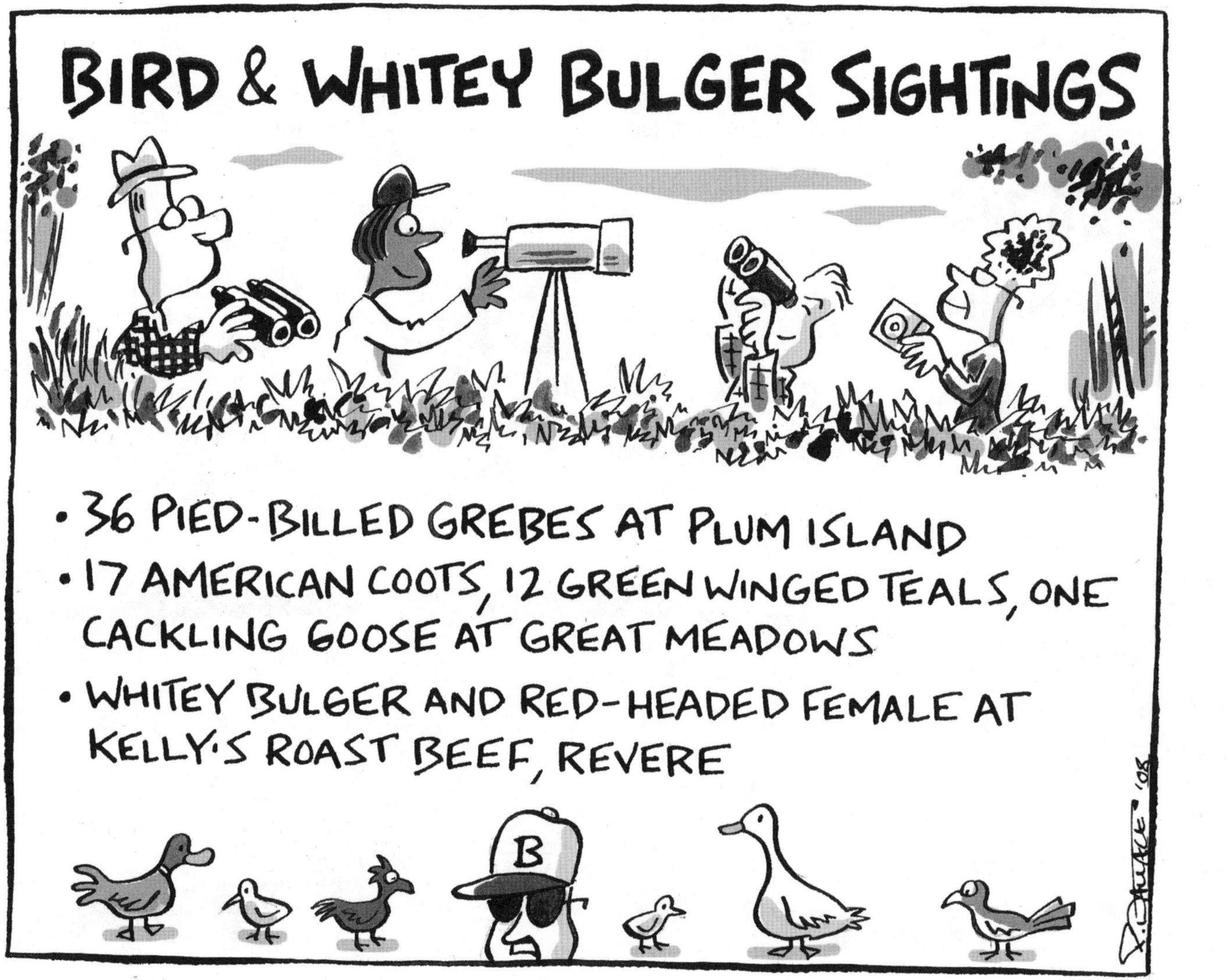
BIRD & WHITEY BULGER SIGHTINGS
• 36 PIED-BILLED GREBES AT PLUM ISLAND
• 17 AMERICAN COOTS, 12 GREEN WINGED TEALS, ONE CACKLING GOOSE AT GREAT MEADOWS
• WHITEY BULGER AND RED-HEADED FEMALE AT KELLY'S ROAST BEEF, REVERE
B

IN THE BEGINNING...

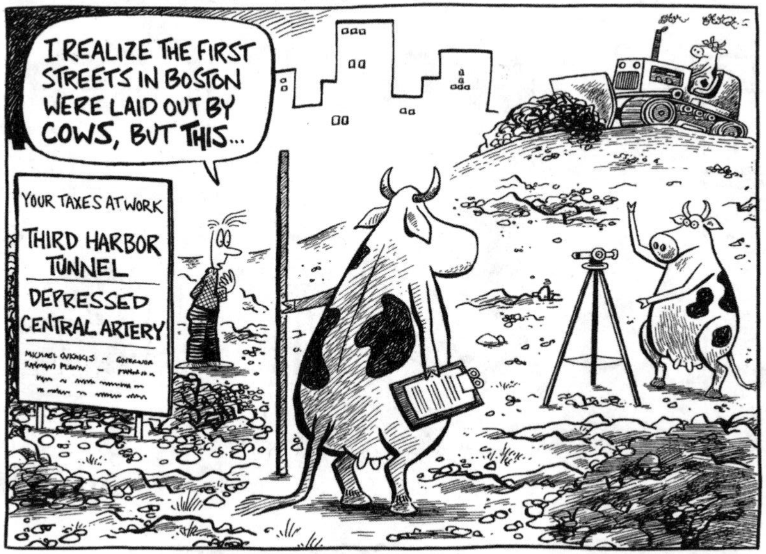

I REALIZE THE FIRST STREETS IN BOSTON WERE LAID OUT BY COWS, BUT THIS...
YOUR TAXES AT WORK
THIRD HARBOR TUNNEL
DEPRESSED CENTRAL ARTERY

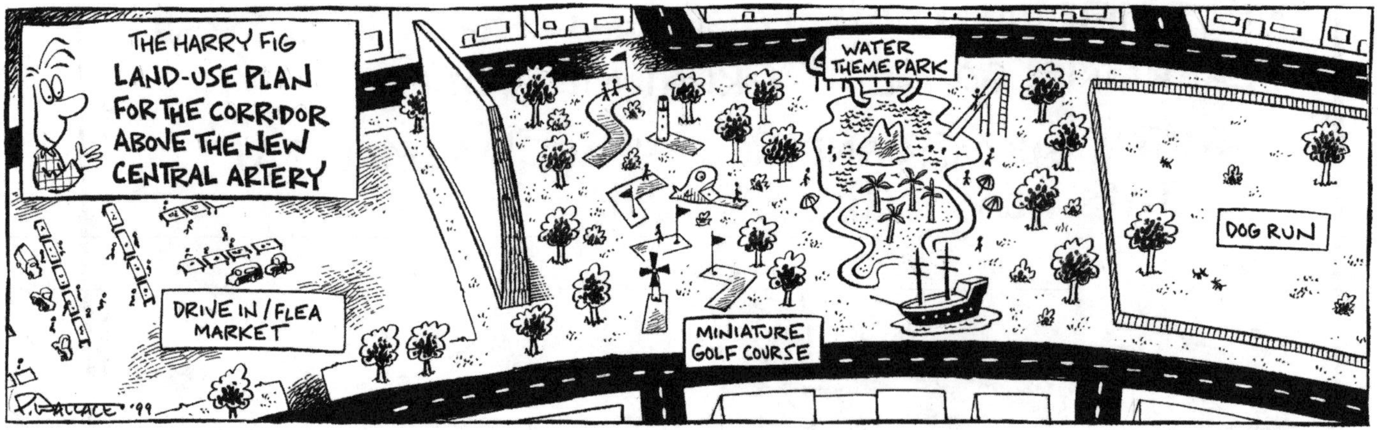

THE HARRY FIG LAND-USE PLAN FOR THE CORRIDOR ABOVE THE NEW CENTRAL ARTERY
DRIVE IN / FLEA MARKET
MINIATURE GOLF COURSE
WATER THEME PARK
DOG RUN
P. WALLACE '99

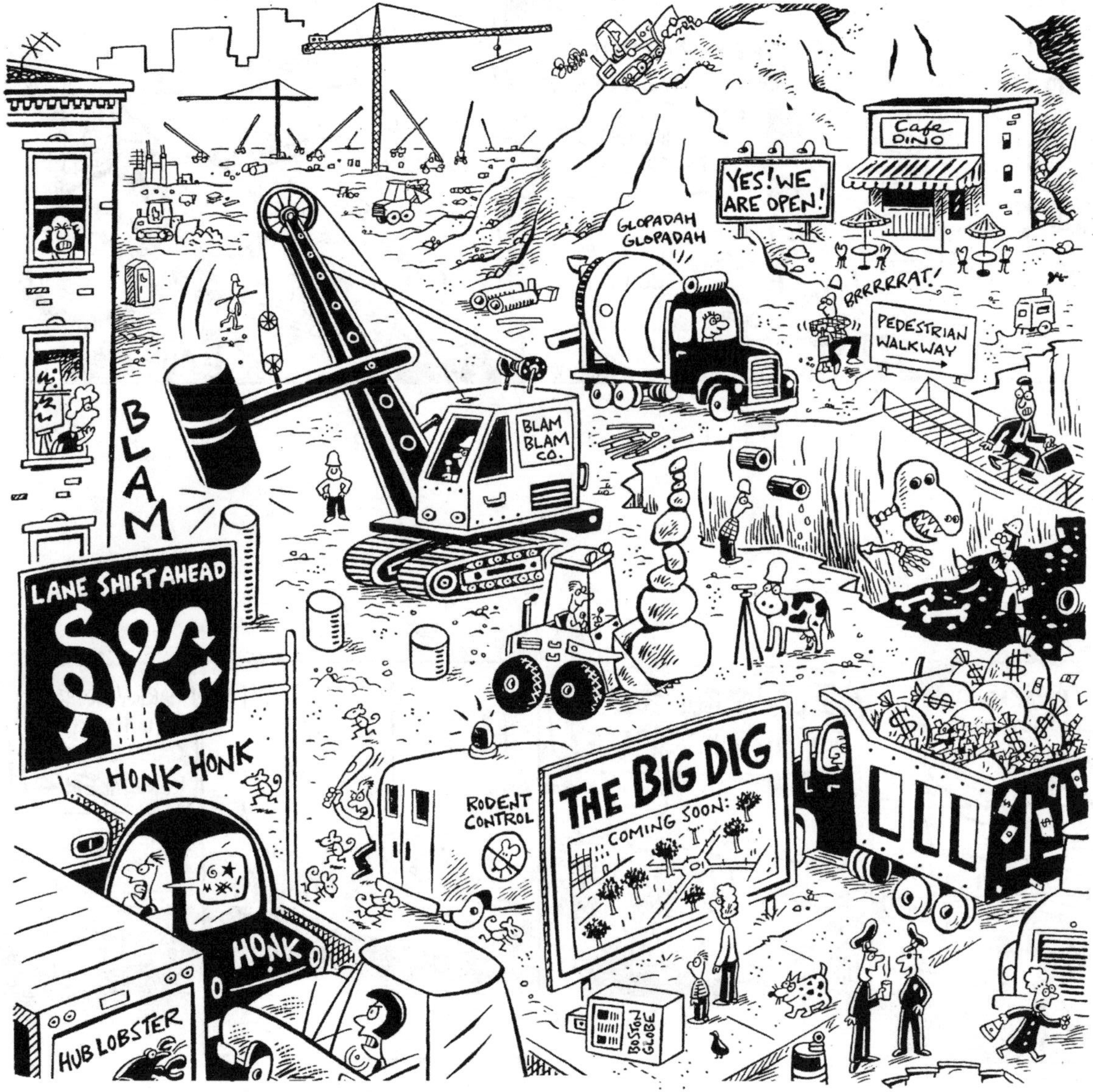

Cafe DINO
YES! WE ARE OPEN!
GLOPADAH GLOPADAH
BRRRRRAT!
PEDESTRIAN WALKWAY
BLAM BLAM CO.
BLAM
LANE SHIFT AHEAD
HONK HONK
RODENT CONTROL
THE BIG DIG
COMING SOON:
HONK
HUB LOBSTER
BOSTON GLOBE

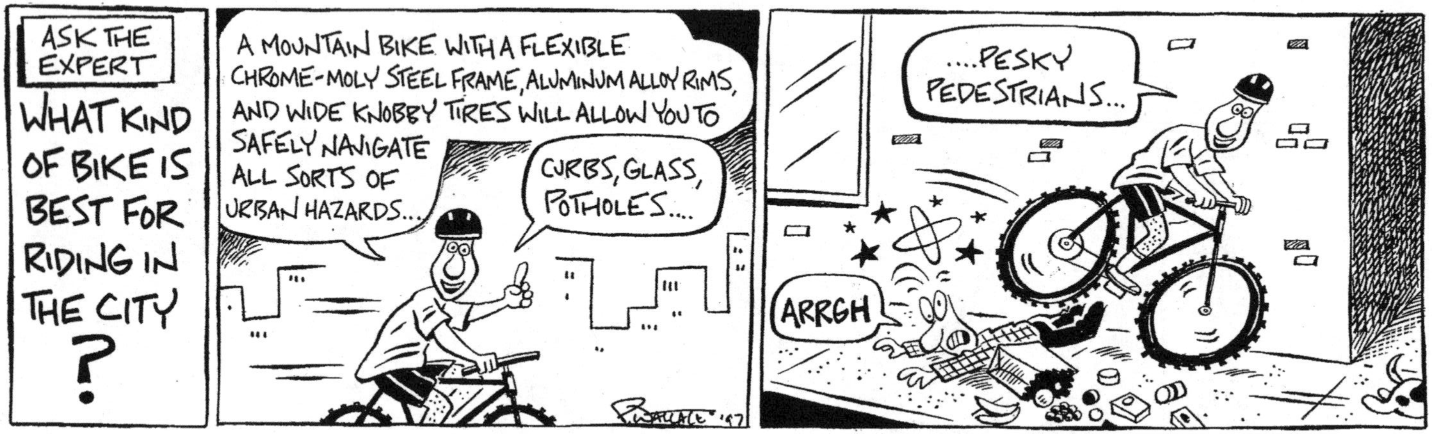
ASK THE EXPERT
WHAT KIND OF BIKE IS BEST FOR RIDING IN THE CITY ?
A MOUNTAIN BIKE WITH A FLEXIBLE CHROME-MOLY STEEL FRAME, ALUMINUM ALLOY RIMS, AND WIDE KNOBBY TIRES WILL ALLOW YOU TO SAFELY NAVIGATE ALL SORTS OF URBAN HAZARDS...
CURBS, GLASS, POTHOLES....
....PESKY PEDESTRIANS...
ARRGH
P. WALLACE '97

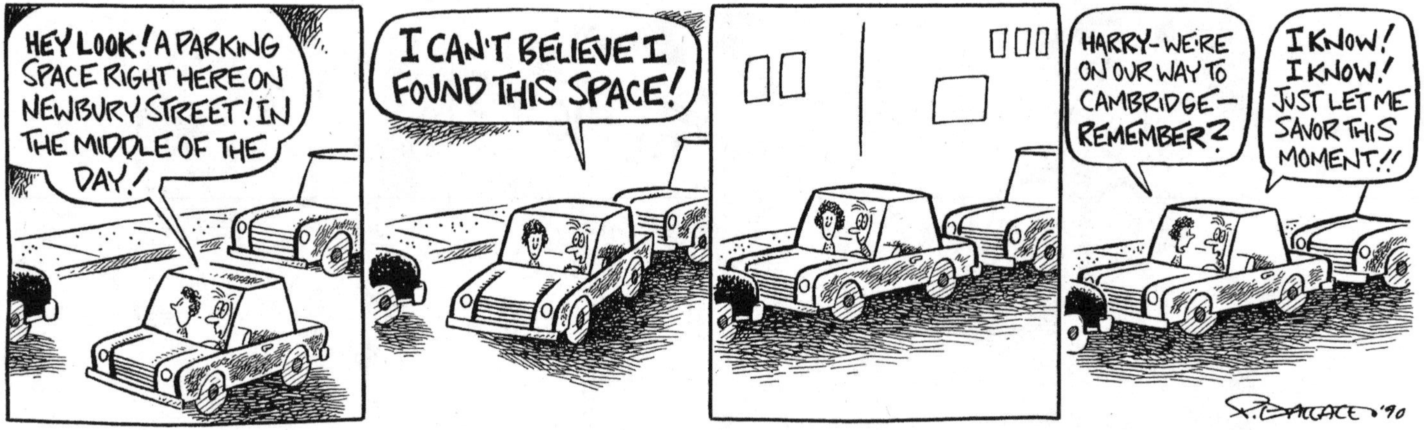
HEY LOOK! A PARKING SPACE RIGHT HERE ON NEWBURY STREET! IN THE MIDDLE OF THE DAY!
I CAN'T BELIEVE I FOUND THIS SPACE!
HARRY- WE'RE ON OUR WAY TO CAMBRIDGE— REMEMBER?
I KNOW! I KNOW! JUST LET ME SAVOR THIS MOMENT!!
P. WALLACE '90

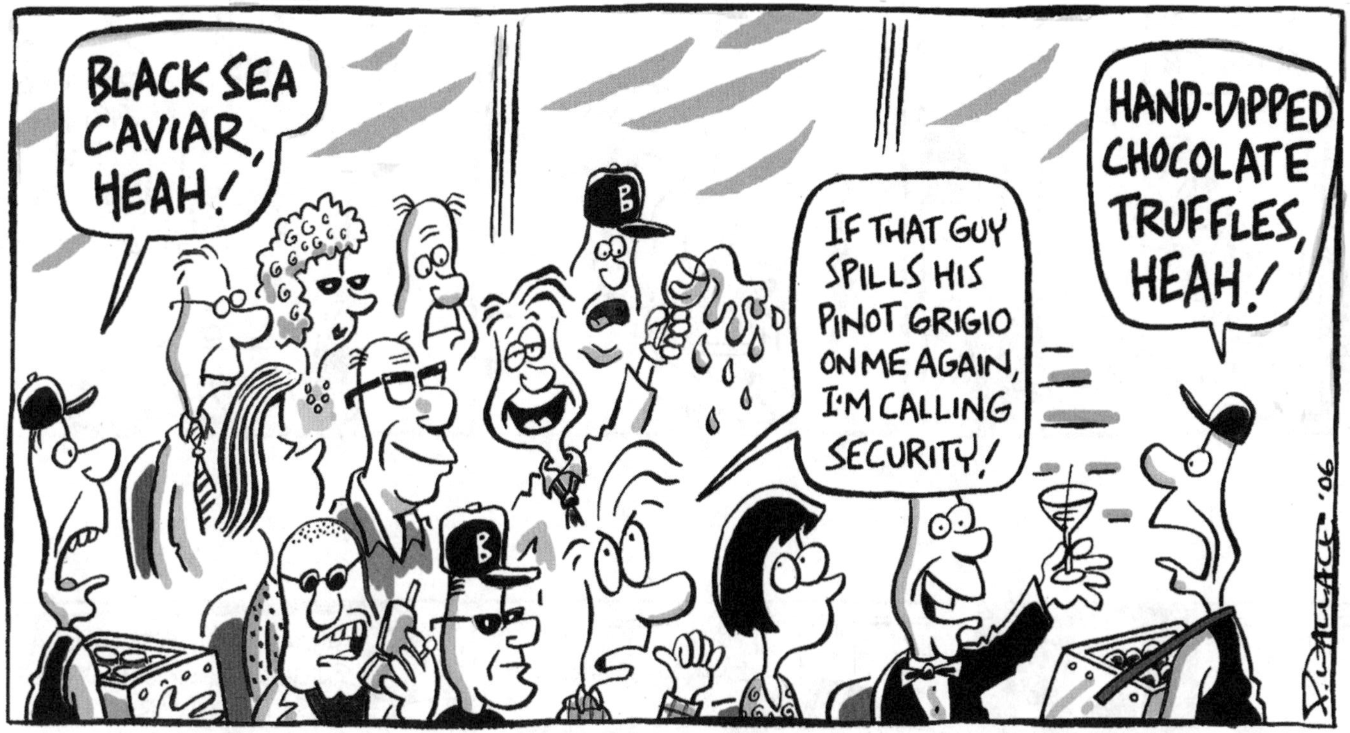
BLACK SEA CAVIAR, HEAH!
IF THAT GUY SPILLS HIS PINOT GRIGIO ON ME AGAIN, I'M CALLING SECURITY!
HAND-DIPPED CHOCOLATE TRUFFLES, HEAH!
'06

HARRY CHECKS OUT THE $297 SEATS AT FENWAY PARK'S EXCLUSIVE **EMC CLUB**

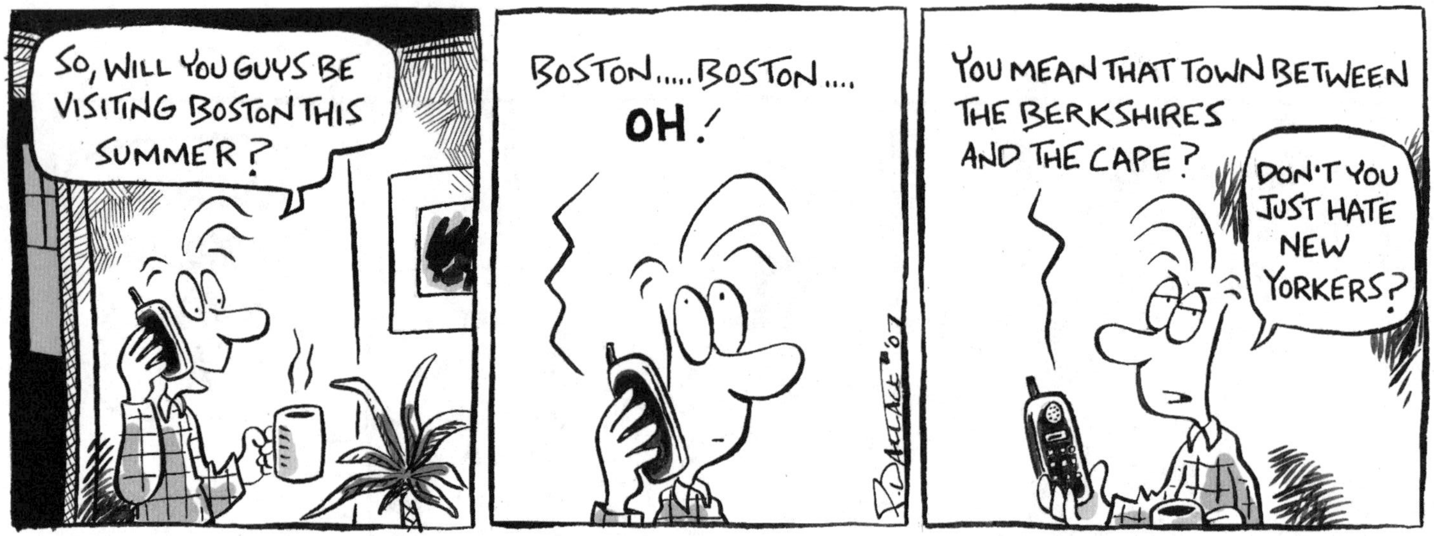
SO, WILL YOU GUYS BE VISITING BOSTON THIS SUMMER?
BOSTON..... BOSTON....
OH!
YOU MEAN THAT TOWN BETWEEN THE BERKSHIRES AND THE CAPE?
DON'T YOU JUST HATE NEW YORKERS?
P. WALLACE '07

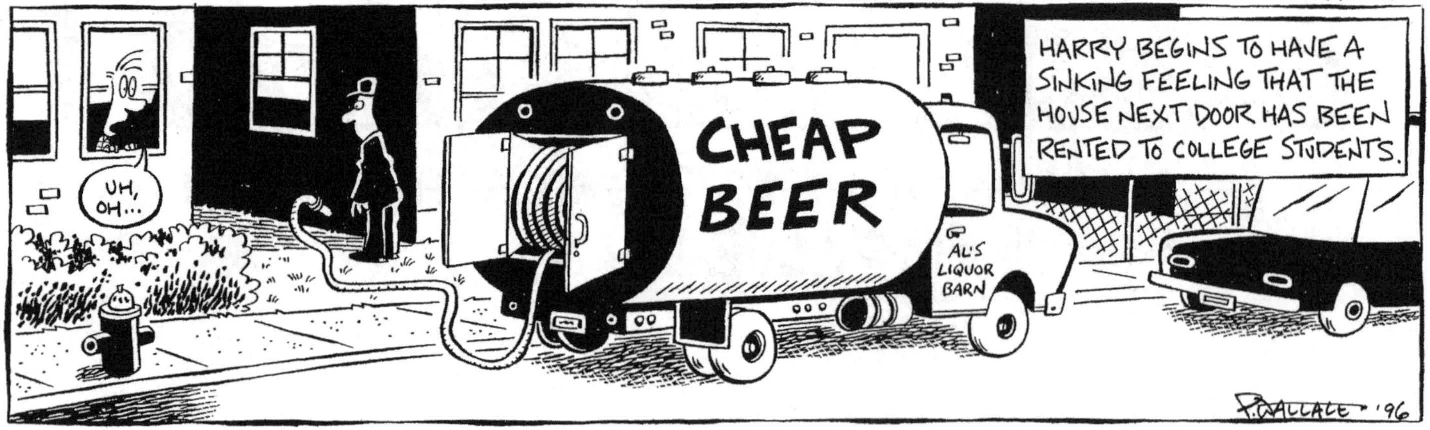
UH, OH...
CHEAP BEER
AL'S LIQUOR BARN
HARRY BEGINS TO HAVE A SINKING FEELING THAT THE HOUSE NEXT DOOR HAS BEEN RENTED TO COLLEGE STUDENTS.
P. WALLACE '96

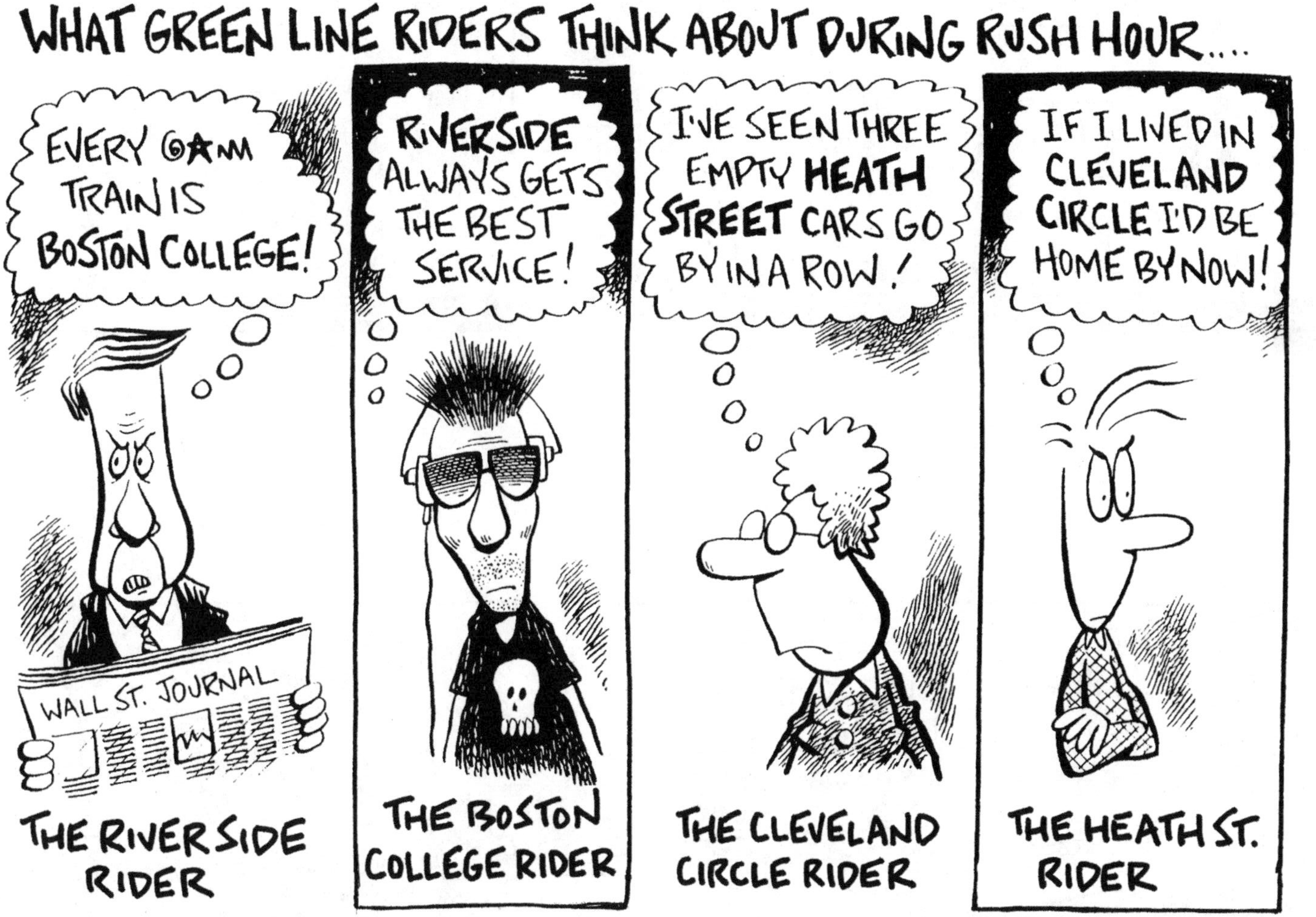
WHAT GREEN LINE RIDERS THINK ABOUT DURING RUSH HOUR....
EVERY G★M TRAIN IS BOSTON COLLEGE!
WALL ST. JOURNAL
THE RIVERSIDE RIDER
RIVERSIDE ALWAYS GETS THE BEST SERVICE!
THE BOSTON COLLEGE RIDER
I'VE SEEN THREE EMPTY HEATH STREET CARS GO BY IN A ROW!
THE CLEVELAND CIRCLE RIDER
IF I LIVED IN CLEVELAND CIRCLE I'D BE HOME BY NOW!
THE HEATH ST. RIDER

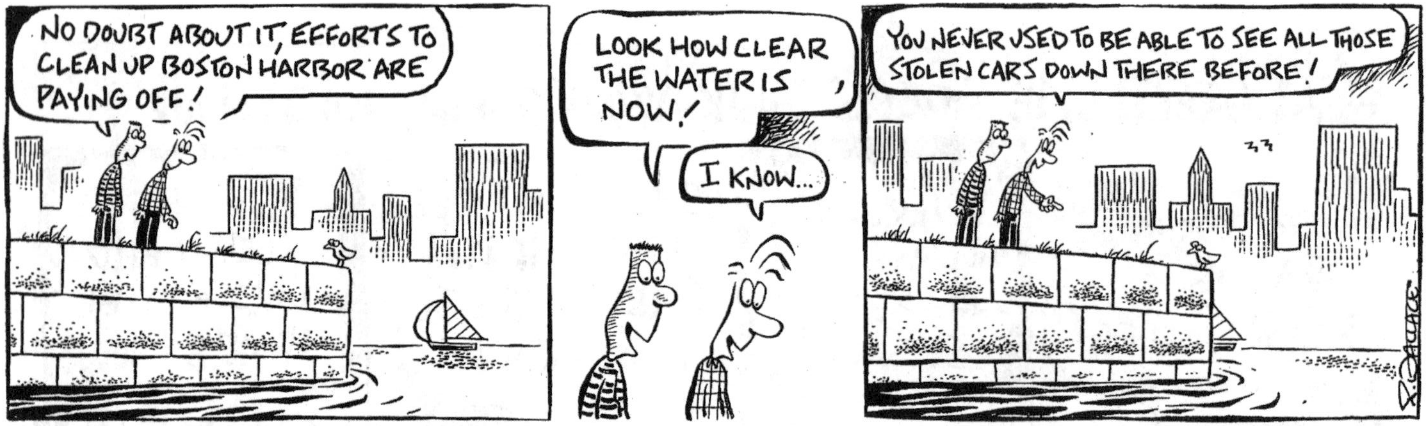
NO DOUBT ABOUT IT, EFFORTS TO CLEAN UP BOSTON HARBOR ARE PAYING OFF!
LOOK HOW CLEAR THE WATER IS NOW!
I KNOW...
YOU NEVER USED TO BE ABLE TO SEE ALL THOSE STOLEN CARS DOWN THERE BEFORE!
R. WALLACE

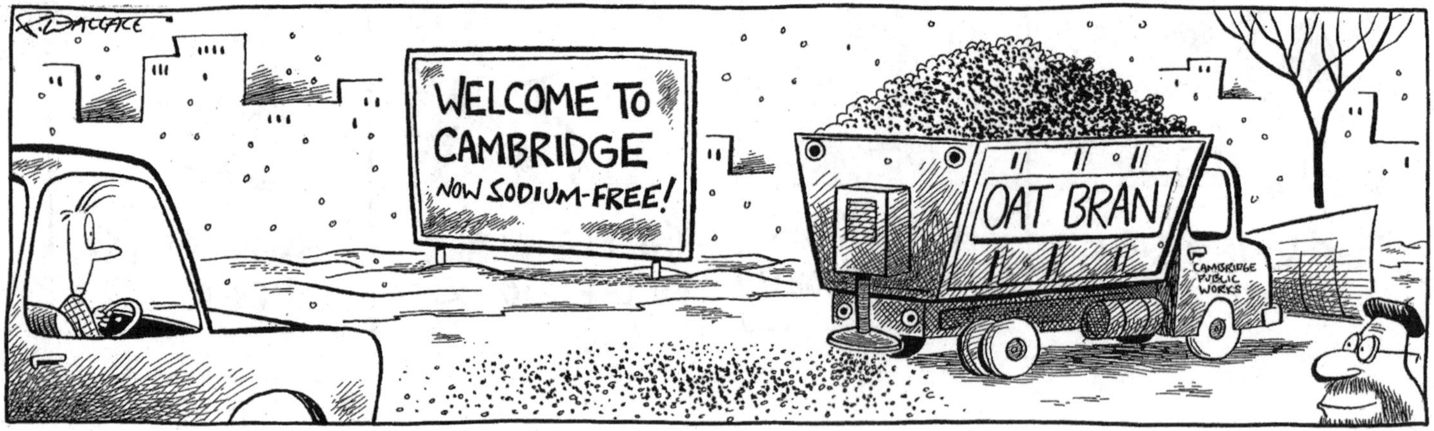
R. WALLACE
WELCOME TO CAMBRIDGE
NOW SODIUM-FREE!
OAT BRAN
CAMBRIDGE PUBLIC WORKS

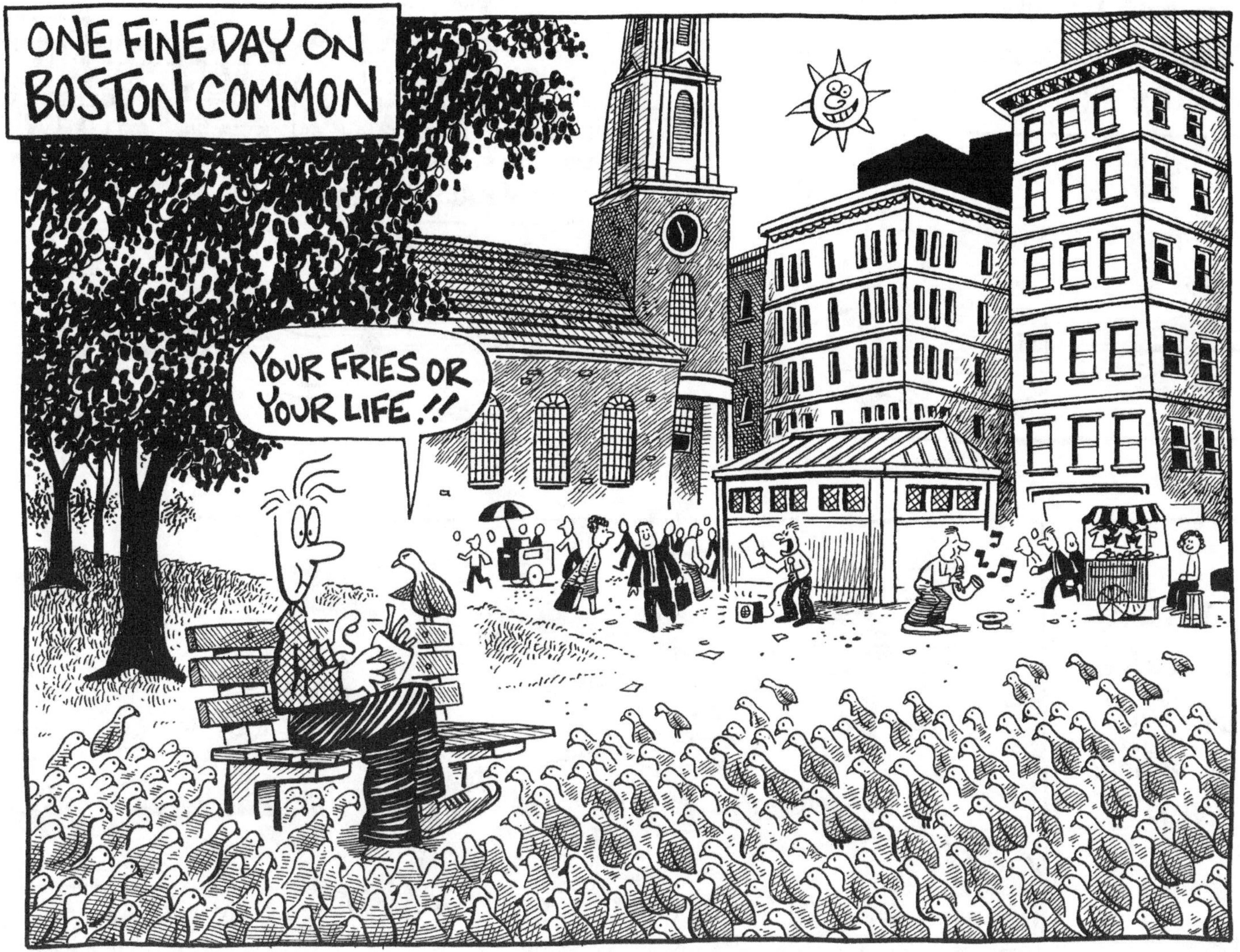
ONE FINE DAY ON BOSTON COMMON
YOUR FRIES OR YOUR LIFE!!

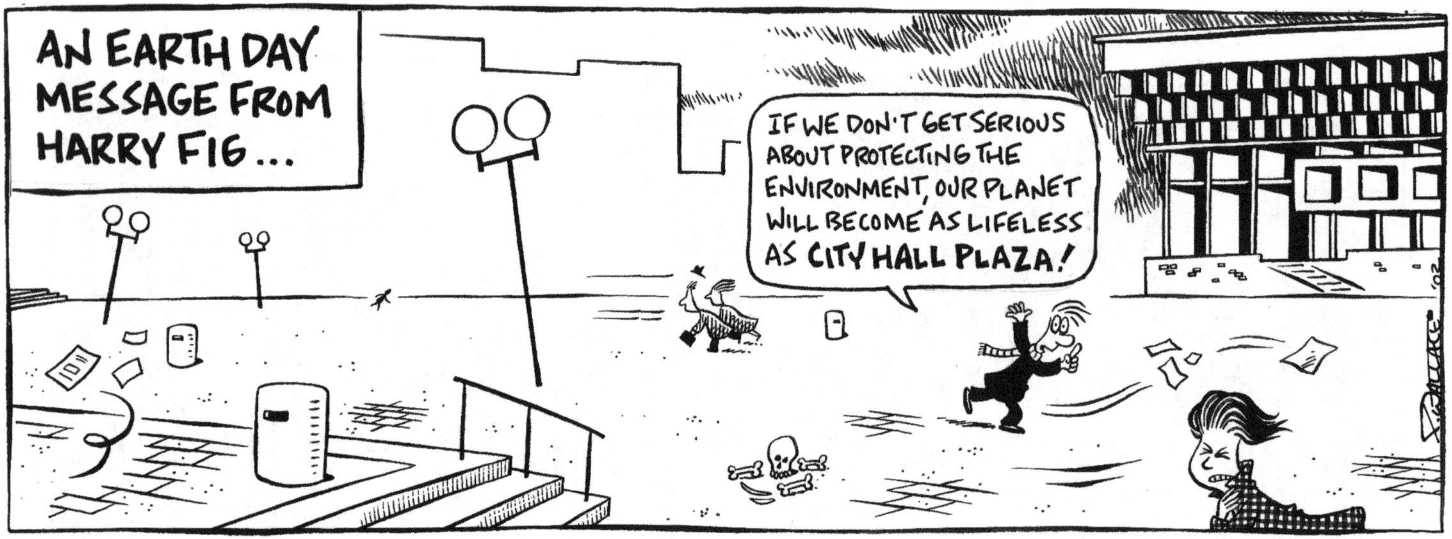
AN EARTH DAY MESSAGE FROM HARRY FIG...
IF WE DON'T GET SERIOUS ABOUT PROTECTING THE ENVIRONMENT, OUR PLANET WILL BECOME AS LIFELESS AS CITY HALL PLAZA!

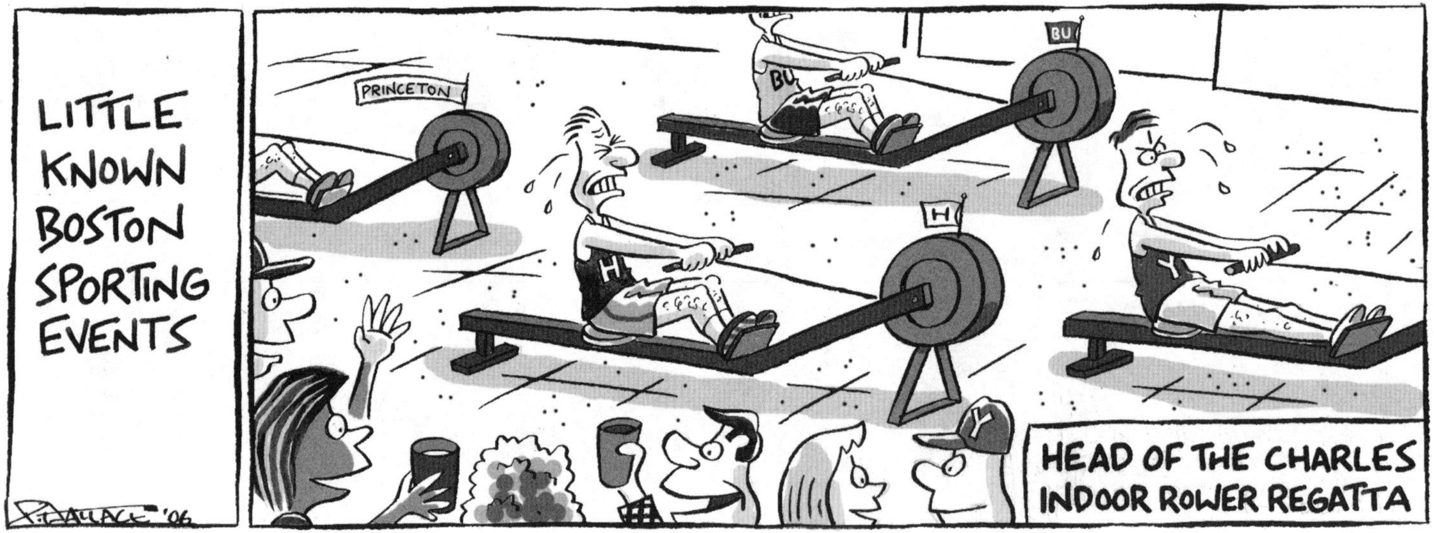
LITTLE KNOWN BOSTON SPORTING EVENTS
PRINCETON
BU
H
Y
HEAD OF THE CHARLES INDOOR ROWER REGATTA

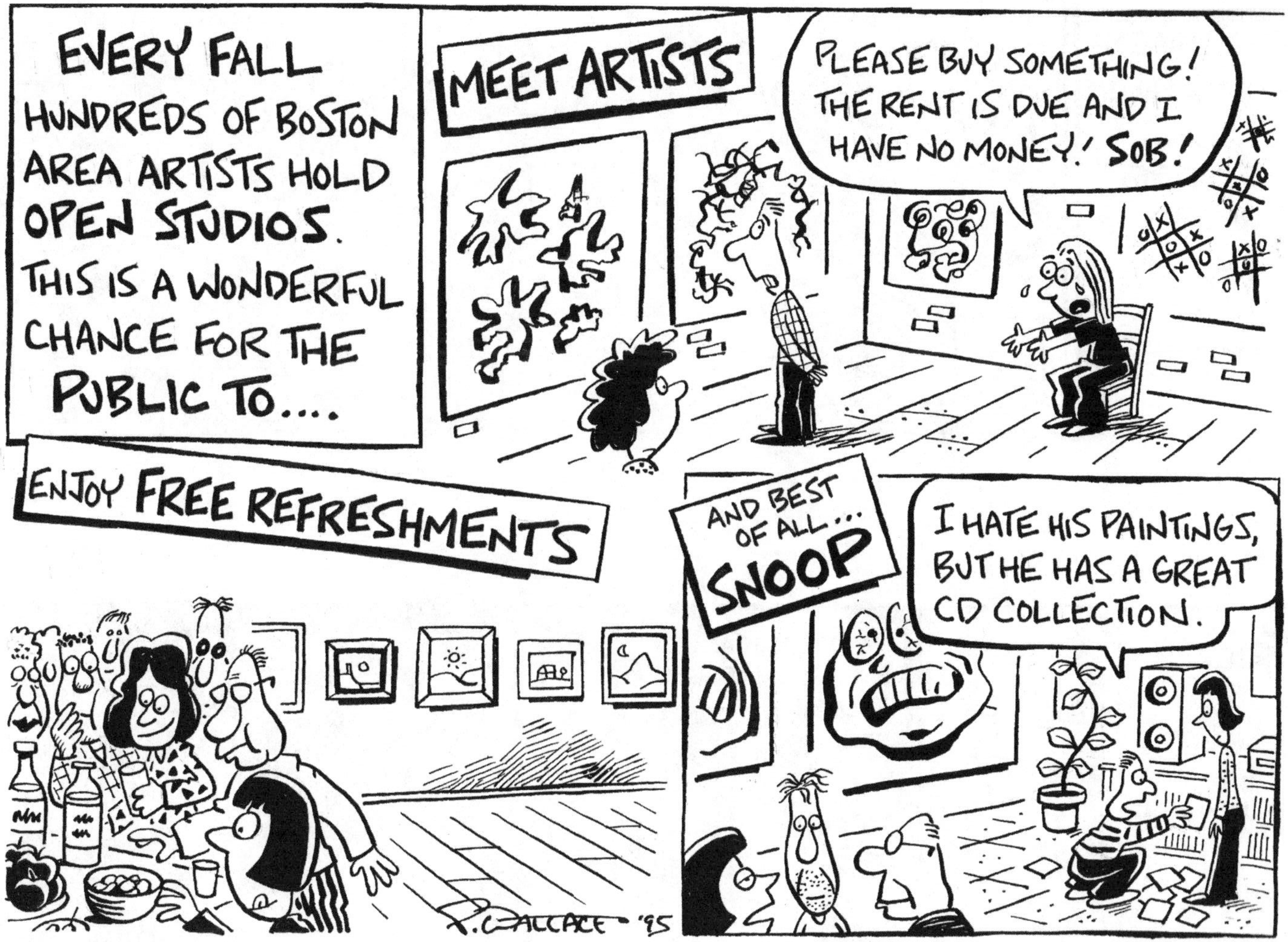
EVERY FALL HUNDREDS OF BOSTON AREA ARTISTS HOLD OPEN STUDIOS. THIS IS A WONDERFUL CHANCE FOR THE PUBLIC TO....
MEET ARTISTS
PLEASE BUY SOMETHING! THE RENT IS DUE AND I HAVE NO MONEY! SOB!
ENJOY FREE REFRESHMENTS
AND BEST OF ALL... SNOOP
I HATE HIS PAINTINGS, BUT HE HAS A GREAT CD COLLECTION.
R. WALLACE '95

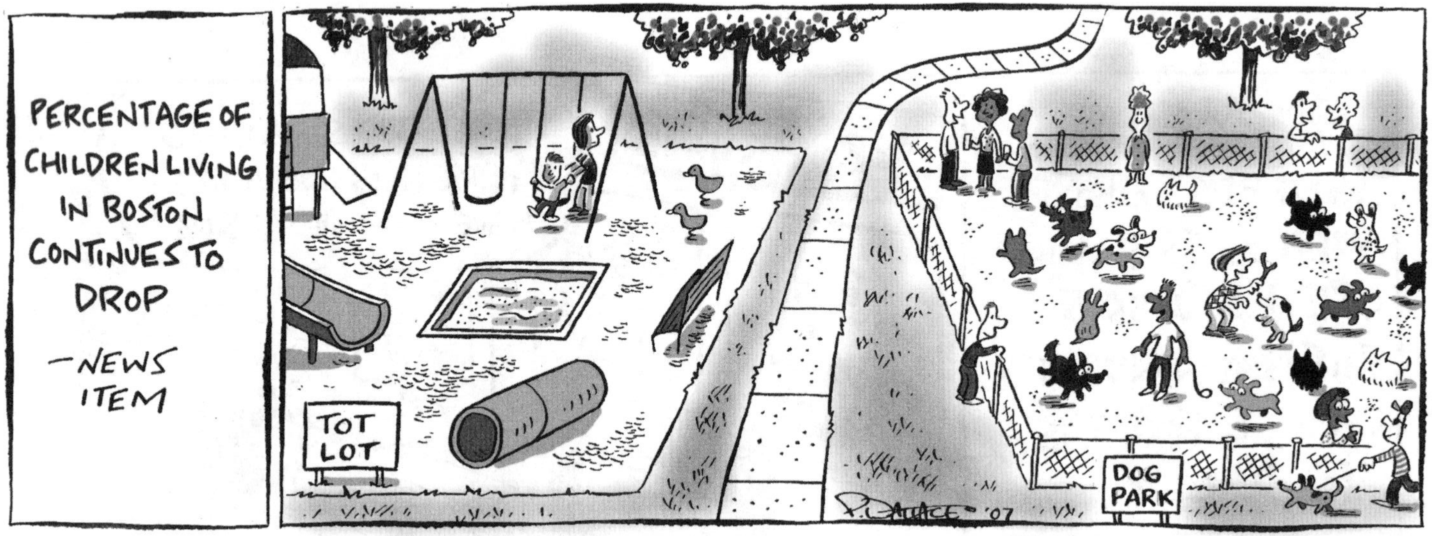
PERCENTAGE OF CHILDREN LIVING IN BOSTON CONTINUES TO DROP
—NEWS ITEM
TOT LOT
DOG PARK
P. WALLACE '07

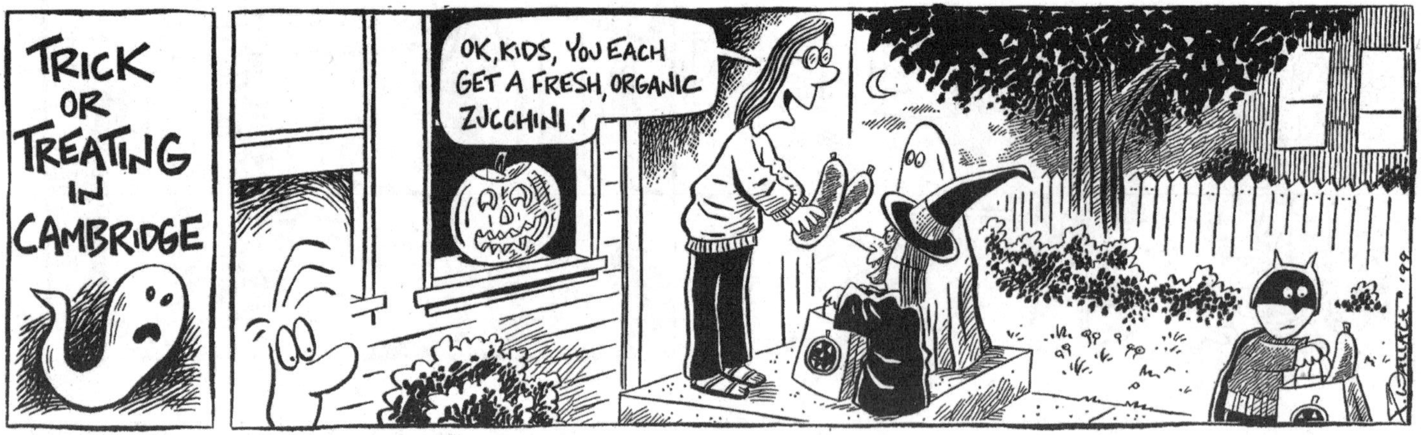
TRICK OR TREATING IN CAMBRIDGE
OK, KIDS, YOU EACH GET A FRESH, ORGANIC ZUCCHINI!

GREAT BOSTON DAREDEVILS

COPLEY PLACE, JUNE 12, 1998

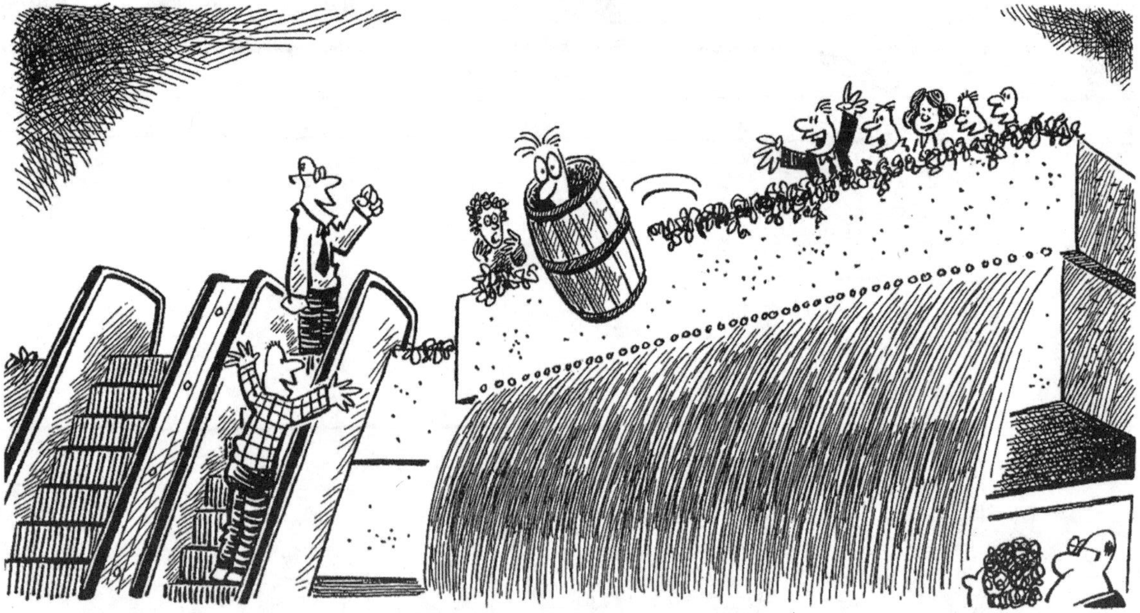

HAROLD FIG BECOMES THE FIRST MAN TO GO OVER THE WESTIN HOTEL WATERFALL IN A BARREL!

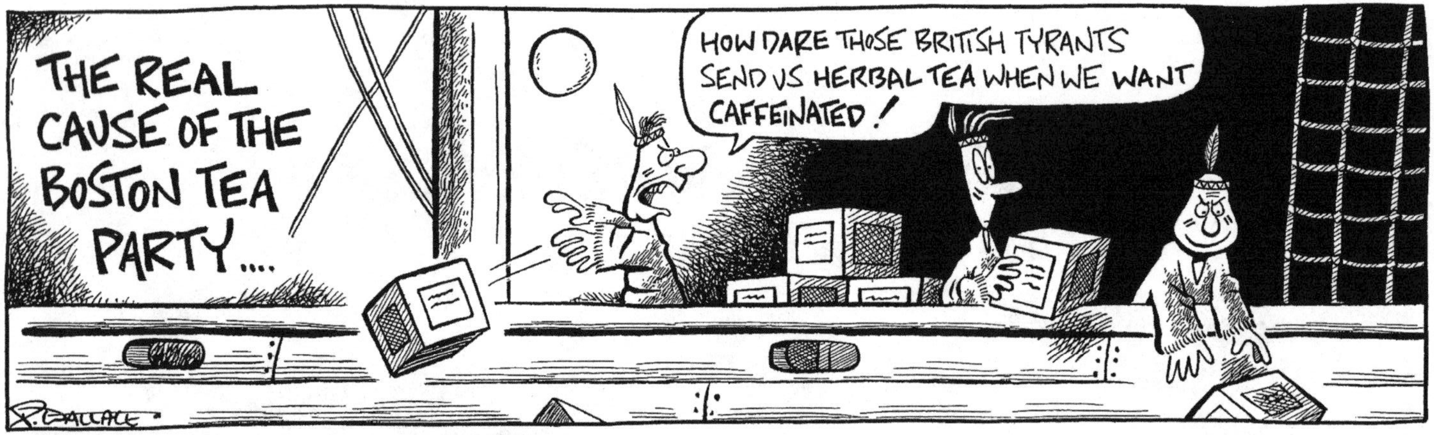
THE REAL CAUSE OF THE BOSTON TEA PARTY....
HOW DARE THOSE BRITISH TYRANTS SEND US HERBAL TEA WHEN WE WANT CAFFEINATED!
P. WALLACE

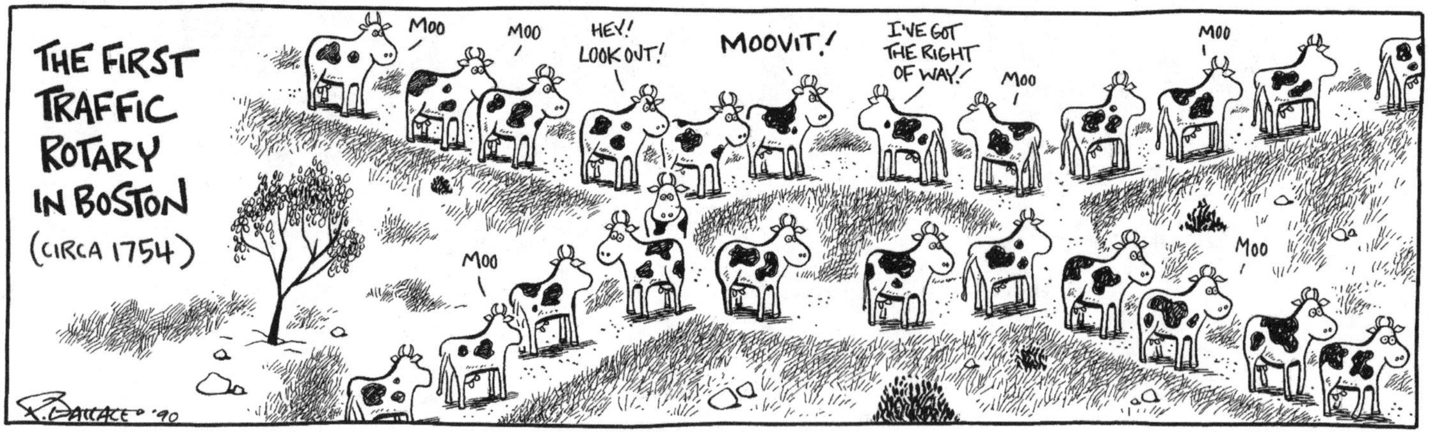
THE FIRST TRAFFIC ROTARY IN BOSTON
(CIRCA 1754)
MOO
MOO
HEY! LOOK OUT!
MOOVIT!
I'VE GOT THE RIGHT OF WAY!
MOO
MOO
MOO
MOO
P. WALLACE '90

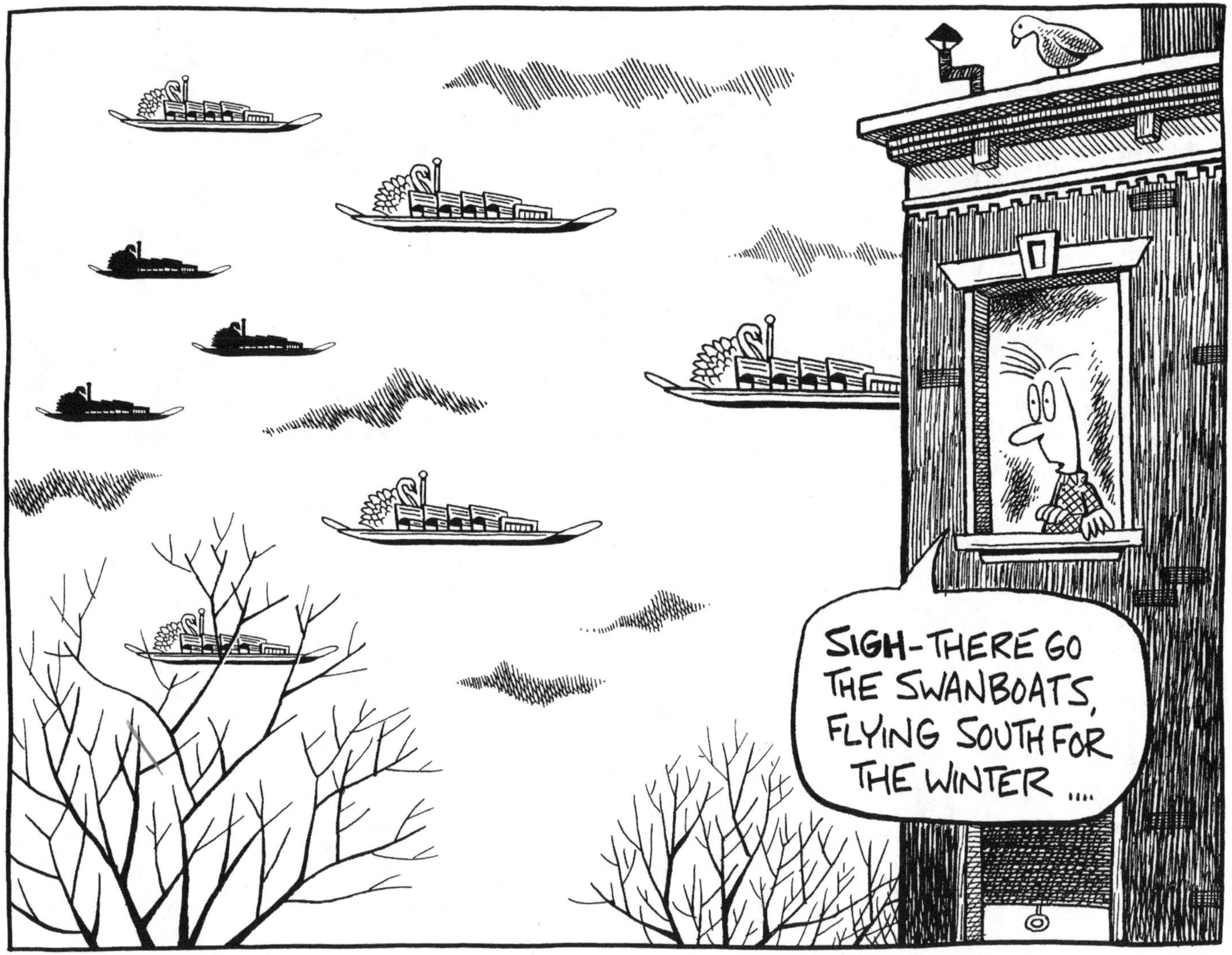
SIGH- THERE GO THE SWANBOATS, FLYING SOUTH FOR THE WINTER ....

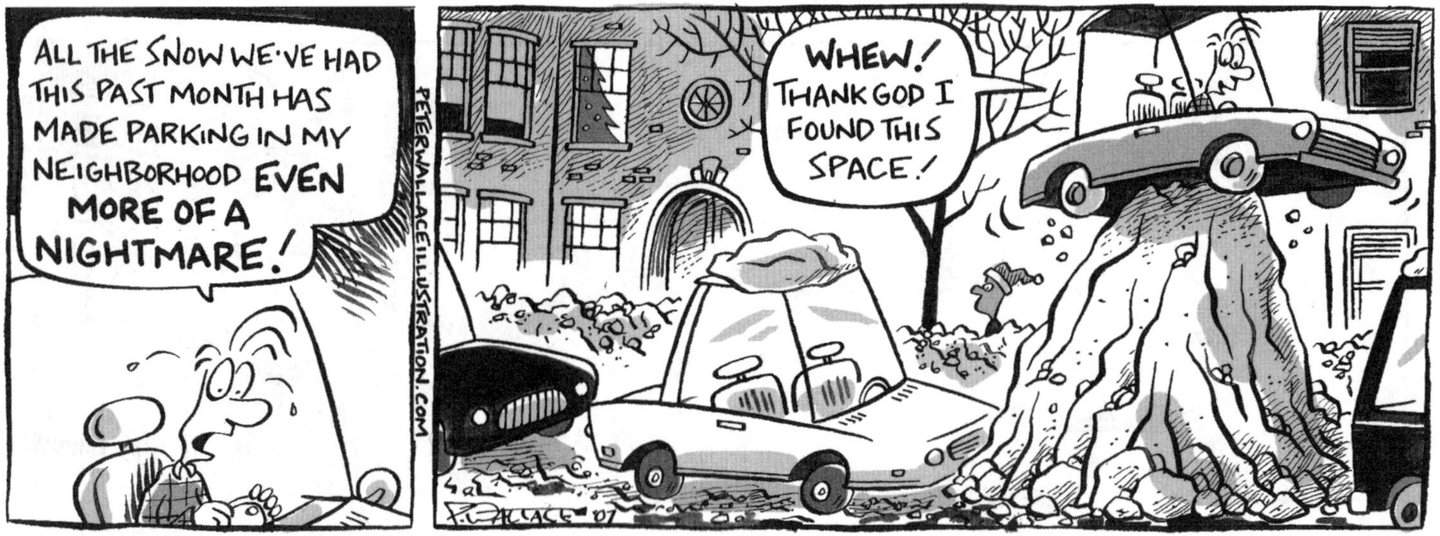
ALL THE SNOW WE'VE HAD THIS PAST MONTH HAS MADE PARKING IN MY NEIGHBORHOOD EVEN MORE OF A NIGHTMARE!
PETERWALLACEILLUSTRATION.COM
WHEW! THANK GOD I FOUND THIS SPACE!
P. WALLACE '07

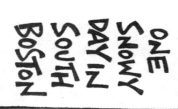

ONE SNOWY DAY IN SOUTH BOSTON

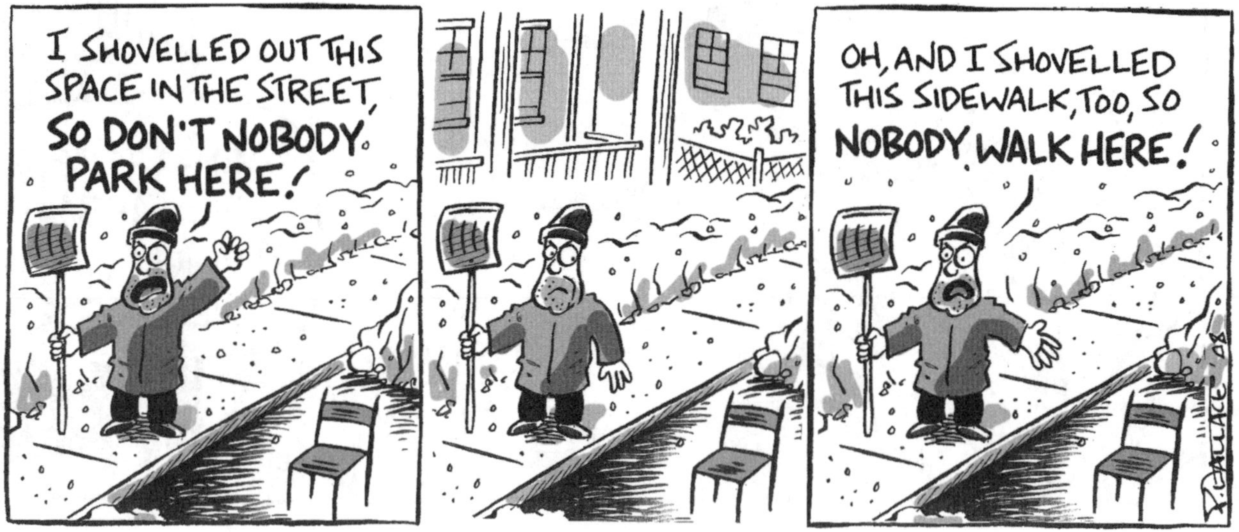
I SHOVELLED OUT THIS SPACE IN THE STREET, SO DON'T NOBODY PARK HERE!
OH, AND I SHOVELLED THIS SIDEWALK, TOO, SO NOBODY WALK HERE!
P. WALLACE '08

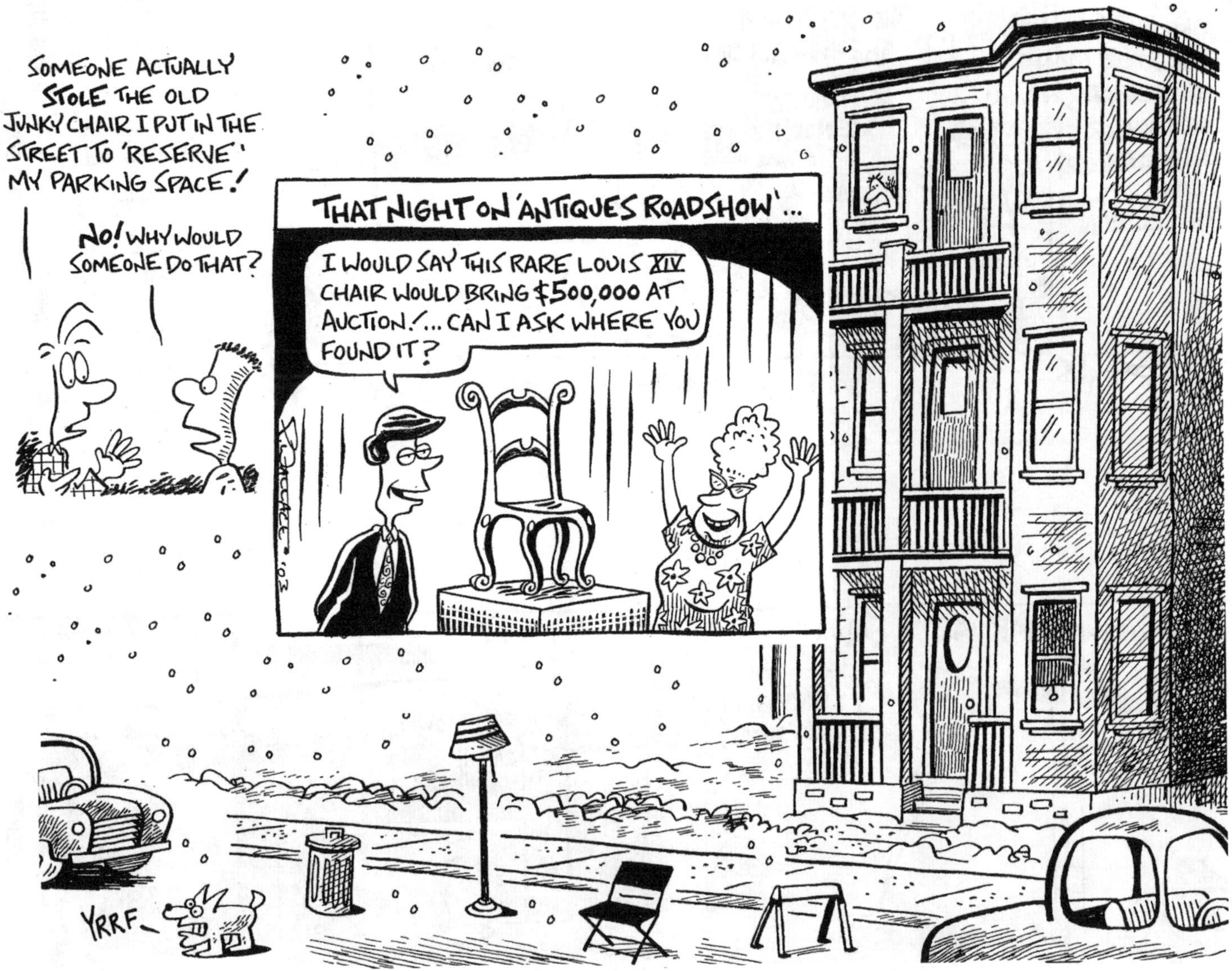

SOMEONE ACTUALLY STOLE THE OLD JUNKY CHAIR I PUT IN THE STREET TO 'RESERVE' MY PARKING SPACE!
NO! WHY WOULD SOMEONE DO THAT?
THAT NIGHT ON 'ANTIQUES ROADSHOW'...
I WOULD SAY THIS RARE LOUIS XIV CHAIR WOULD BRING $500,000 AT AUCTION!... CAN I ASK WHERE YOU FOUND IT?
YRRF
P. WALLACE '03

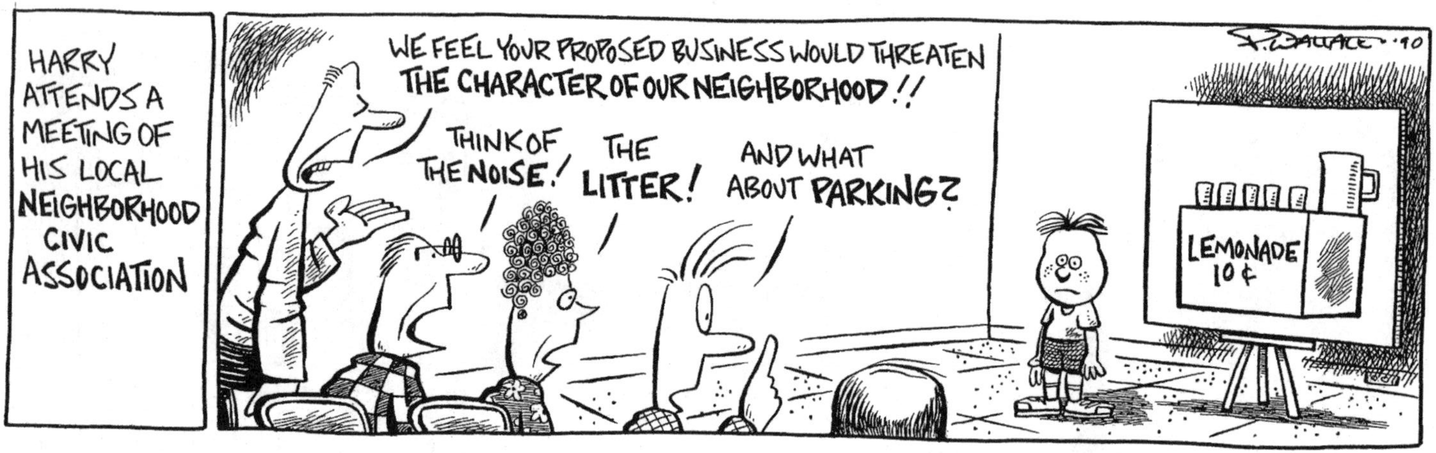
HARRY ATTENDS A MEETING OF HIS LOCAL NEIGHBORHOOD CIVIC ASSOCIATION
WE FEEL YOUR PROPOSED BUSINESS WOULD THREATEN THE CHARACTER OF OUR NEIGHBORHOOD!!
THINK OF THE NOISE!
THE LITTER!
AND WHAT ABOUT PARKING?
LEMONADE 10¢
R. WALLACE '90

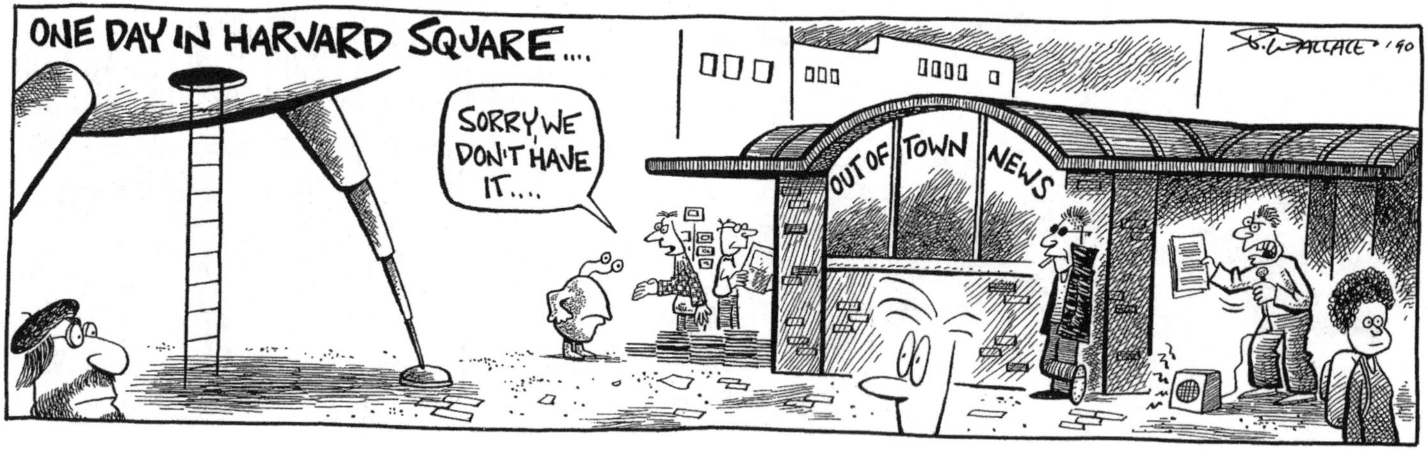
ONE DAY IN HARVARD SQUARE....
SORRY, WE DON'T HAVE IT....
OUT OF TOWN NEWS
R. WALLACE '90

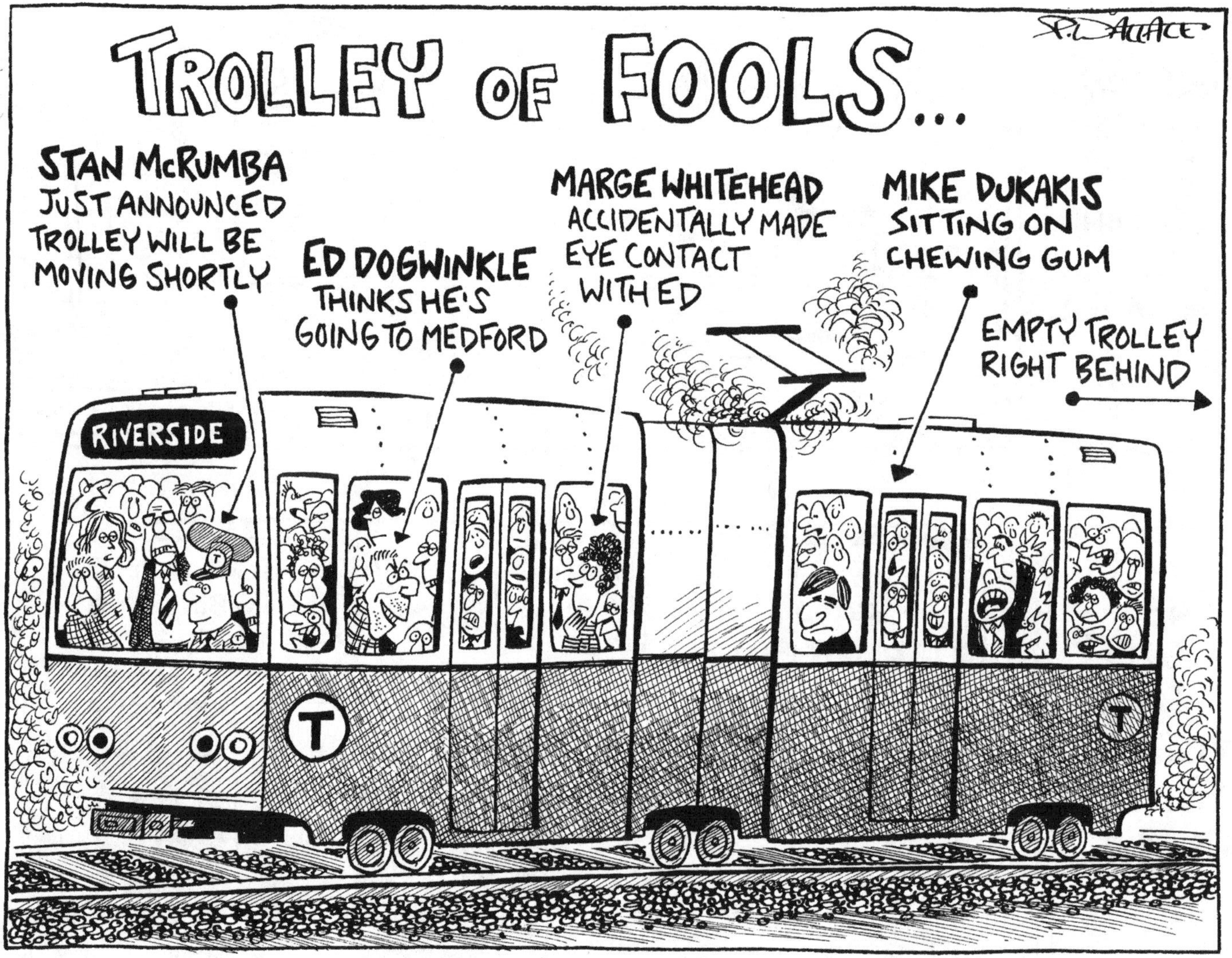
P. WALLACE
TROLLEY OF FOOLS...
STAN McRUMBA JUST ANNOUNCED TROLLEY WILL BE MOVING SHORTLY
ED DOGWINKLE THINKS HE'S GOING TO MEDFORD
MARGE WHITEHEAD ACCIDENTALLY MADE EYE CONTACT WITH ED
MIKE DUKAKIS SITTING ON CHEWING GUM
EMPTY TROLLEY RIGHT BEHIND
RIVERSIDE
T

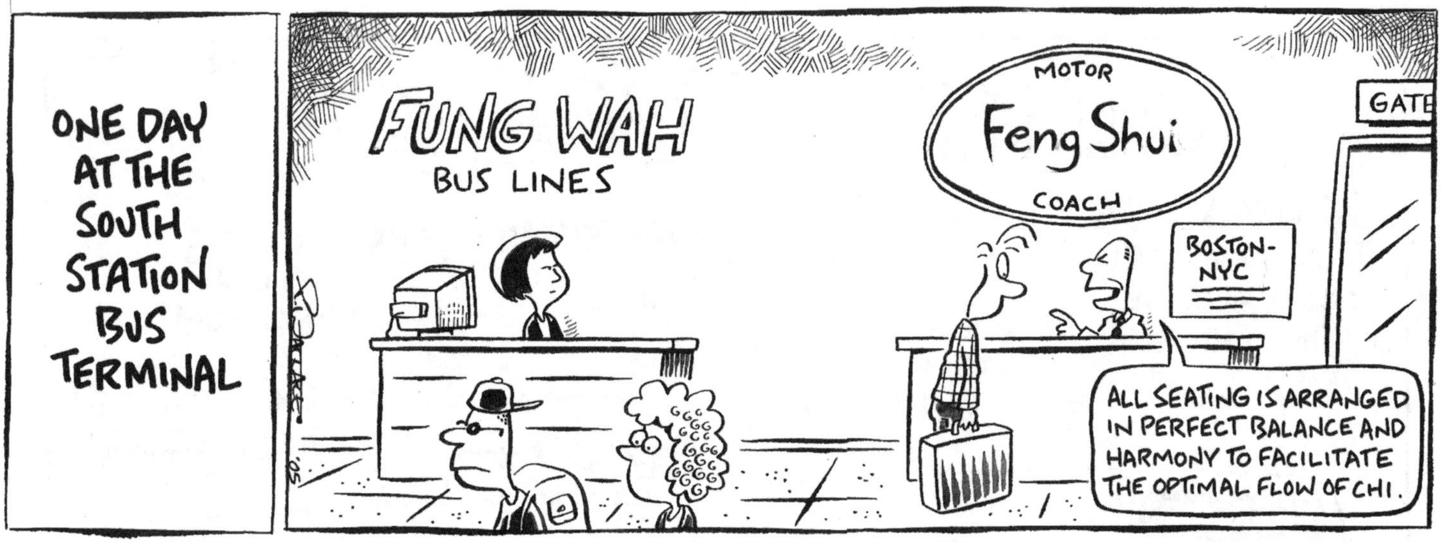
ONE DAY AT THE SOUTH STATION BUS TERMINAL
FUNG WAH BUS LINES
MOTOR Feng Shui COACH
BOSTON-NYC
GATE
ALL SEATING IS ARRANGED IN PERFECT BALANCE AND HARMONY TO FACILITATE THE OPTIMAL FLOW OF CHI.

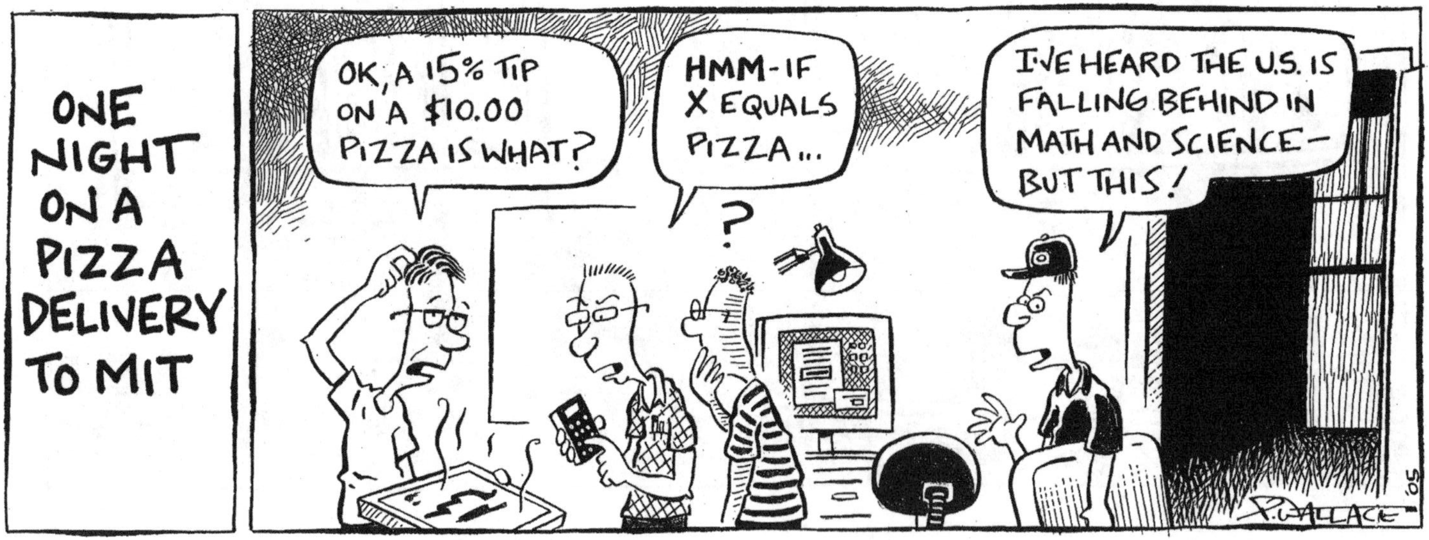
ONE NIGHT ON A PIZZA DELIVERY TO MIT
OK, A 15% TIP ON A $10.00 PIZZA IS WHAT?
HMM-IF X EQUALS PIZZA...
?
I'VE HEARD THE U.S. IS FALLING BEHIND IN MATH AND SCIENCE— BUT THIS!
P. WALLACE '05

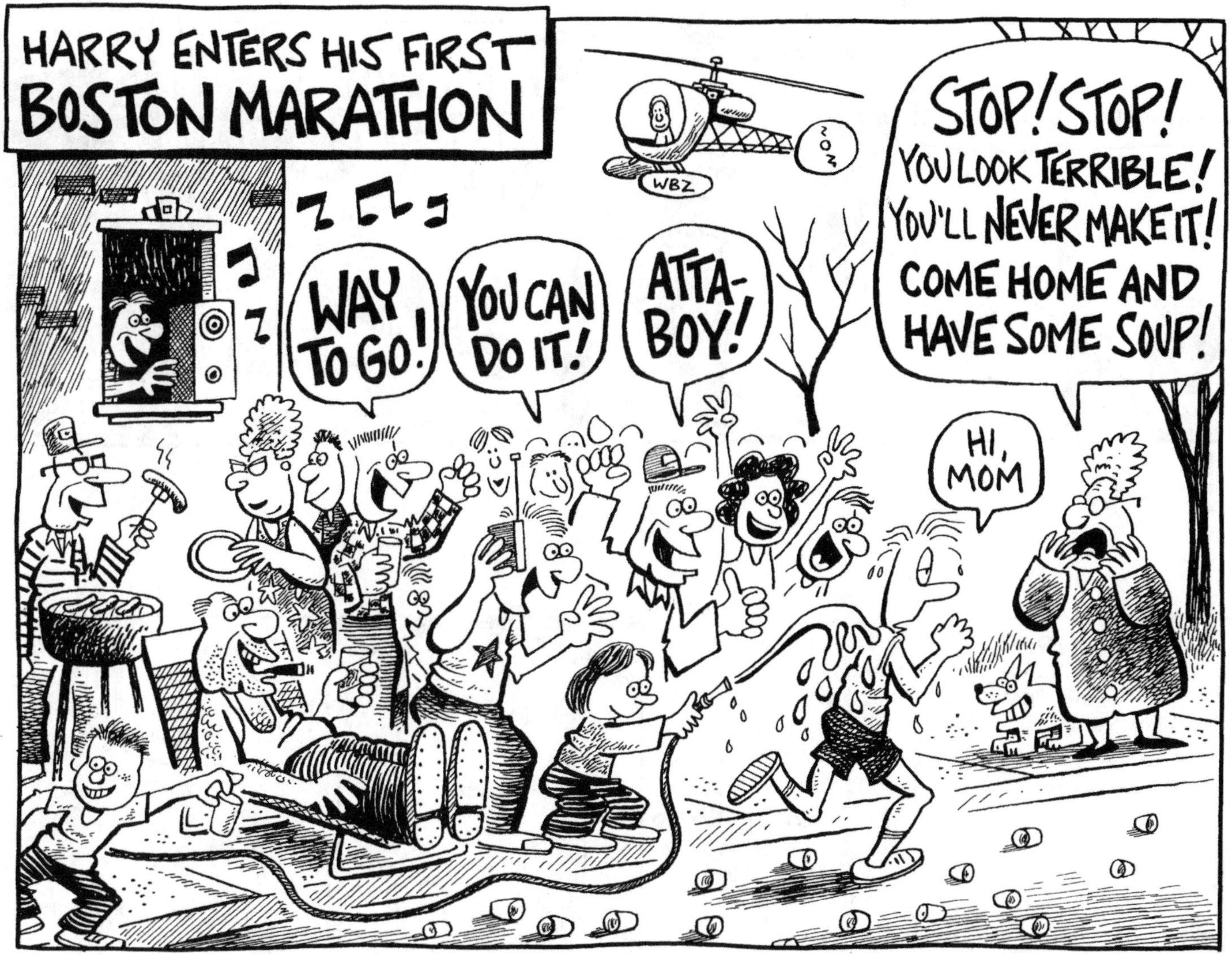
HARRY ENTERS HIS FIRST BOSTON MARATHON
WBZ
WAY TO GO!
YOU CAN DO IT!
ATTA-BOY!
STOP! STOP! YOU LOOK TERRIBLE! YOU'LL NEVER MAKE IT! COME HOME AND HAVE SOME SOUP!
HI, MOM

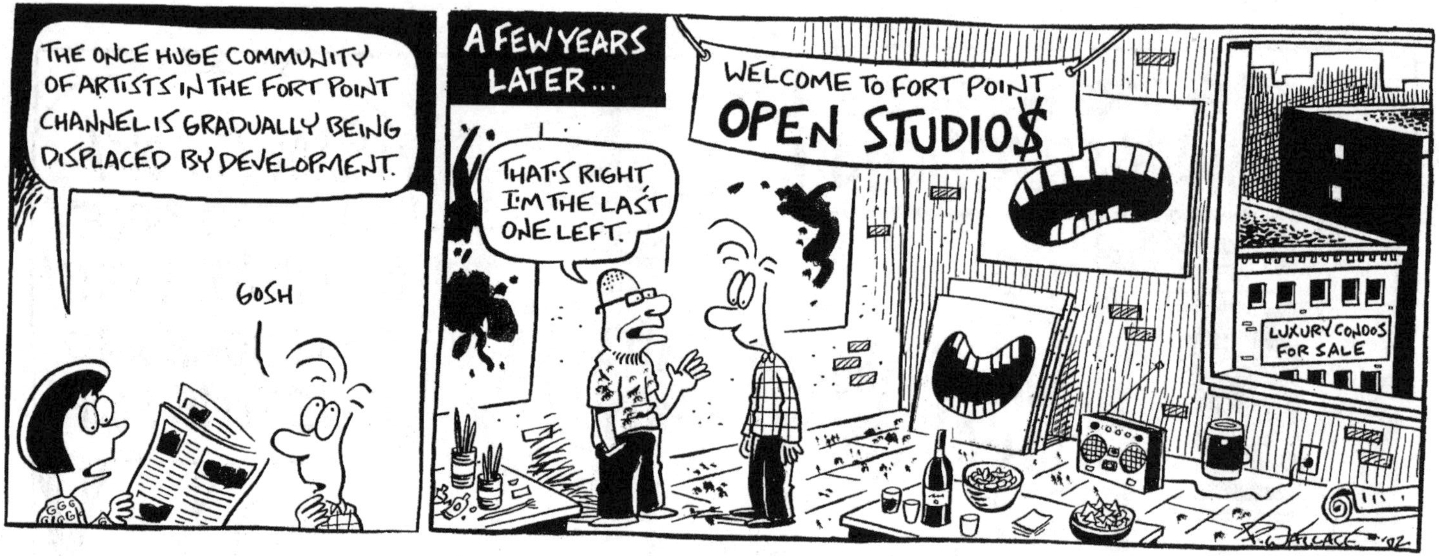
THE ONCE HUGE COMMUNITY OF ARTISTS IN THE FORT POINT CHANNEL IS GRADUALLY BEING DISPLACED BY DEVELOPMENT.
GOSH
A FEW YEARS LATER...
WELCOME TO FORT POINT OPEN STUDIO$
THAT'S RIGHT. I'M THE LAST ONE LEFT.
LUXURY CONDOS FOR SALE

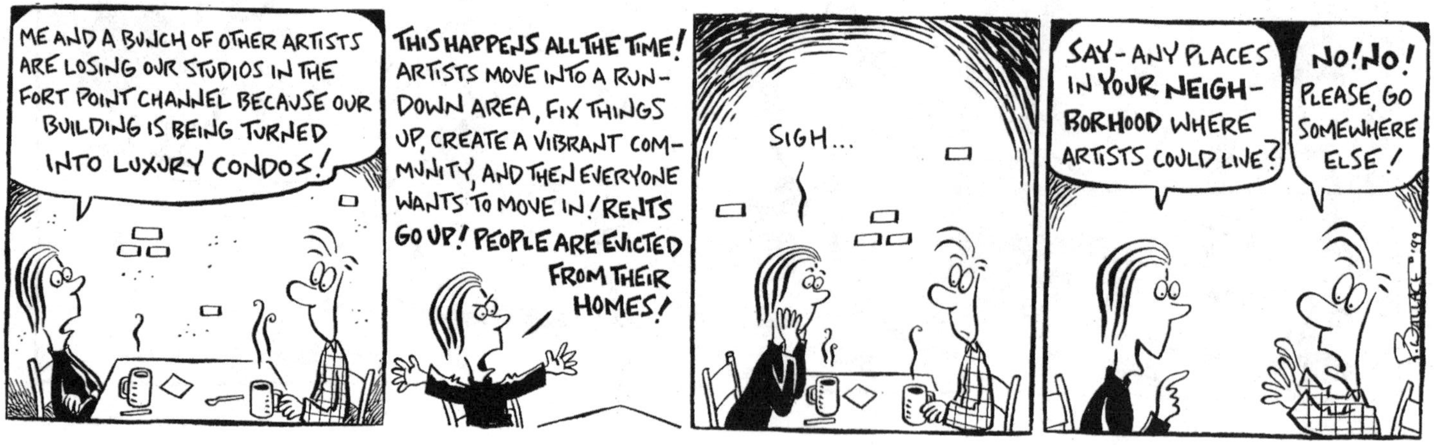
ME AND A BUNCH OF OTHER ARTISTS ARE LOSING OUR STUDIOS IN THE FORT POINT CHANNEL BECAUSE OUR BUILDING IS BEING TURNED INTO LUXURY CONDOS!
THIS HAPPENS ALL THE TIME! ARTISTS MOVE INTO A RUN-DOWN AREA, FIX THINGS UP, CREATE A VIBRANT COMMUNITY, AND THEN EVERYONE WANTS TO MOVE IN! RENTS GO UP! PEOPLE ARE EVICTED FROM THEIR HOMES!
SIGH...
SAY-ANY PLACES IN YOUR NEIGHBORHOOD WHERE ARTISTS COULD LIVE?
NO! NO! PLEASE, GO SOMEWHERE ELSE!

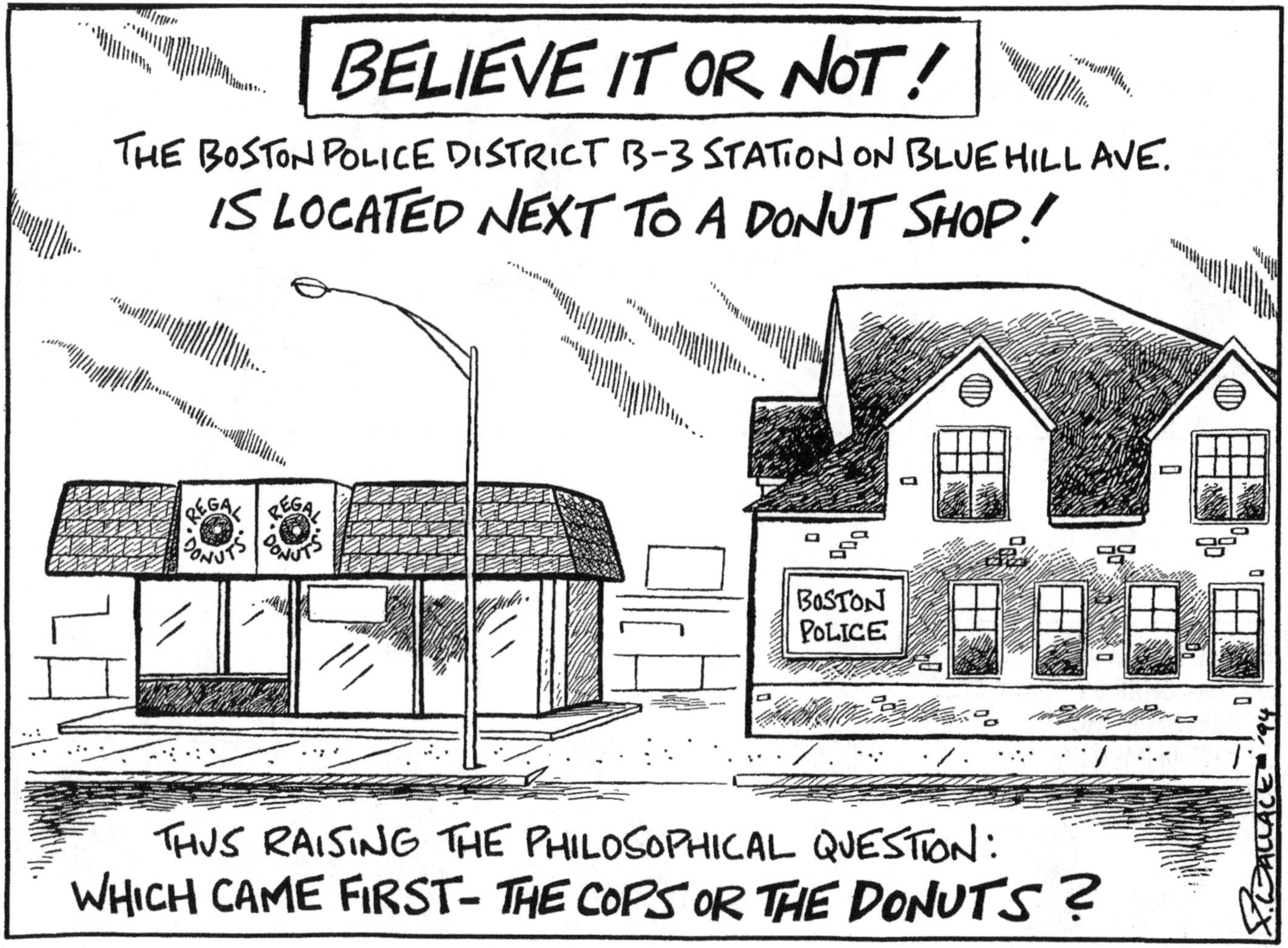
BELIEVE IT OR NOT!
THE BOSTON POLICE DISTRICT B-3 STATION ON BLUE HILL AVE.
IS LOCATED NEXT TO A DONUT SHOP!
REGAL DONUTS
REGAL DONUTS
BOSTON POLICE
THUS RAISING THE PHILOSOPHICAL QUESTION:
WHICH CAME FIRST- THE COPS OR THE DONUTS?

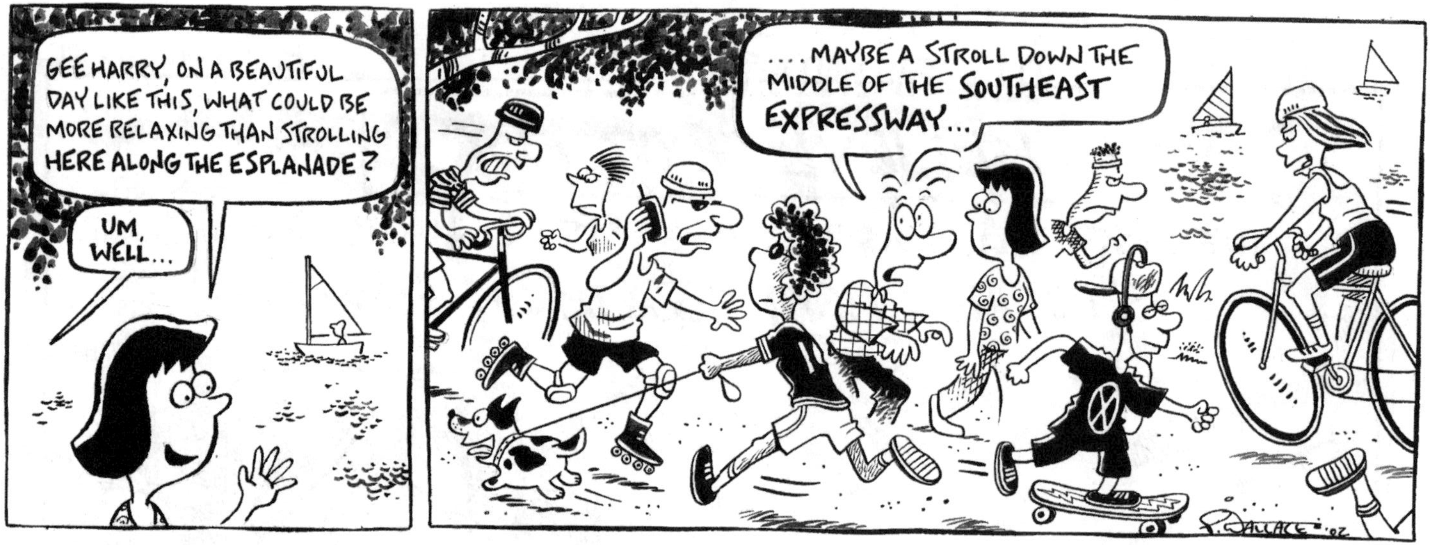
GEE HARRY, ON A BEAUTIFUL DAY LIKE THIS, WHAT COULD BE MORE RELAXING THAN STROLLING HERE ALONG THE ESPLANADE?
UM, WELL...
....MAYBE A STROLL DOWN THE MIDDLE OF THE SOUTHEAST EXPRESSWAY...
P. WALLACE '02

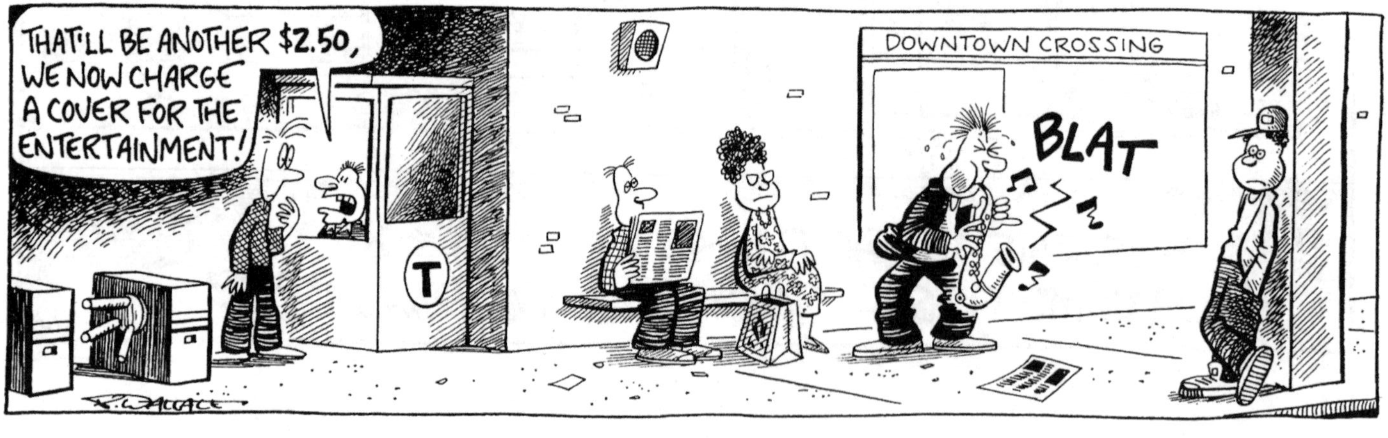
THAT'LL BE ANOTHER $2.50, WE NOW CHARGE A COVER FOR THE ENTERTAINMENT!
T
DOWNTOWN CROSSING
BLAT
P. WALLACE

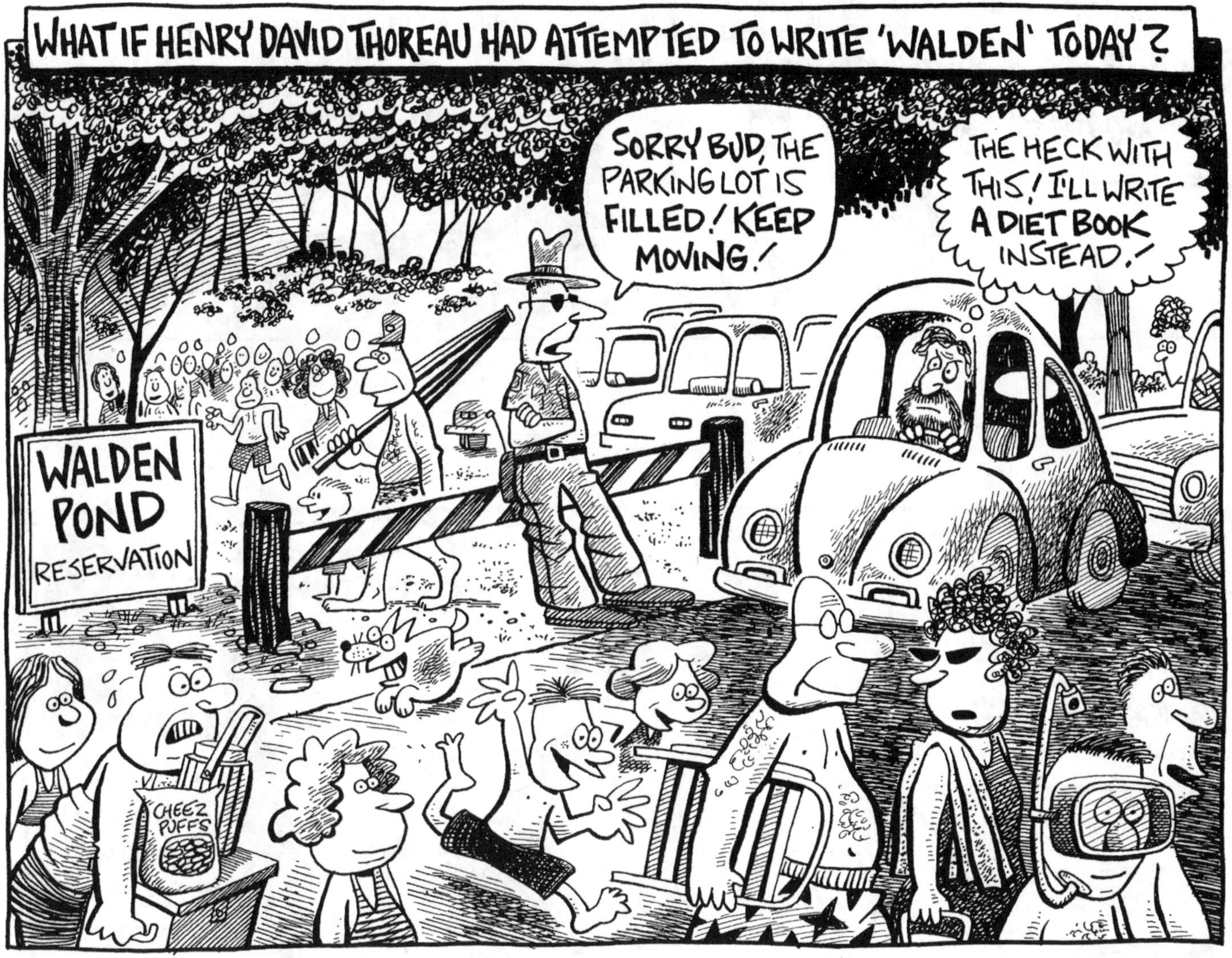
WHAT IF HENRY DAVID THOREAU HAD ATTEMPTED TO WRITE 'WALDEN' TODAY?
SORRY BUD, THE PARKING LOT IS FILLED! KEEP MOVING!
THE HECK WITH THIS! I'LL WRITE A DIET BOOK INSTEAD!
WALDEN POND RESERVATION
CHEEZ PUFFS

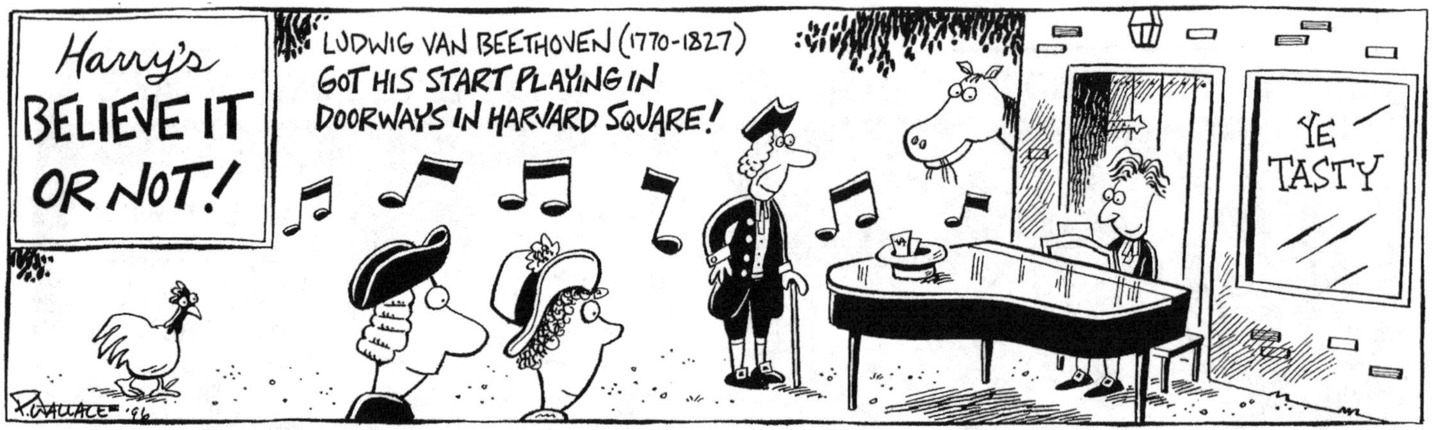
Harry's BELIEVE IT OR NOT!
LUDWIG VAN BEETHOVEN (1770-1827) GOT HIS START PLAYING IN DOORWAYS IN HARVARD SQUARE!
YE TASTY
P. WALLACE '96

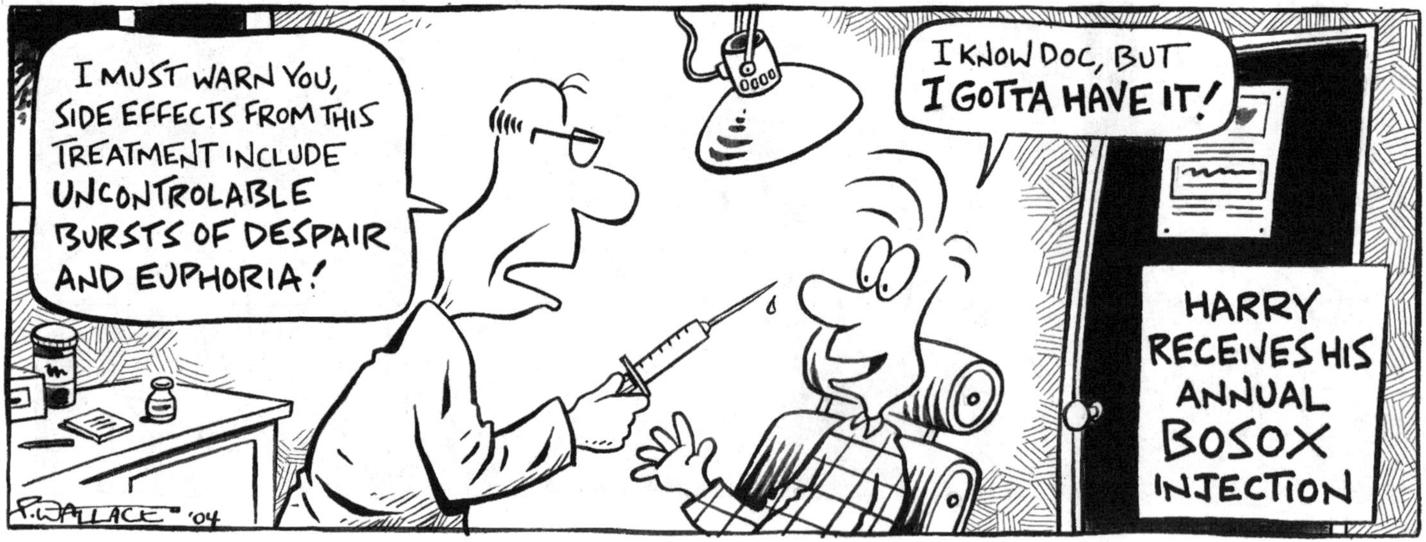
I MUST WARN YOU, SIDE EFFECTS FROM THIS TREATMENT INCLUDE UNCONTROLABLE BURSTS OF DESPAIR AND EUPHORIA!
I KNOW DOC, BUT I GOTTA HAVE IT!
HARRY RECEIVES HIS ANNUAL BOSOX INJECTION
P. WALLACE '04

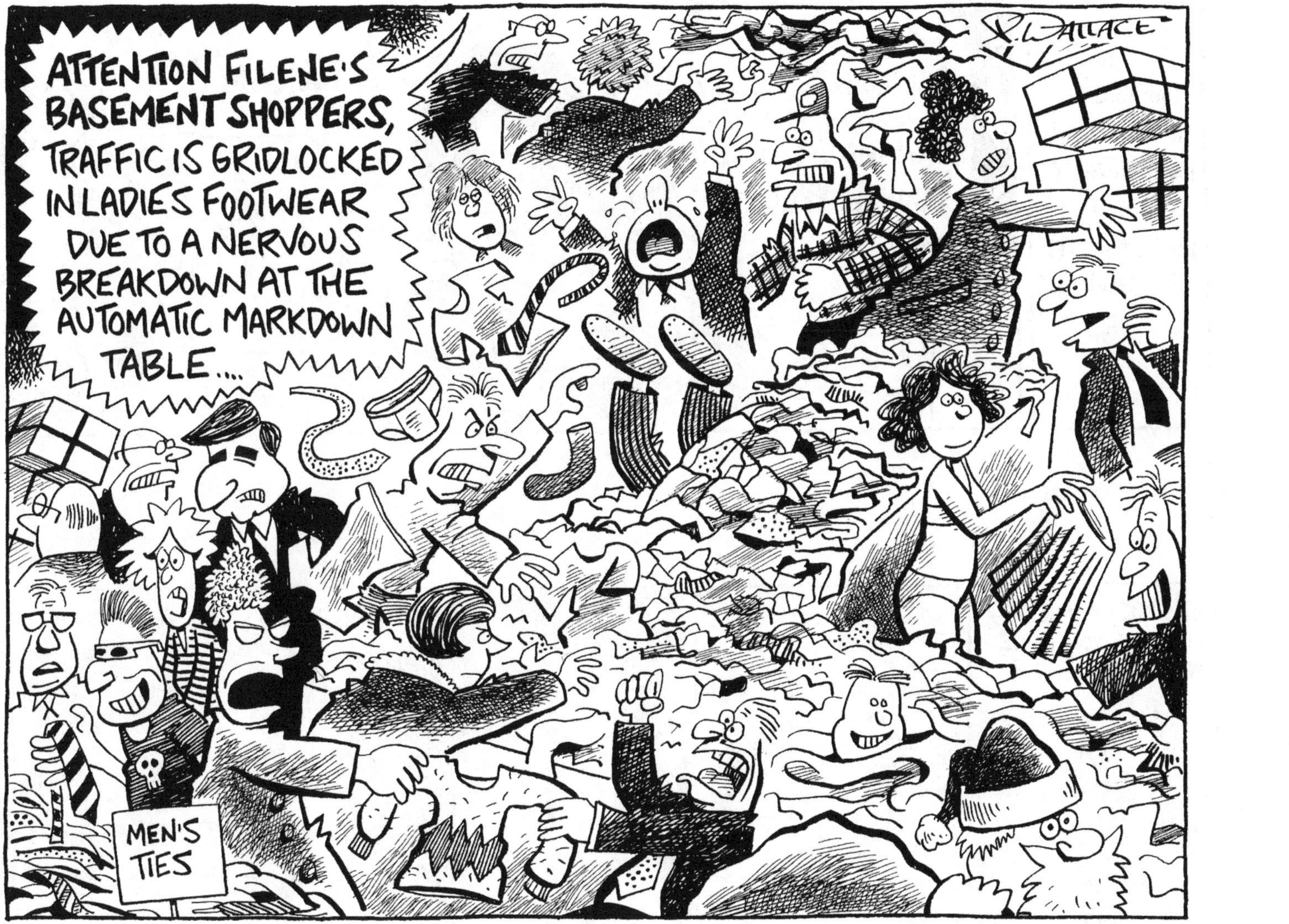
ATTENTION FILENE'S BASEMENT SHOPPERS, TRAFFIC IS GRIDLOCKED IN LADIES FOOTWEAR DUE TO A NERVOUS BREAKDOWN AT THE AUTOMATIC MARKDOWN TABLE....
MEN'S TIES
R. WALLACE

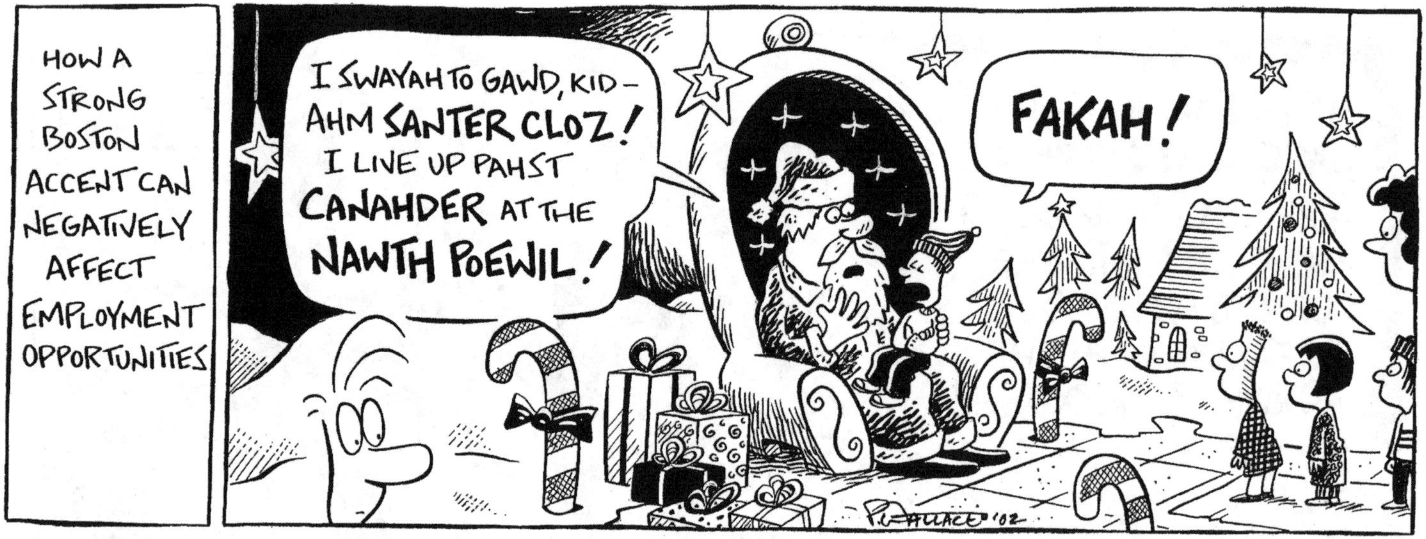
HOW A STRONG BOSTON ACCENT CAN NEGATIVELY AFFECT EMPLOYMENT OPPORTUNITIES
I SWAYAH TO GAWD, KID — AHM SANTER CLOZ! I LIVE UP PAHST CANAHDER AT THE NAWTH POEWIL!
FAKAH!

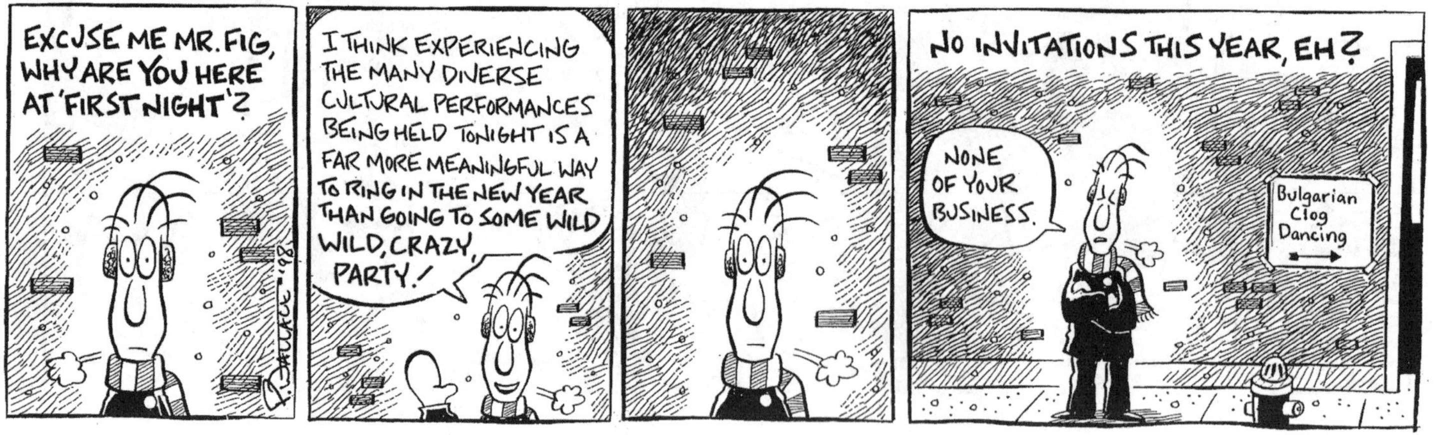
EXCUSE ME MR. FIG, WHY ARE YOU HERE AT 'FIRST NIGHT'?
I THINK EXPERIENCING THE MANY DIVERSE CULTURAL PERFORMANCES BEING HELD TONIGHT IS A FAR MORE MEANINGFUL WAY TO RING IN THE NEW YEAR THAN GOING TO SOME WILD WILD, CRAZY, PARTY!
NO INVITATIONS THIS YEAR, EH?
NONE OF YOUR BUSINESS.
Bulgarian Clog Dancing

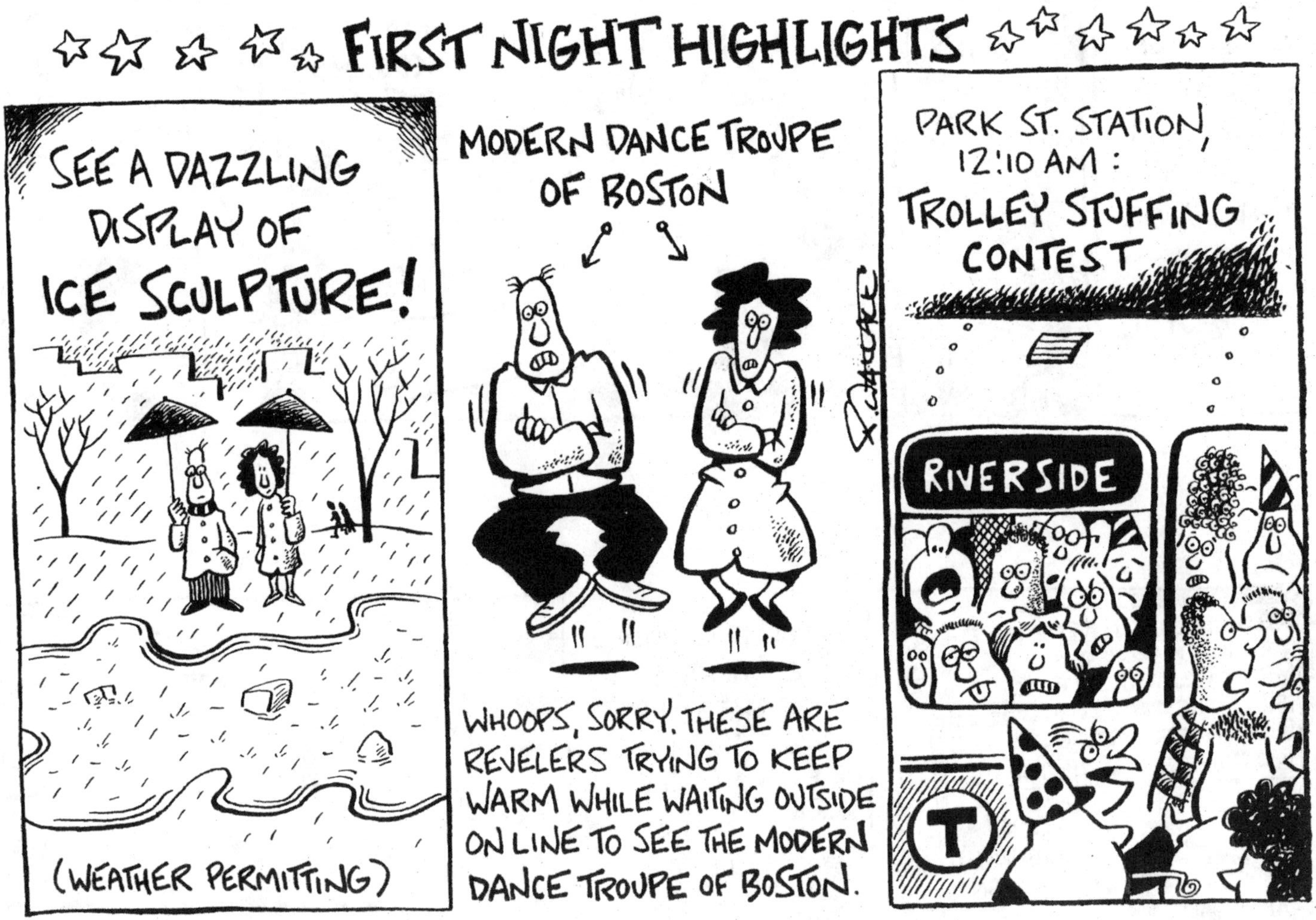
FIRST NIGHT HIGHLIGHTS
SEE A DAZZLING DISPLAY OF ICE SCULPTURE!
(WEATHER PERMITTING)
MODERN DANCE TROUPE OF BOSTON
WHOOPS, SORRY. THESE ARE REVELERS TRYING TO KEEP WARM WHILE WAITING OUTSIDE ON LINE TO SEE THE MODERN DANCE TROUPE OF BOSTON.
PARK ST. STATION, 12:10 AM: TROLLEY STUFFING CONTEST
RIVERSIDE
T

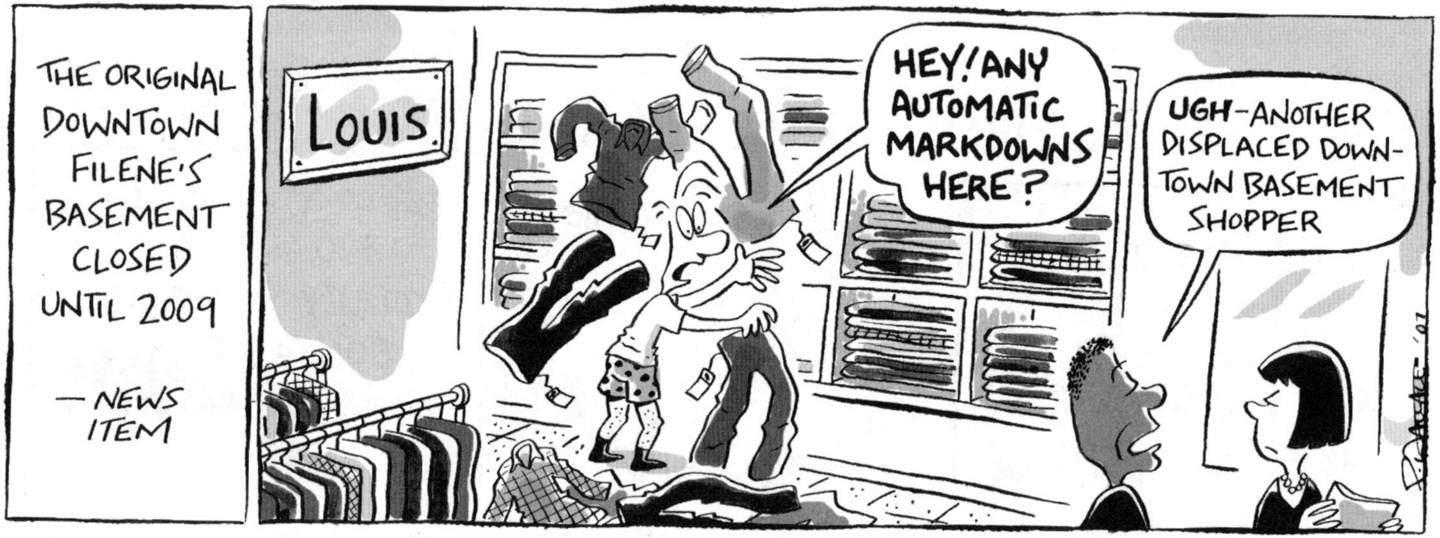
THE ORIGINAL DOWNTOWN FILENE'S BASEMENT CLOSED UNTIL 2009
— NEWS ITEM
LOUIS
HEY! ANY AUTOMATIC MARKDOWNS HERE?
UGH-ANOTHER DISPLACED DOWN-TOWN BASEMENT SHOPPER

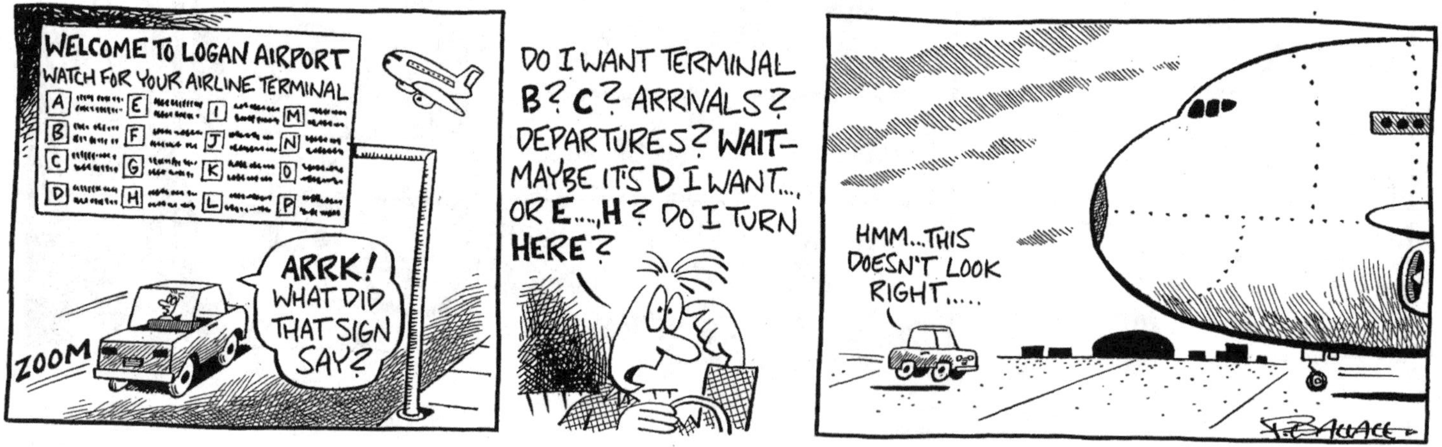
WELCOME TO LOGAN AIRPORT
WATCH FOR YOUR AIRLINE TERMINAL
A E I M B F J N C G K O D H L P
ARRK! WHAT DID THAT SIGN SAY?
ZOOM
DO I WANT TERMINAL B? C? ARRIVALS? DEPARTURES? WAIT-MAYBE IT'S D I WANT..., OR E...,H? DO I TURN HERE?
HMM...THIS DOESN'T LOOK RIGHT.....

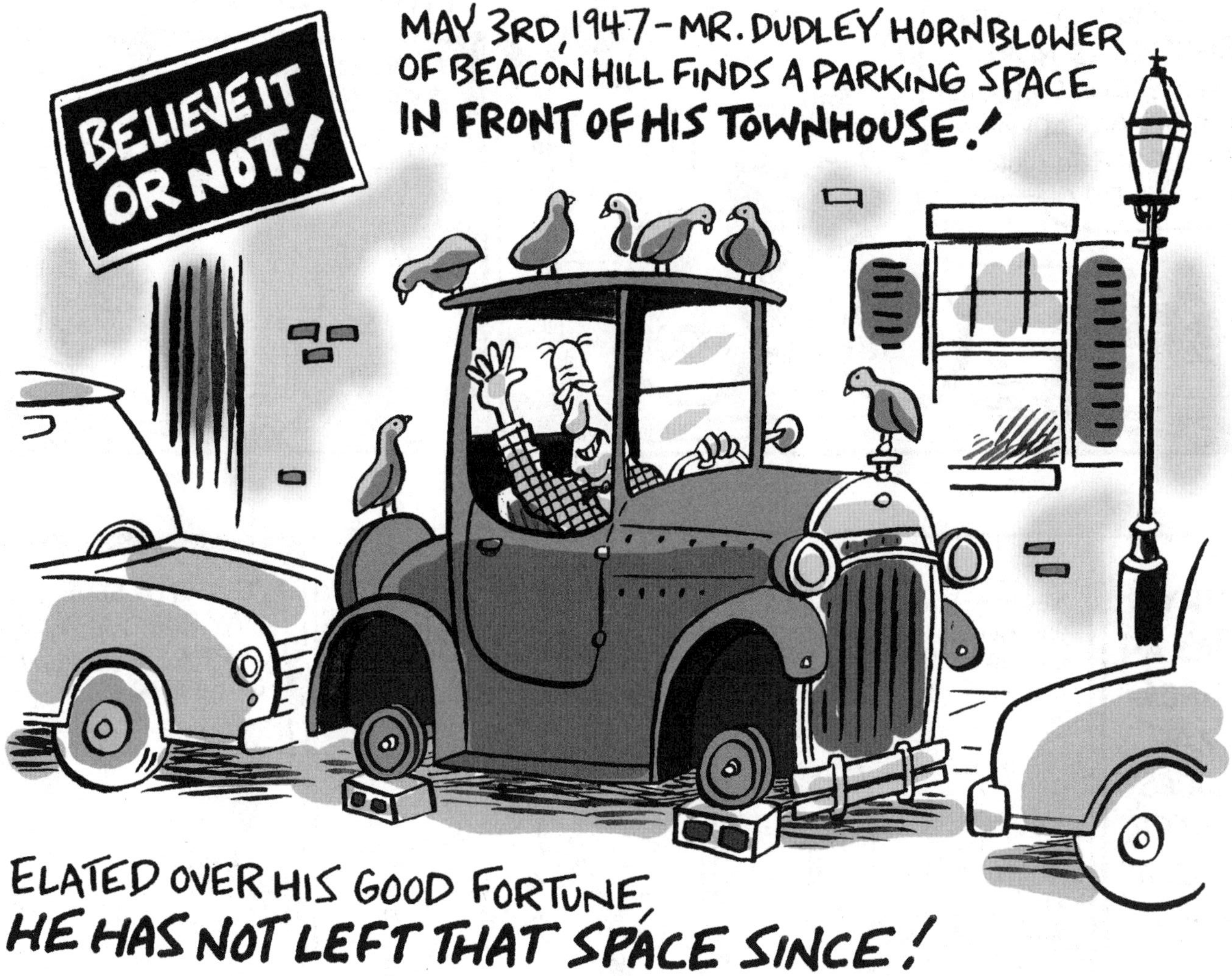
BELIEVE IT OR NOT!
MAY 3RD, 1947 – MR. DUDLEY HORNBLOWER OF BEACON HILL FINDS A PARKING SPACE IN FRONT OF HIS TOWNHOUSE!
ELATED OVER HIS GOOD FORTUNE, HE HAS NOT LEFT THAT SPACE SINCE!

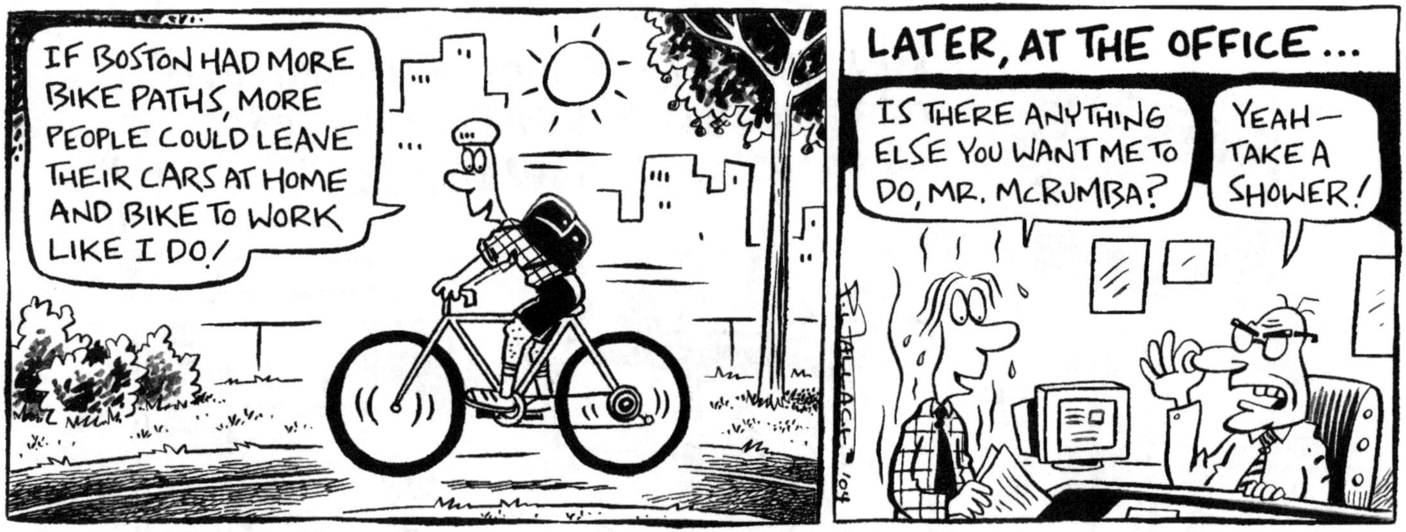
IF BOSTON HAD MORE BIKE PATHS, MORE PEOPLE COULD LEAVE THEIR CARS AT HOME AND BIKE TO WORK LIKE I DO!
LATER, AT THE OFFICE...
IS THERE ANYTHING ELSE YOU WANT ME TO DO, MR. MCRUMBA?
YEAH— TAKE A SHOWER!

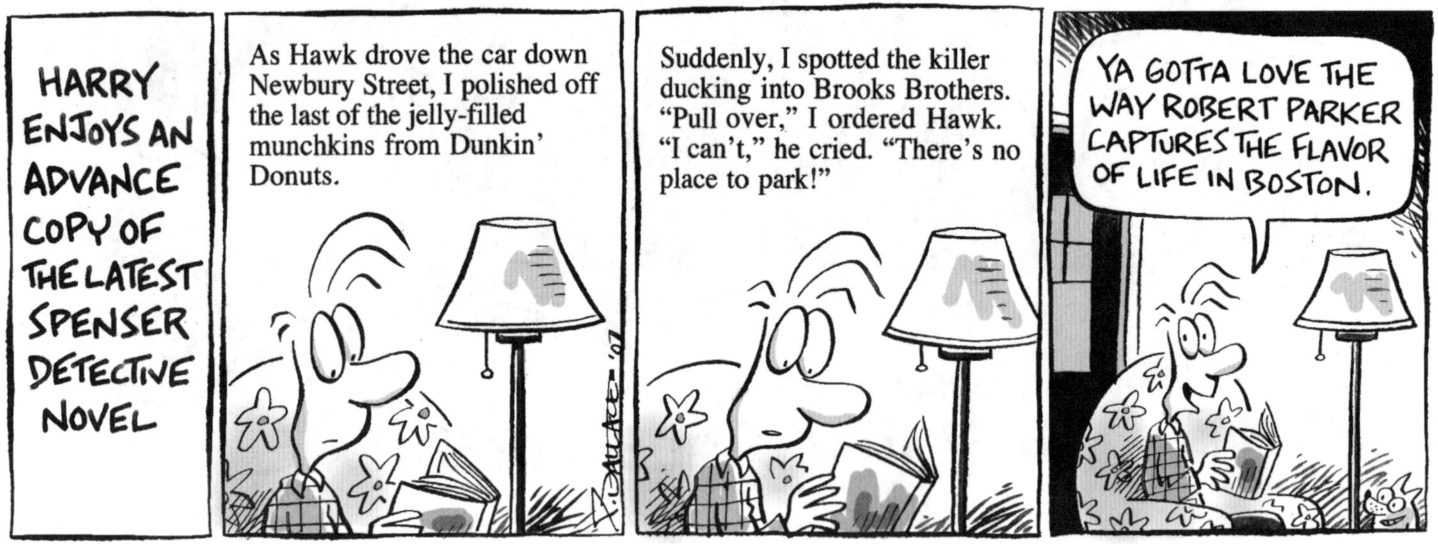
HARRY ENJOYS AN ADVANCE COPY OF THE LATEST SPENSER DETECTIVE NOVEL
As Hawk drove the car down Newbury Street, I polished off the last of the jelly-filled munchkins from Dunkin' Donuts.
Suddenly, I spotted the killer ducking into Brooks Brothers. "Pull over," I ordered Hawk. "I can't," he cried. "There's no place to park!"
YA GOTTA LOVE THE WAY ROBERT PARKER CAPTURES THE FLAVOR OF LIFE IN BOSTON.

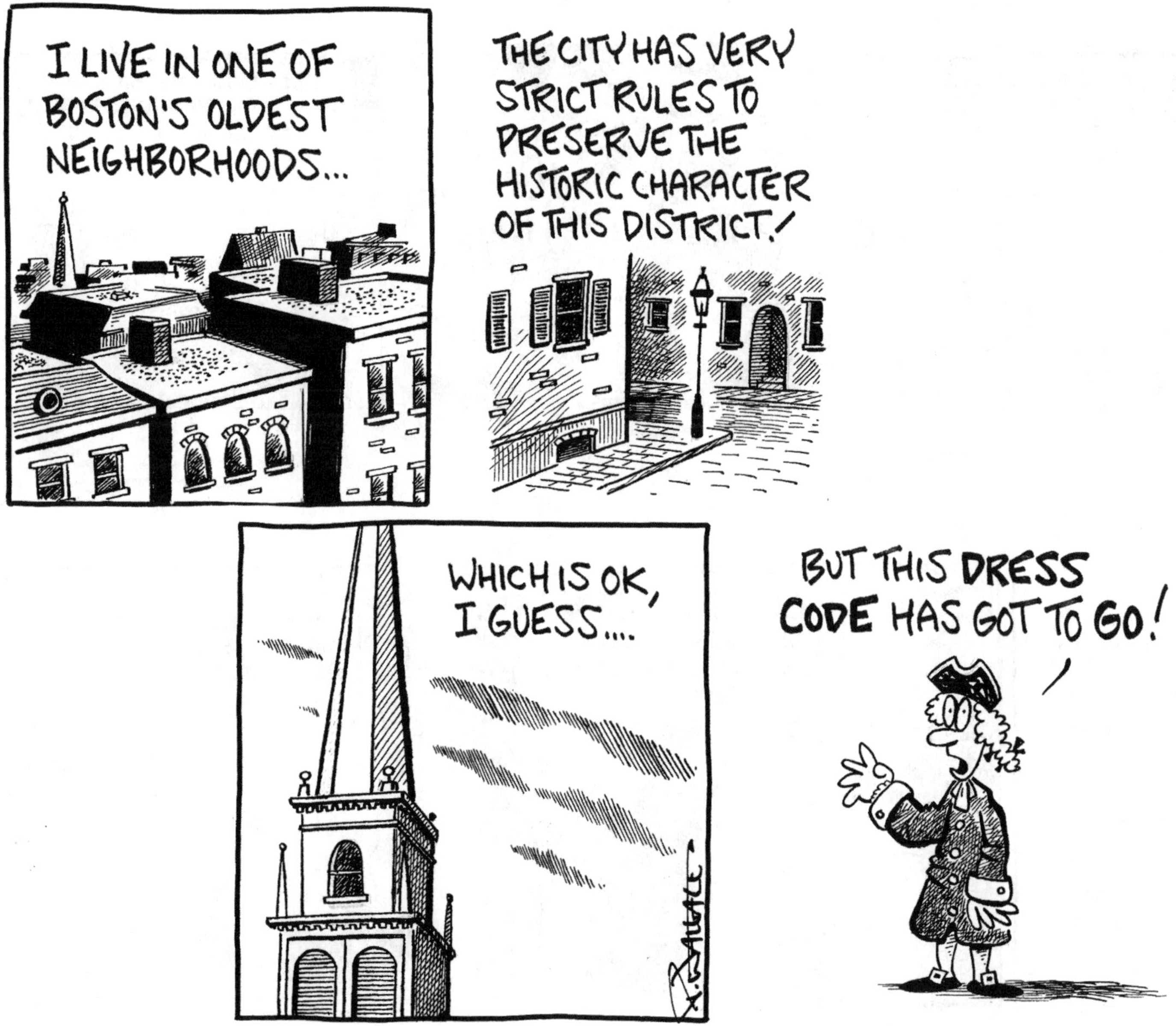
I LIVE IN ONE OF BOSTON'S OLDEST NEIGHBORHOODS...
THE CITY HAS VERY STRICT RULES TO PRESERVE THE HISTORIC CHARACTER OF THIS DISTRICT!
WHICH IS OK, I GUESS....
BUT THIS DRESS CODE HAS GOT TO GO!

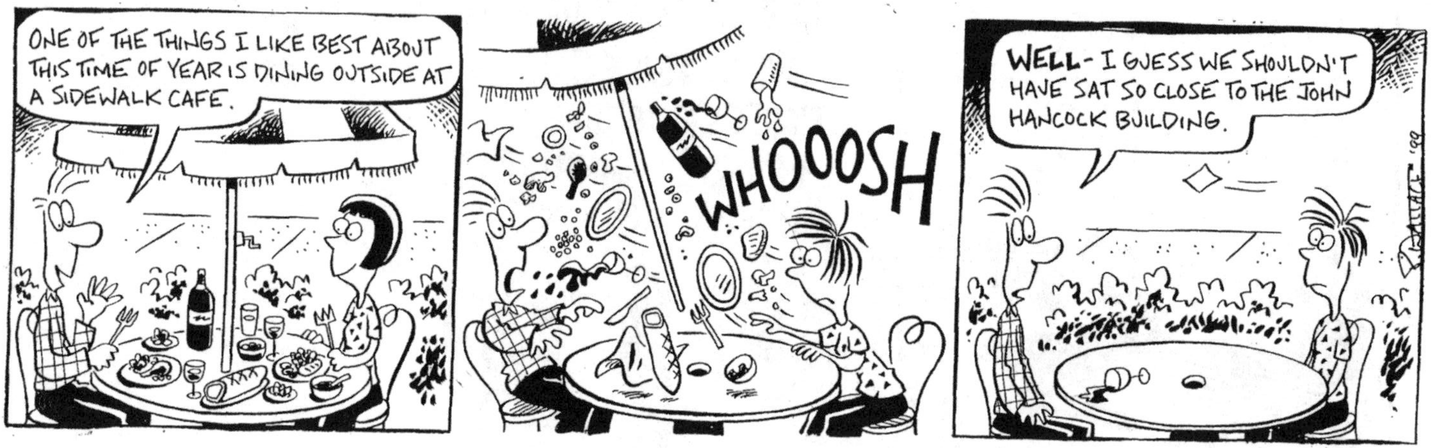
ONE OF THE THINGS I LIKE BEST ABOUT THIS TIME OF YEAR IS DINING OUTSIDE AT A SIDEWALK CAFE.
WHOOOSH
WELL- I GUESS WE SHOULDN'T HAVE SAT SO CLOSE TO THE JOHN HANCOCK BUILDING.

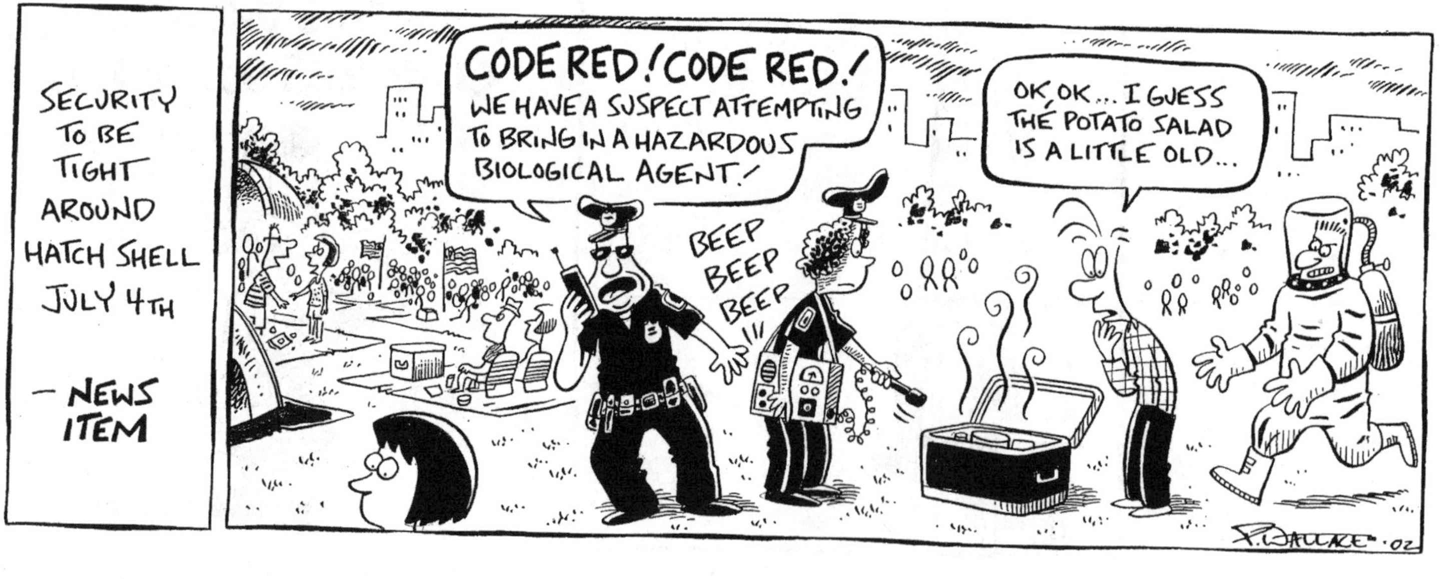
SECURITY TO BE TIGHT AROUND HATCH SHELL JULY 4TH
– NEWS ITEM
CODE RED! CODE RED! WE HAVE A SUSPECT ATTEMPTING TO BRING IN A HAZARDOUS BIOLOGICAL AGENT!
BEEP BEEP BEEP
OK, OK... I GUESS THE POTATO SALAD IS A LITTLE OLD...

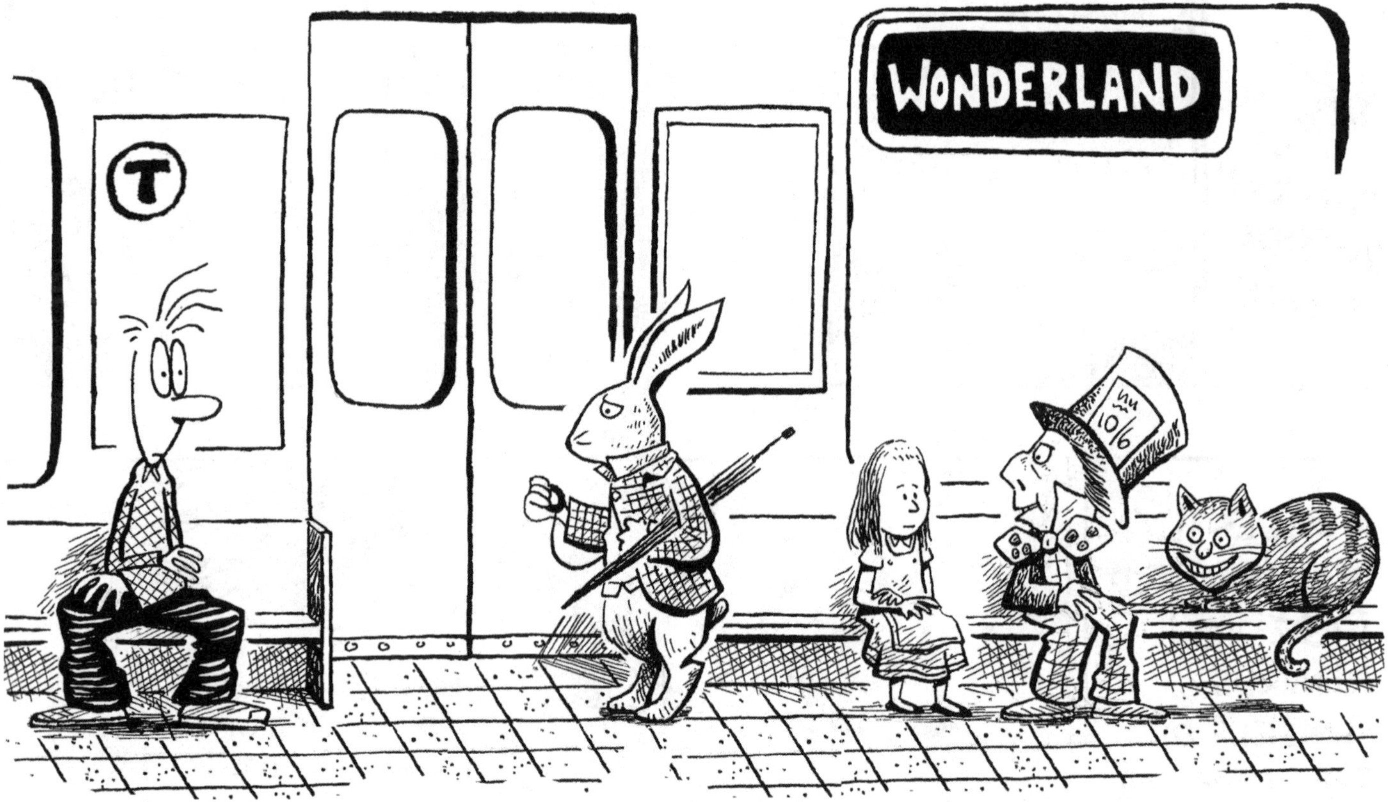
WONDERLAND
T
10/6

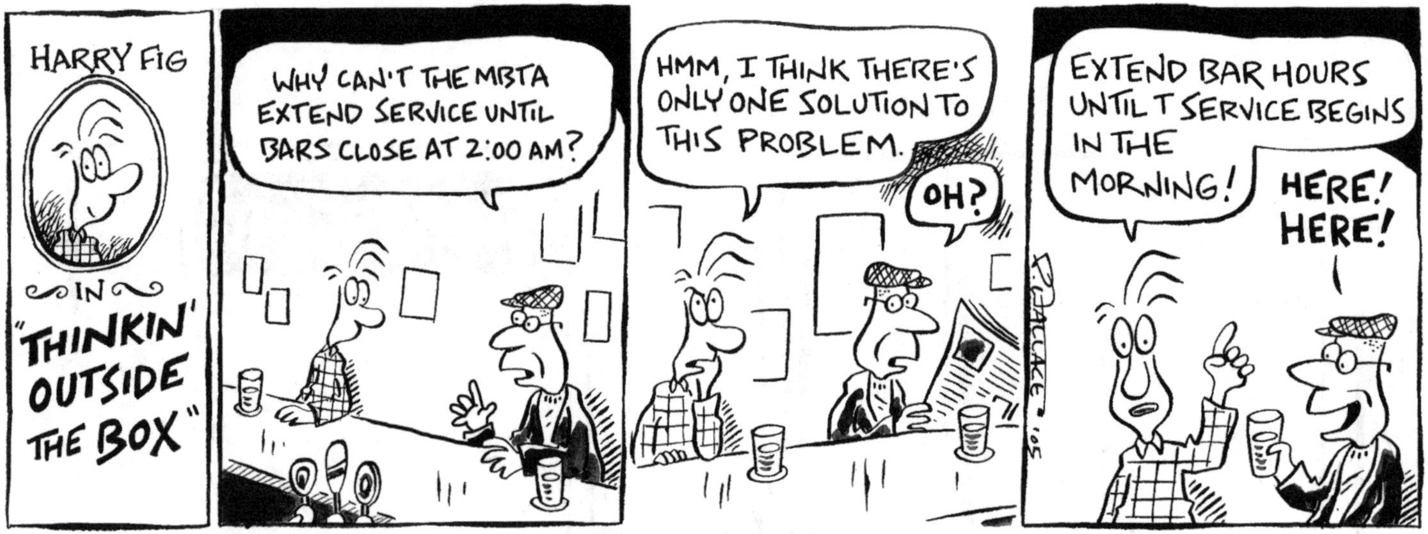
HARRY FIG
IN
"THINKIN' OUTSIDE THE BOX"
WHY CAN'T THE MBTA EXTEND SERVICE UNTIL BARS CLOSE AT 2:00 AM?
HMM, I THINK THERE'S ONLY ONE SOLUTION TO THIS PROBLEM.
OH?
EXTEND BAR HOURS UNTIL T SERVICE BEGINS IN THE MORNING!
HERE! HERE!

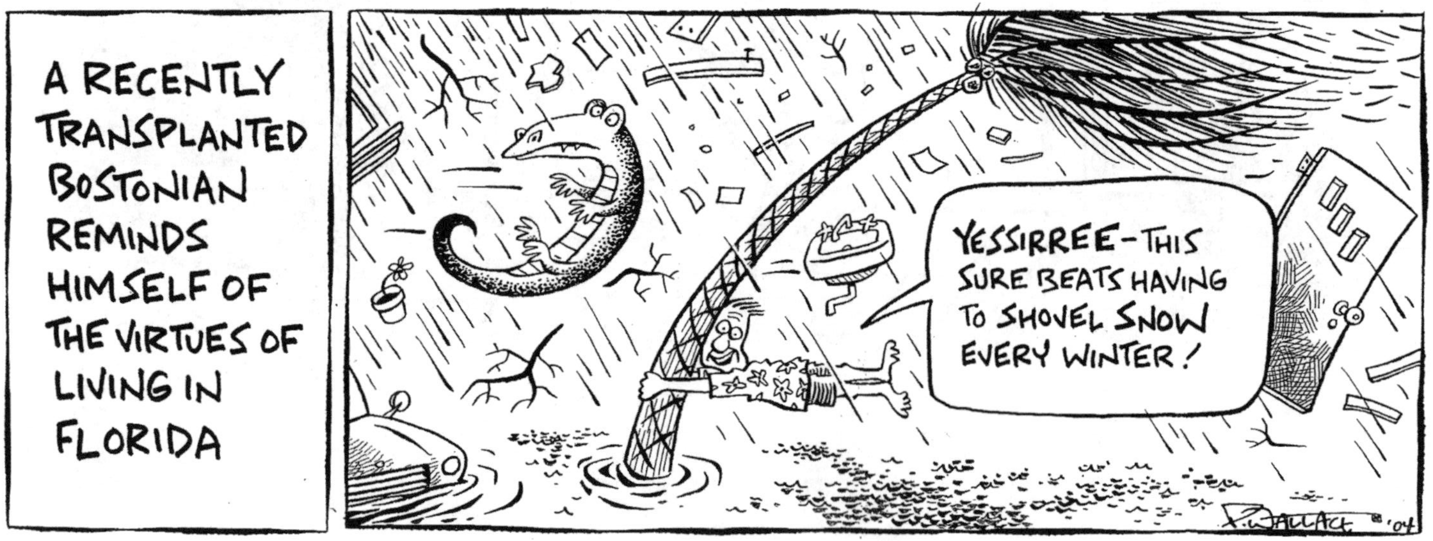
A RECENTLY TRANSPLANTED BOSTONIAN REMINDS HIMSELF OF THE VIRTUES OF LIVING IN FLORIDA
YESSIRREE - THIS SURE BEATS HAVING TO SHOVEL SNOW EVERY WINTER!

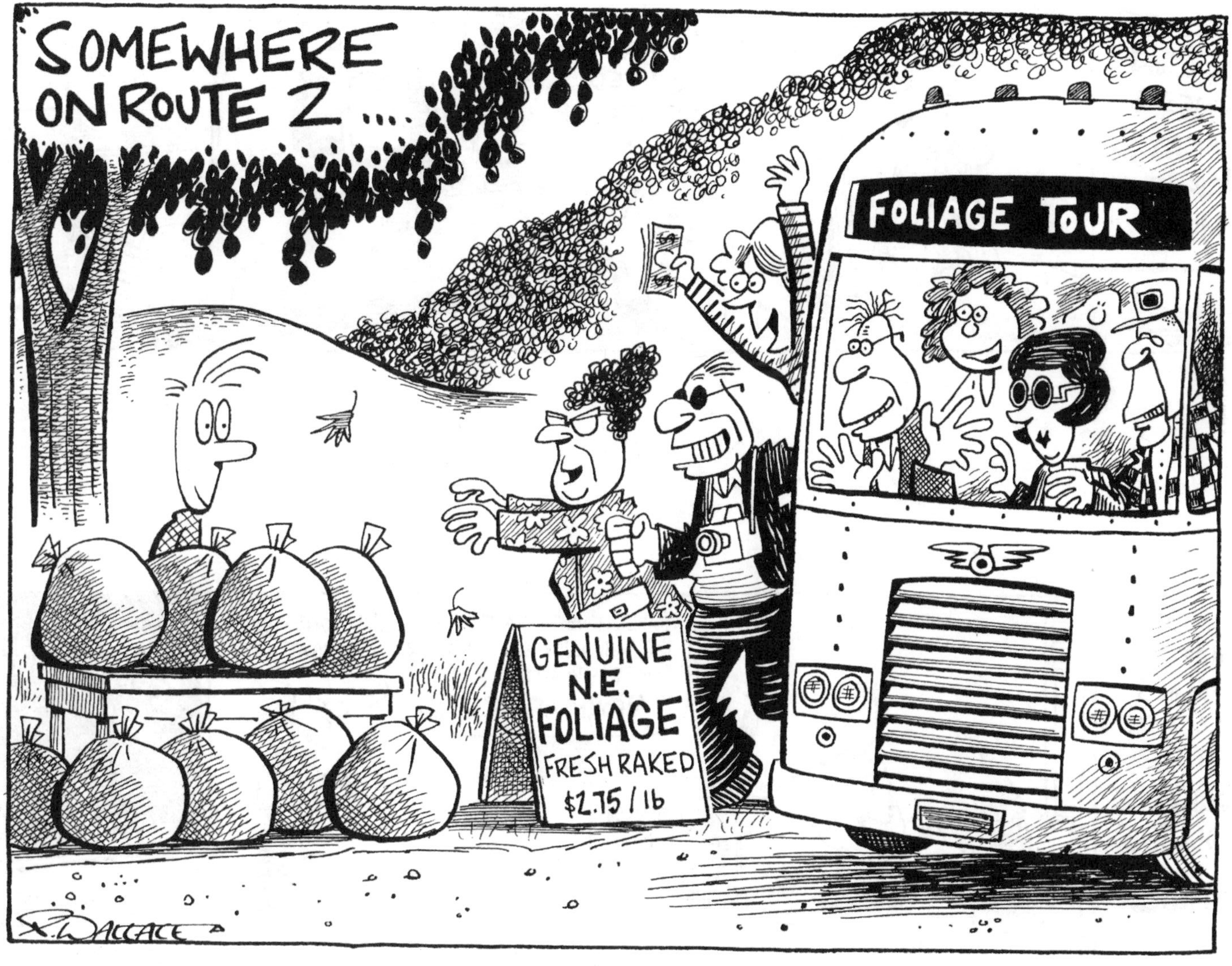
SOMEWHERE ON ROUTE 2 ....
FOLIAGE TOUR
GENUINE N.E. FOLIAGE FRESH RAKED $2.75 / lb
R. WALLACE

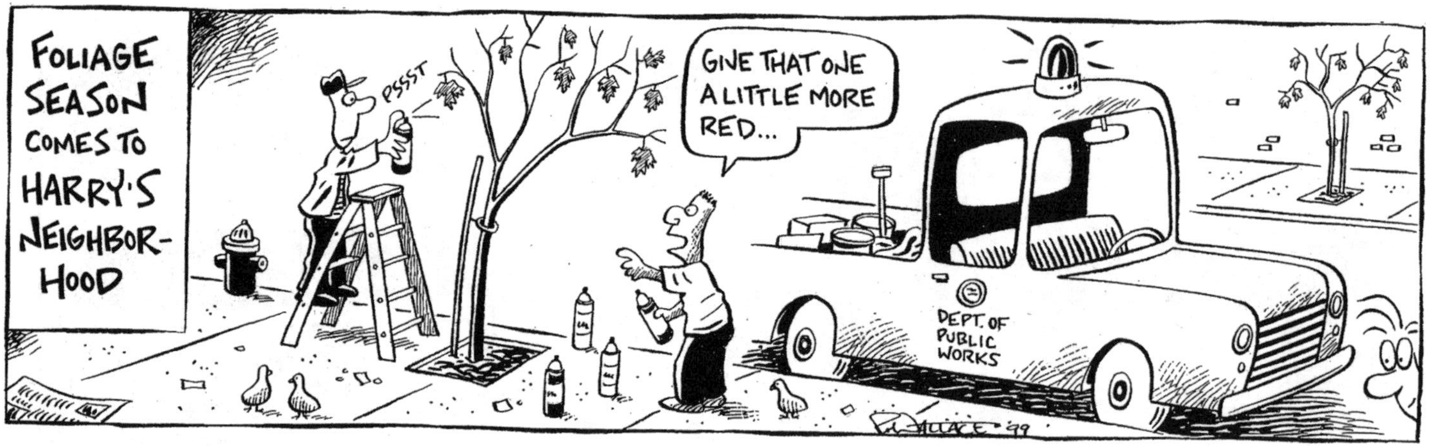
FOLIAGE SEASON COMES TO HARRY'S NEIGHBOR-HOOD
PSSST
GIVE THAT ONE A LITTLE MORE RED...
DEPT. OF PUBLIC WORKS

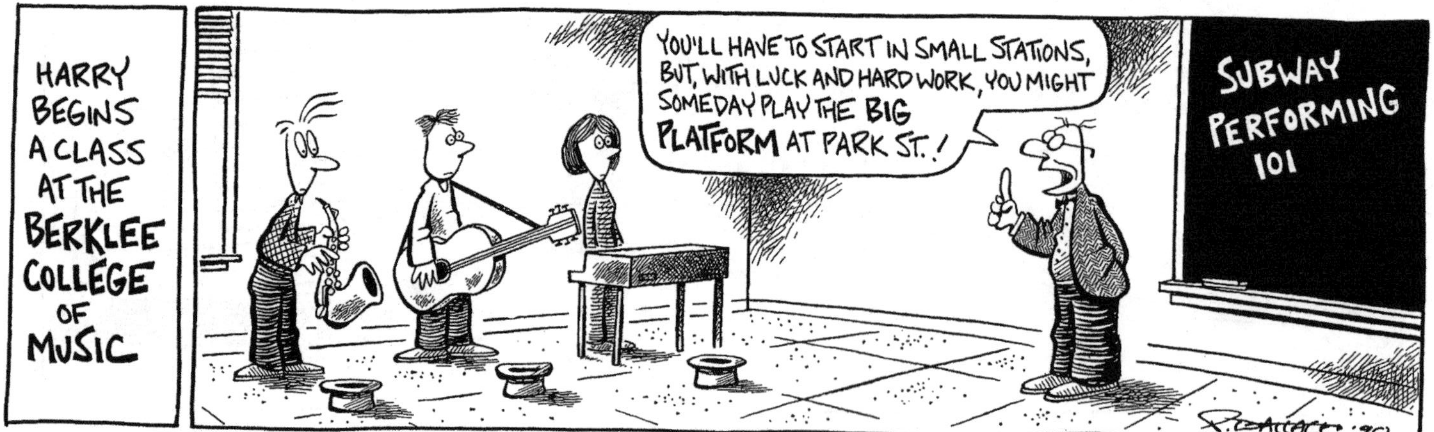
HARRY BEGINS A CLASS AT THE BERKLEE COLLEGE OF MUSIC
YOU'LL HAVE TO START IN SMALL STATIONS, BUT, WITH LUCK AND HARD WORK, YOU MIGHT SOMEDAY PLAY THE BIG PLATFORM AT PARK ST.!
SUBWAY PERFORMING 101

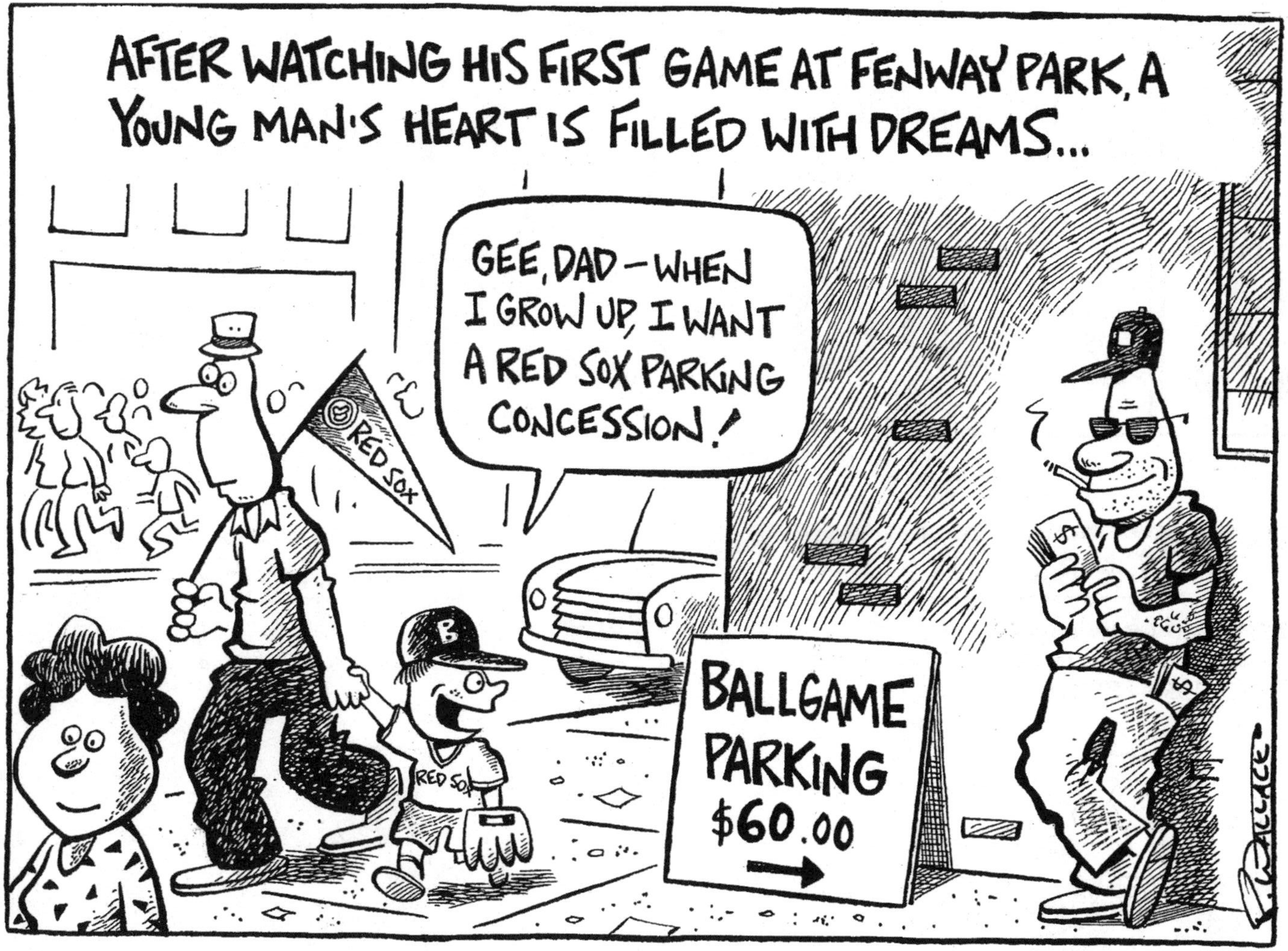
AFTER WATCHING HIS FIRST GAME AT FENWAY PARK, A YOUNG MAN'S HEART IS FILLED WITH DREAMS...
GEE, DAD—WHEN I GROW UP, I WANT A RED SOX PARKING CONCESSION!
RED SOX
RED SOX
BALLGAME PARKING $60.00

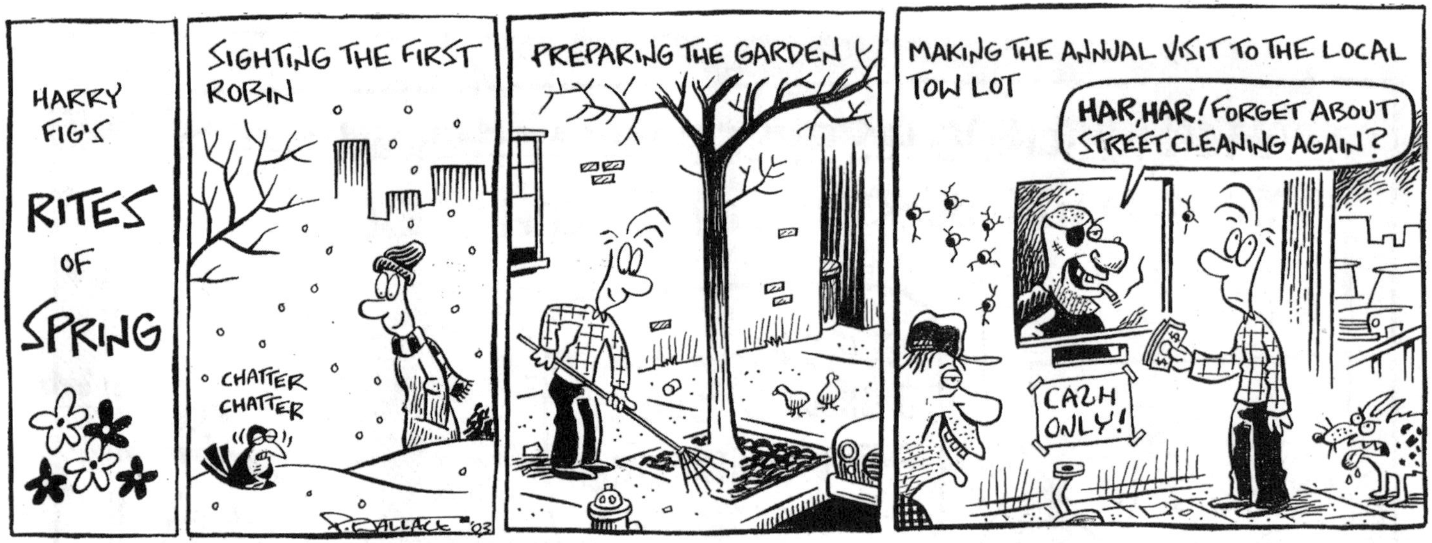
HARRY FIG'S
RITES OF SPRING
SIGHTING THE FIRST ROBIN
CHATTER CHATTER
P. WALLACE '03
PREPARING THE GARDEN
MAKING THE ANNUAL VISIT TO THE LOCAL TOW LOT
HAR, HAR! FORGET ABOUT STREET CLEANING AGAIN?
CASH ONLY!

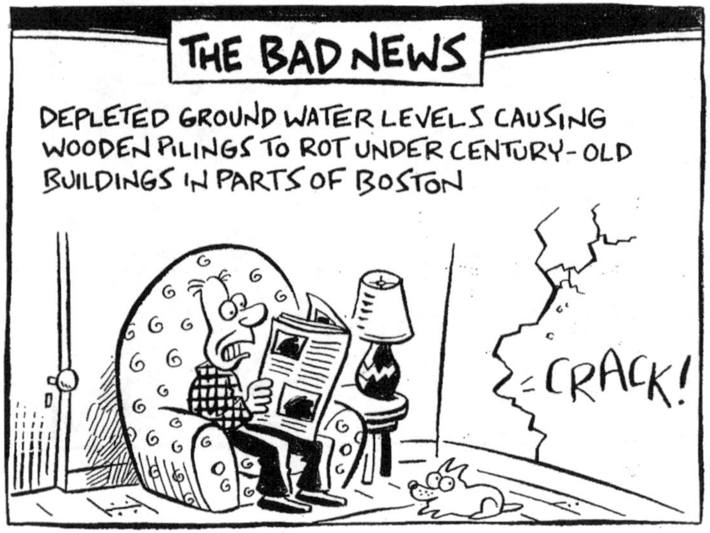
THE BAD NEWS
DEPLETED GROUND WATER LEVELS CAUSING WOODEN PILINGS TO ROT UNDER CENTURY-OLD BUILDINGS IN PARTS OF BOSTON
CRACK!

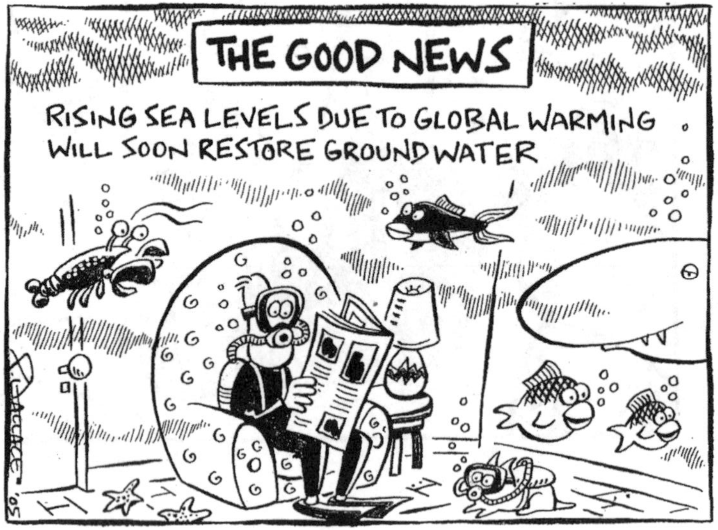
THE GOOD NEWS
RISING SEA LEVELS DUE TO GLOBAL WARMING WILL SOON RESTORE GROUND WATER
P. WALLACE '05

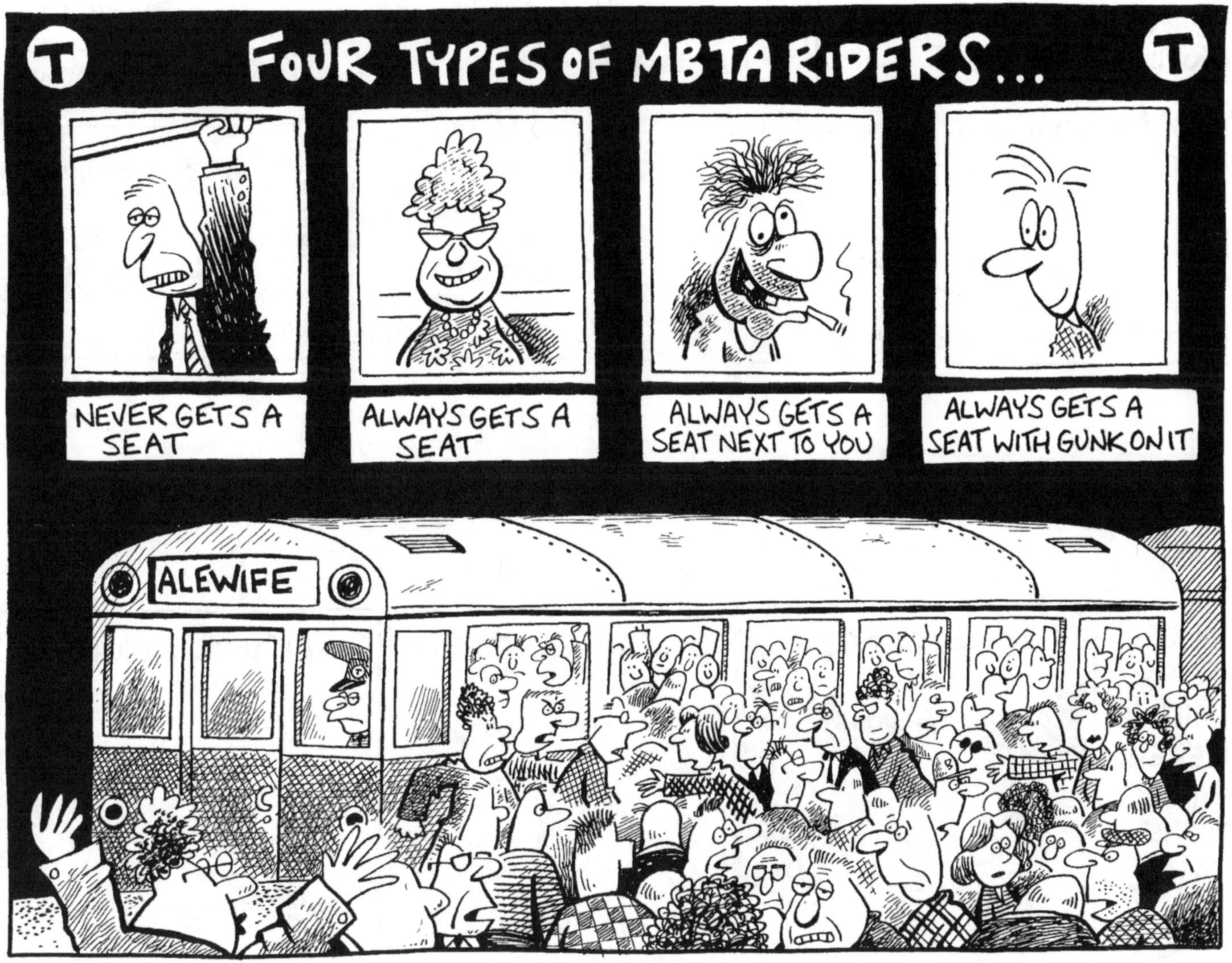
FOUR TYPES OF MBTA RIDERS...
NEVER GETS A SEAT
ALWAYS GETS A SEAT
ALWAYS GETS A SEAT NEXT TO YOU
ALWAYS GETS A SEAT WITH GUNK ON IT
ALEWIFE

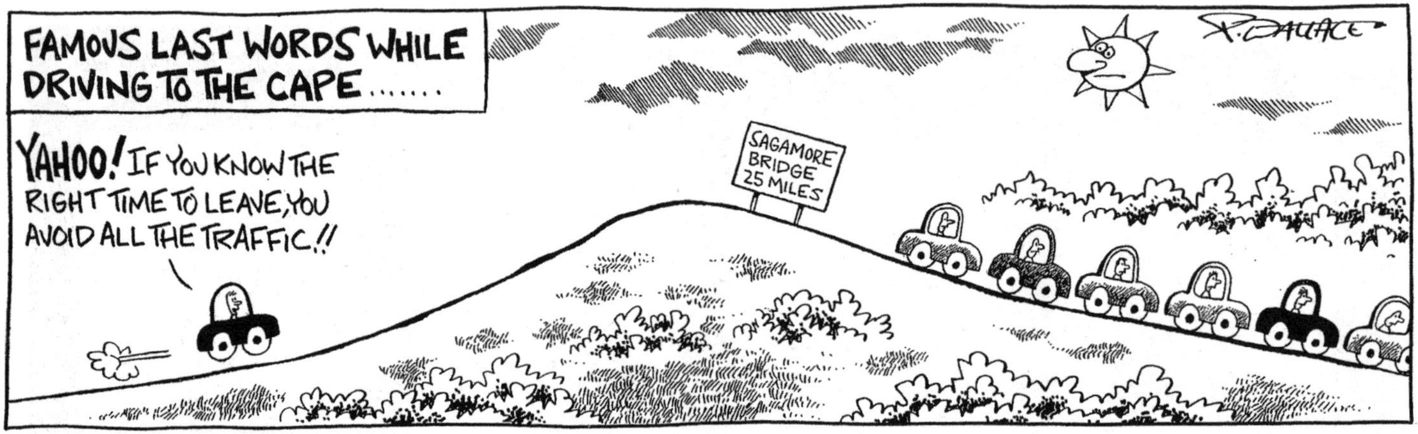

FAMOUS LAST WORDS WHILE DRIVING TO THE CAPE.......
YAHOO! IF YOU KNOW THE RIGHT TIME TO LEAVE, YOU AVOID ALL THE TRAFFIC!!
SAGAMORE BRIDGE 25 MILES
P. WALLACE

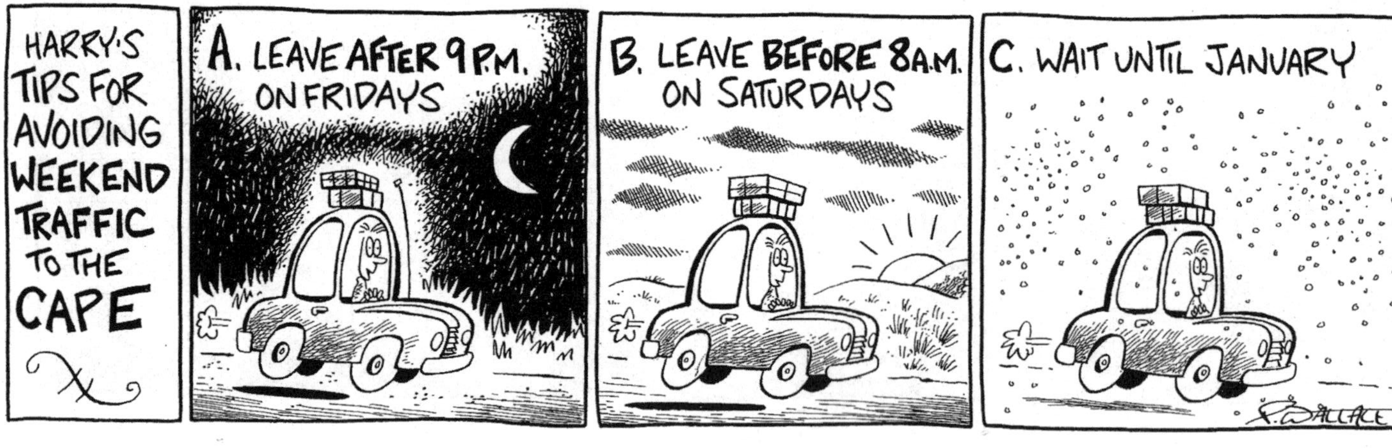

HARRY'S TIPS FOR AVOIDING WEEKEND TRAFFIC TO THE CAPE
A. LEAVE AFTER 9 P.M. ON FRIDAYS
B. LEAVE BEFORE 8 A.M. ON SATURDAYS
C. WAIT UNTIL JANUARY
P. WALLACE

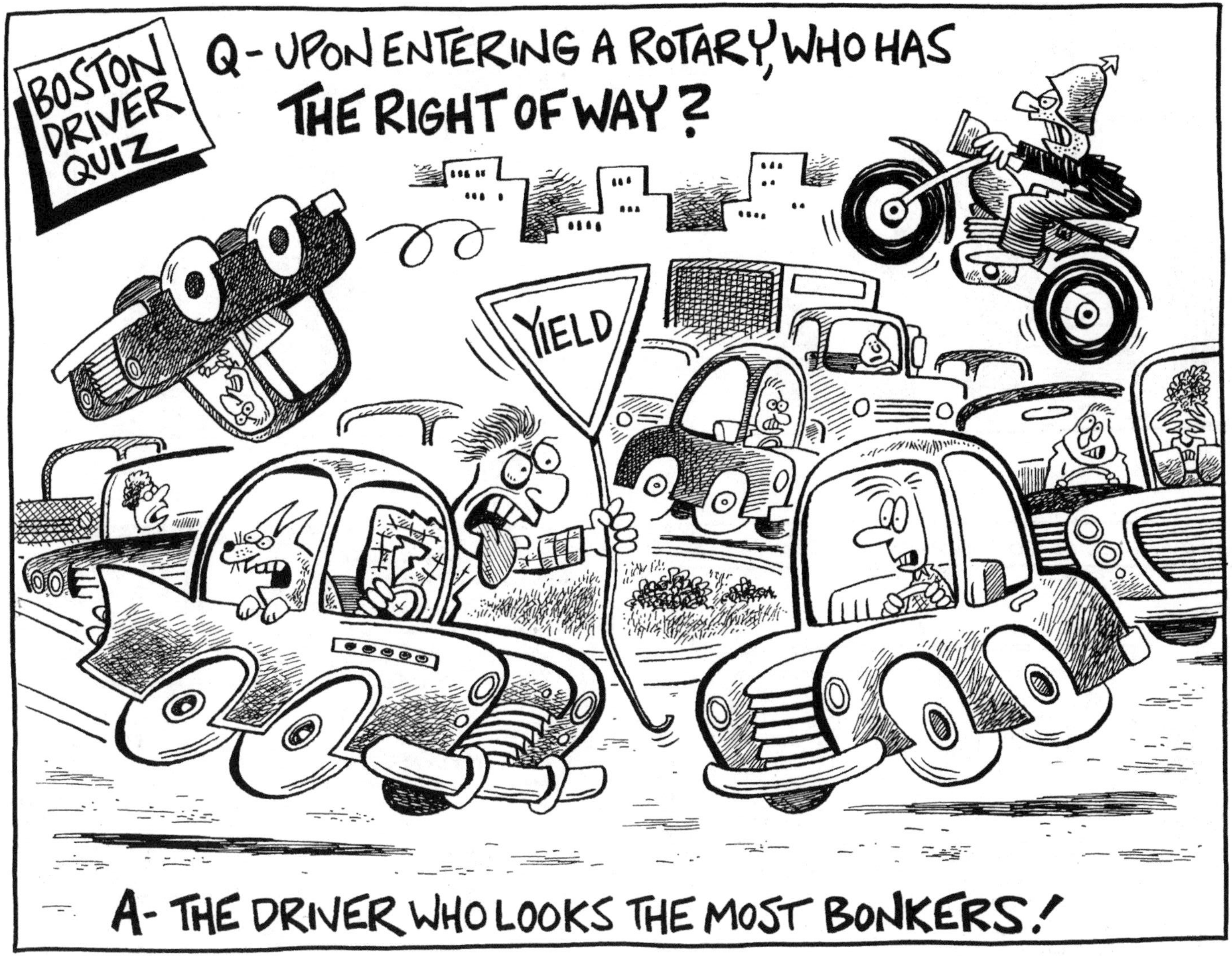
BOSTON DRIVER QUIZ
Q - UPON ENTERING A ROTARY, WHO HAS THE RIGHT OF WAY?
YIELD
A- THE DRIVER WHO LOOKS THE MOST BONKERS!

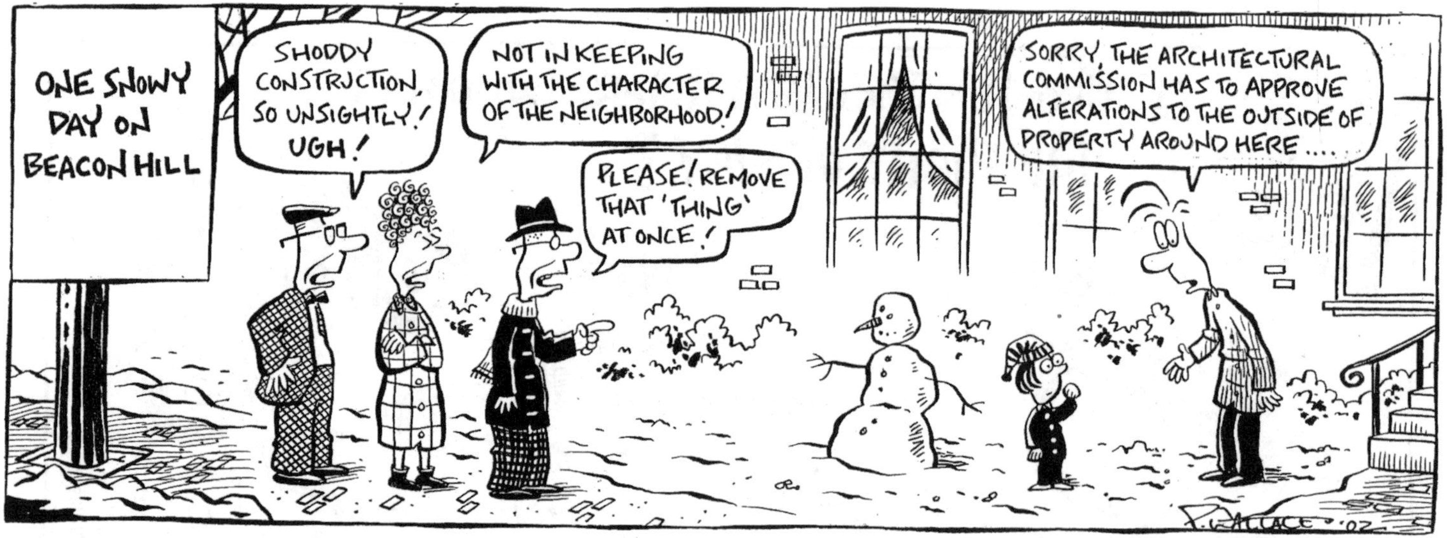
ONE SNOWY DAY ON BEACON HILL
SHODDY CONSTRUCTION, SO UNSIGHTLY! UGH!
NOT IN KEEPING WITH THE CHARACTER OF THE NEIGHBORHOOD!
PLEASE! REMOVE THAT 'THING' AT ONCE!
SORRY, THE ARCHITECTURAL COMMISSION HAS TO APPROVE ALTERATIONS TO THE OUTSIDE OF PROPERTY AROUND HERE....
P. WALLACE '02

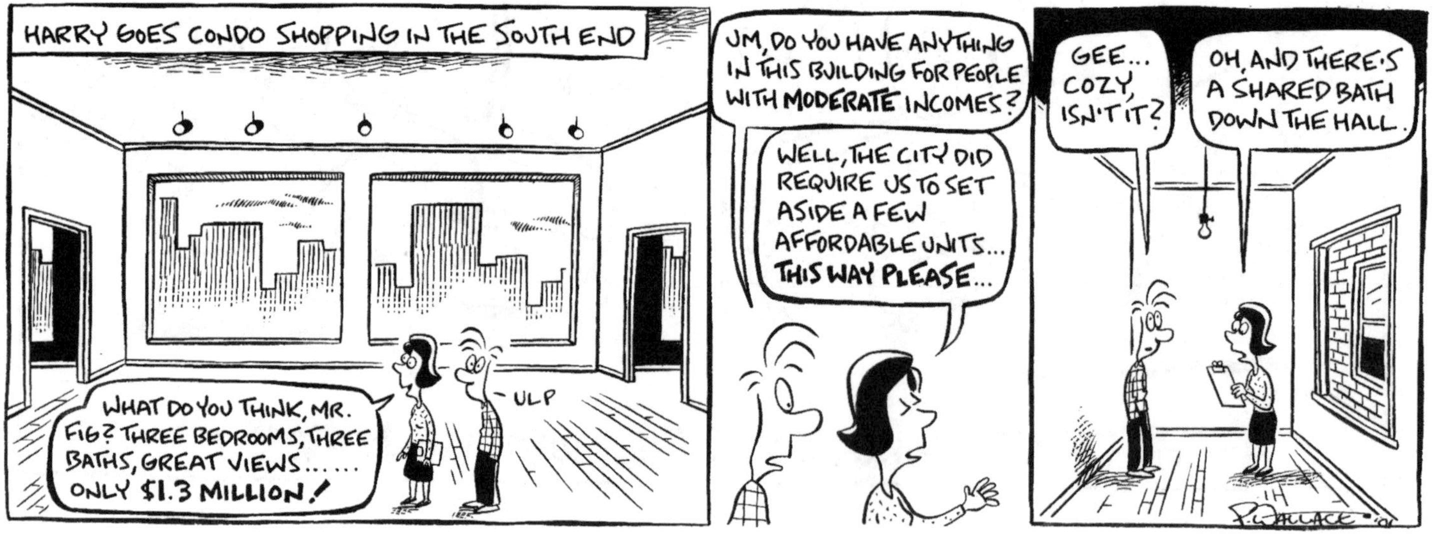
HARRY GOES CONDO SHOPPING IN THE SOUTH END
WHAT DO YOU THINK, MR. FIG? THREE BEDROOMS, THREE BATHS, GREAT VIEWS...... ONLY $1.3 MILLION!
ULP
UM, DO YOU HAVE ANYTHING IN THIS BUILDING FOR PEOPLE WITH MODERATE INCOMES?
WELL, THE CITY DID REQUIRE US TO SET ASIDE A FEW AFFORDABLE UNITS... THIS WAY PLEASE...
GEE... COZY, ISN'T IT?
OH, AND THERE'S A SHARED BATH DOWN THE HALL.

ONE BAD THING ABOUT ALL THE COLLEGE STUDENTS LIVING IN BOSTON IS THEIR ROWDY BEHAVIOR!
UGH - AND THOSE MIT KIDS ARE THE WORST!
HEY! KEEP IT DOWN OUT THERE!

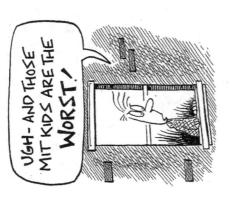

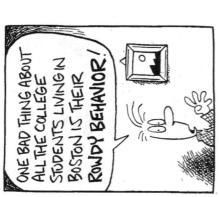

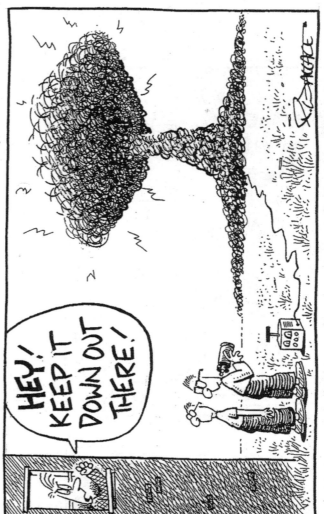

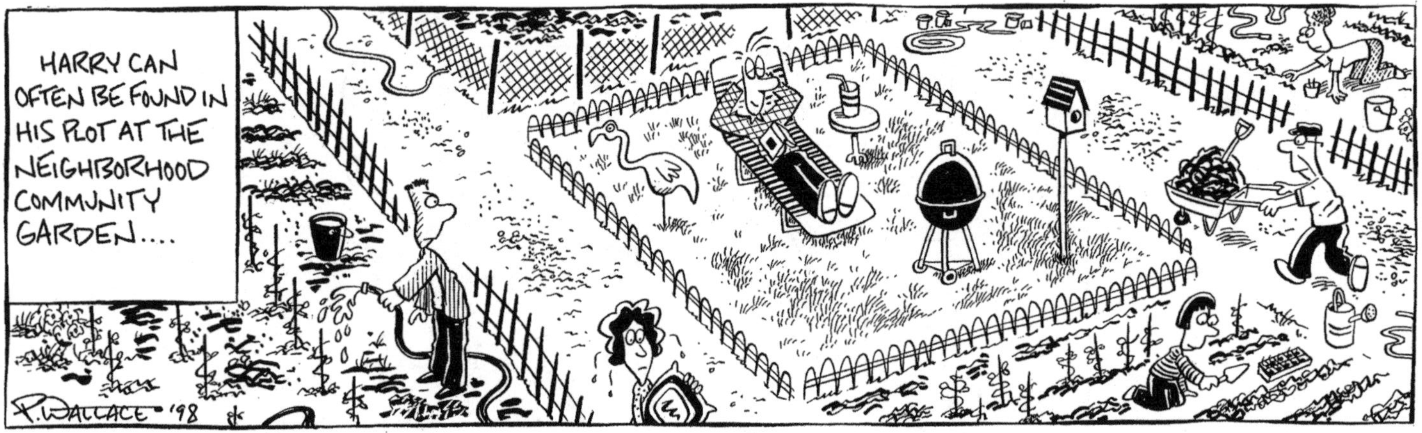
HARRY CAN OFTEN BE FOUND IN HIS PLOT AT THE NEIGHBORHOOD COMMUNITY GARDEN....
P. WALLACE '98

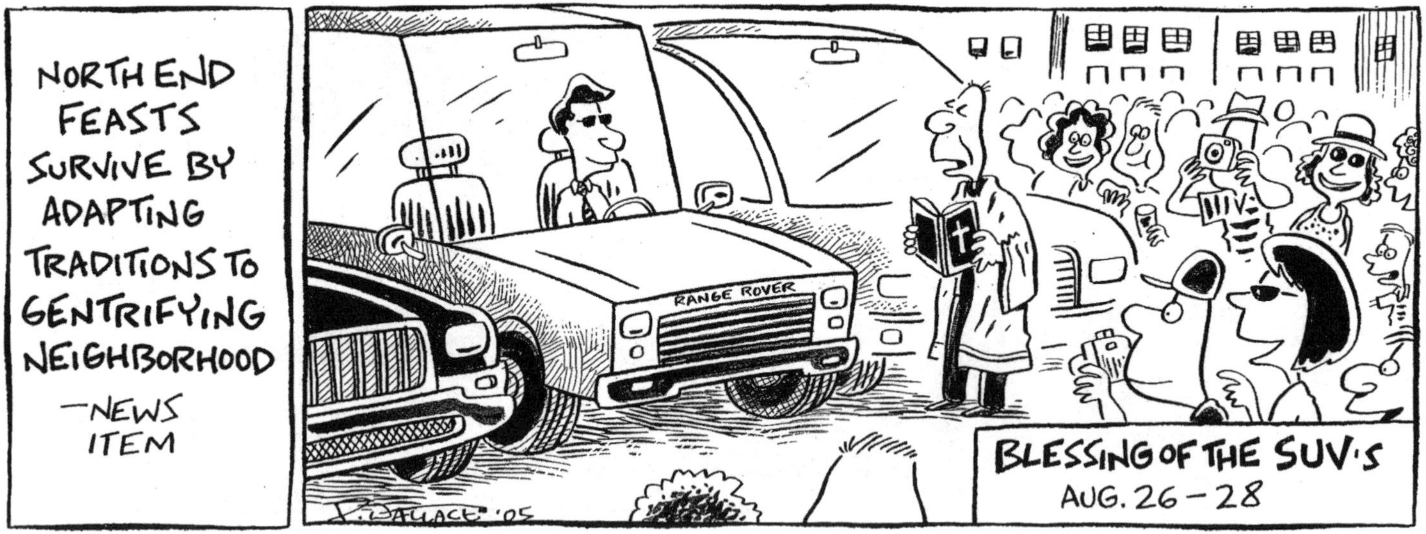
NORTH END FEASTS SURVIVE BY ADAPTING TRADITIONS TO GENTRIFYING NEIGHBORHOOD
—NEWS ITEM
RANGE ROVER
BLESSING OF THE SUV's
AUG. 26 – 28
P. WALLACE '05

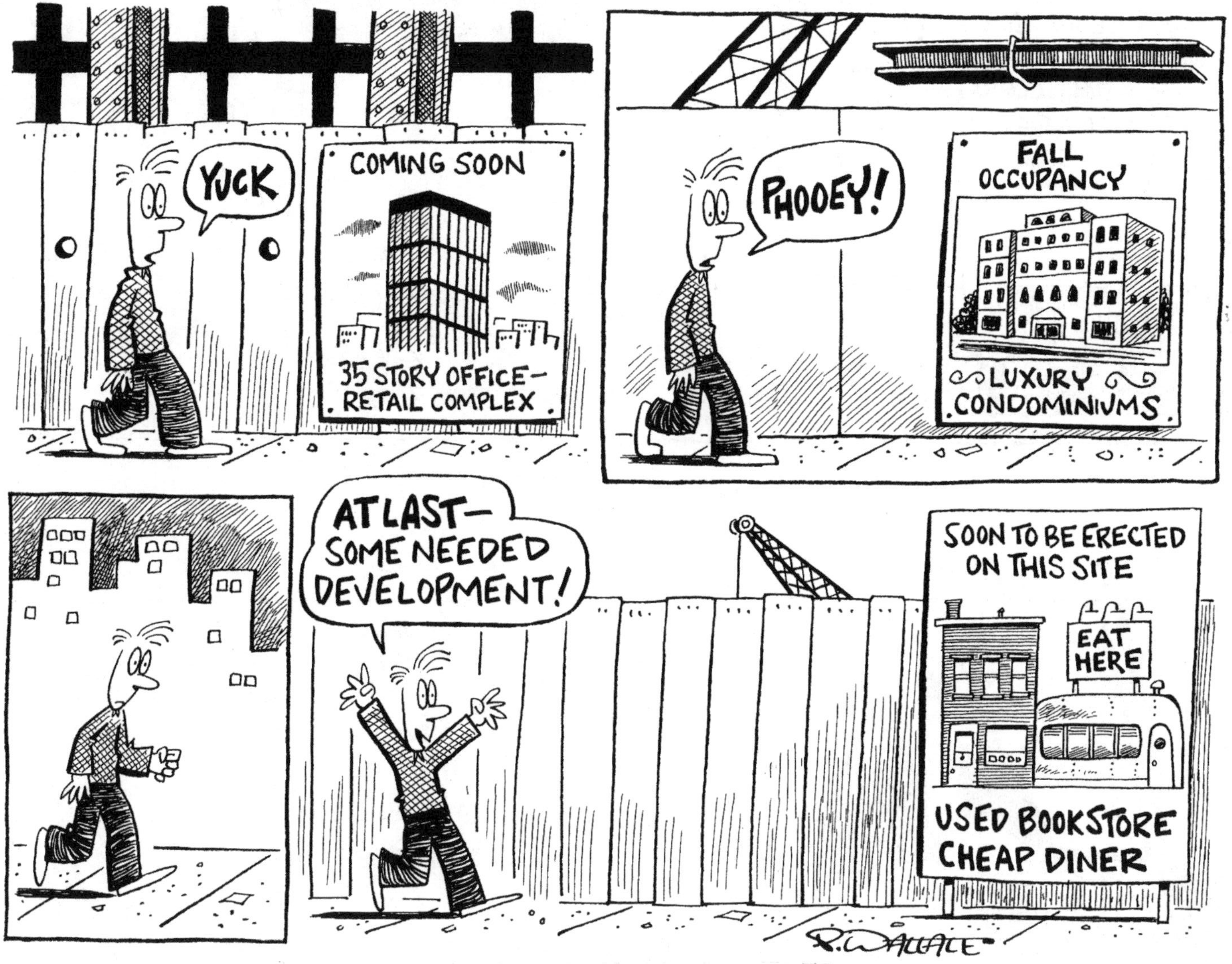
YUCK
COMING SOON
35 STORY OFFICE-
RETAIL COMPLEX
PHOOEY!
FALL
OCCUPANCY
LUXURY
CONDOMINIUMS
AT LAST—
SOME NEEDED
DEVELOPMENT!
SOON TO BE ERECTED
ON THIS SITE
EAT
HERE
USED BOOKSTORE
CHEAP DINER
R. WALLACE

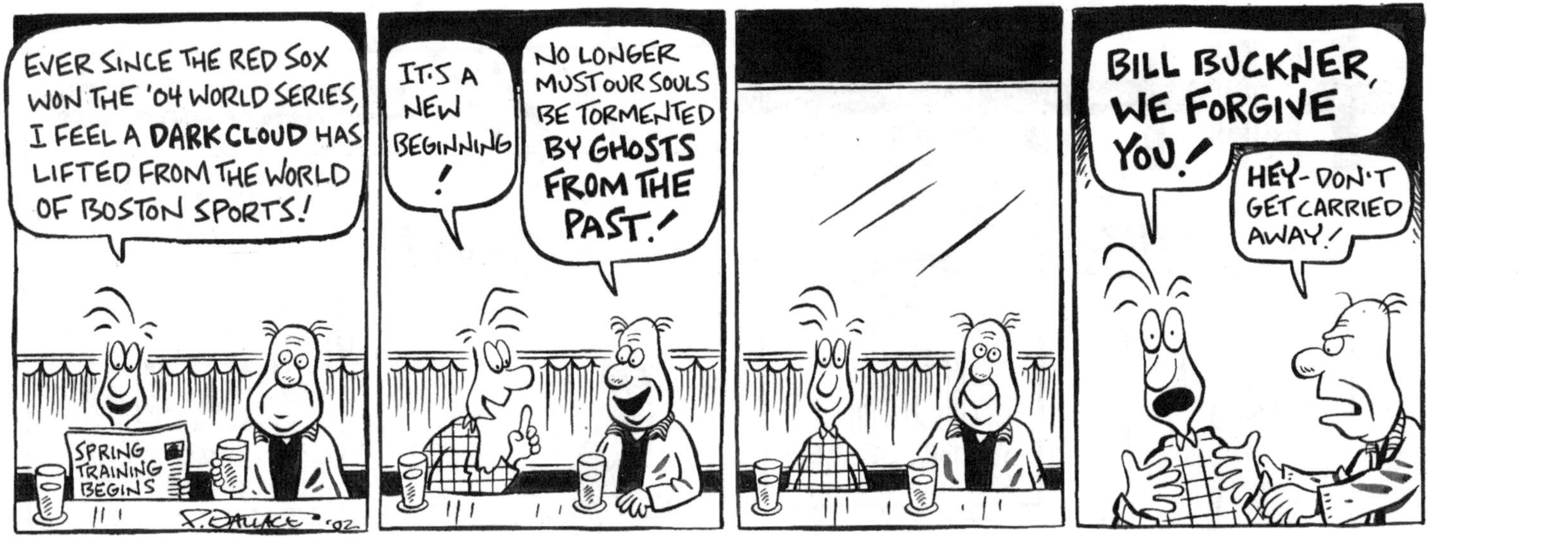
EVER SINCE THE RED SOX WON THE '04 WORLD SERIES, I FEEL A DARK CLOUD HAS LIFTED FROM THE WORLD OF BOSTON SPORTS!
SPRING TRAINING BEGINS
IT'S A NEW BEGINNING!
NO LONGER MUST OUR SOULS BE TORMENTED BY GHOSTS FROM THE PAST!
BILL BUCKNER, WE FORGIVE YOU!
HEY- DON'T GET CARRIED AWAY!

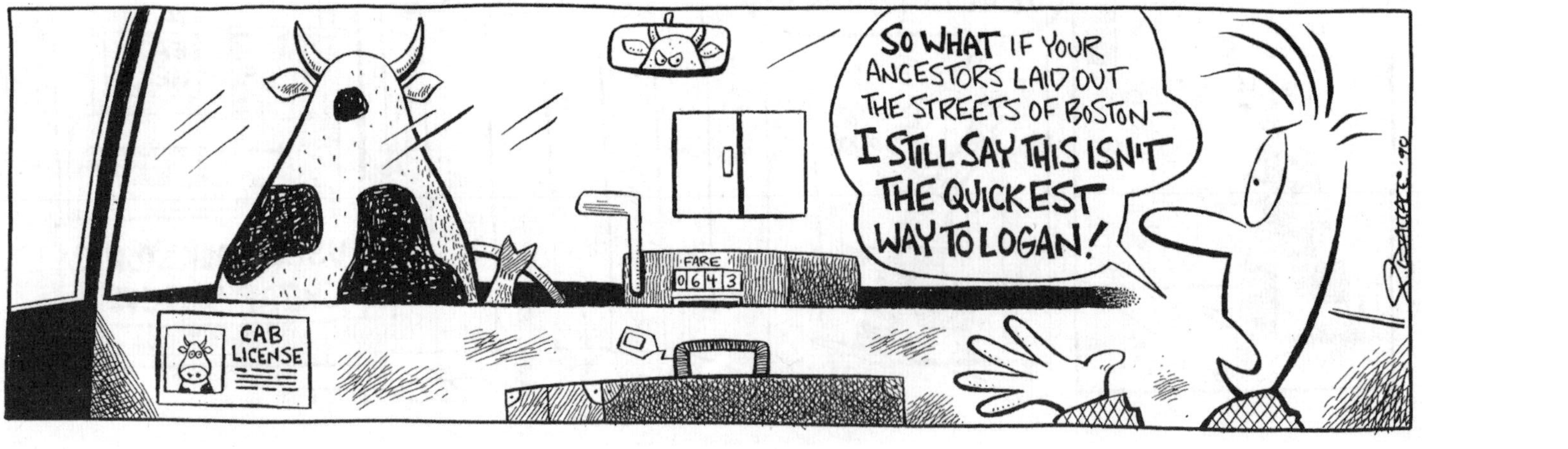
CAB LICENSE
FARE
0643
SO WHAT IF YOUR ANCESTORS LAID OUT THE STREETS OF BOSTON— I STILL SAY THIS ISN'T THE QUICKEST WAY TO LOGAN!

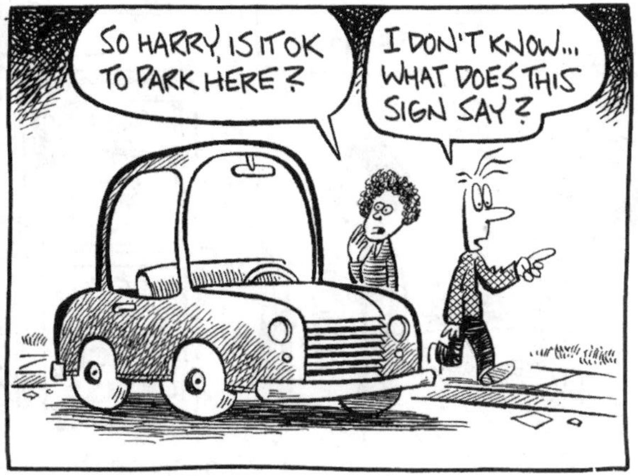
SO HARRY, IS IT OK TO PARK HERE?
I DON'T KNOW... WHAT DOES THIS SIGN SAY?

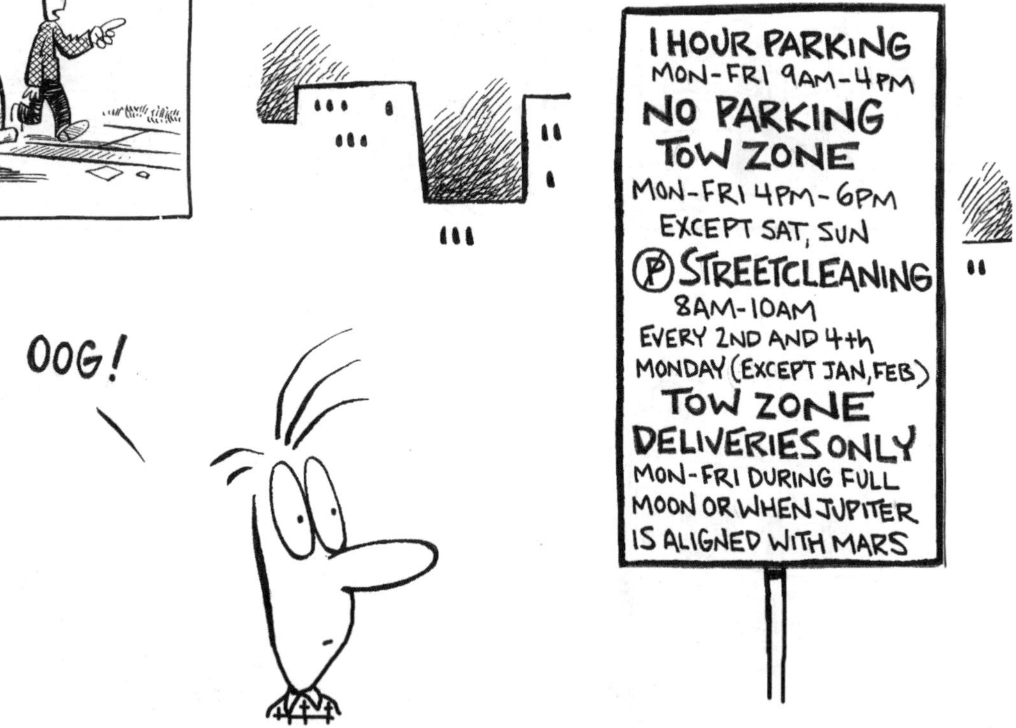
I HOUR PARKING
MON-FRI 9AM-4PM
NO PARKING
TOW ZONE
MON-FRI 4PM-6PM
EXCEPT SAT, SUN
Ⓟ STREETCLEANING
8AM-10AM
EVERY 2ND AND 4th
MONDAY (EXCEPT JAN, FEB)
TOW ZONE
DELIVERIES ONLY
MON-FRI DURING FULL
MOON OR WHEN JUPITER
IS ALIGNED WITH MARS
OOG!

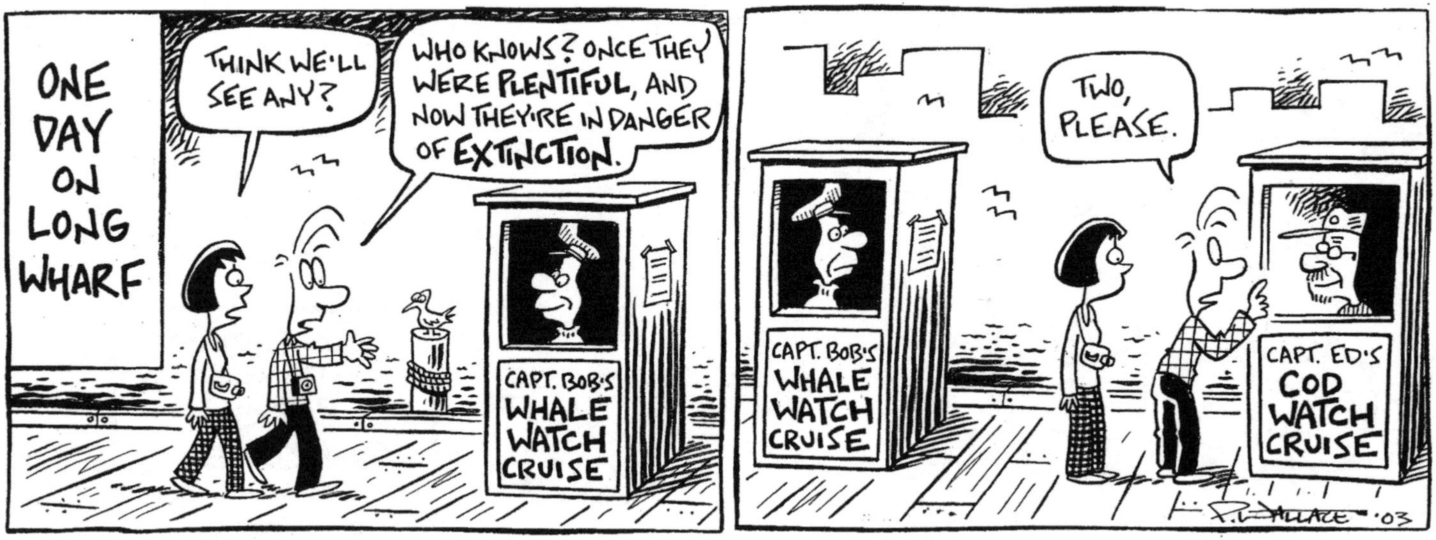
ONE DAY ON LONG WHARF
THINK WE'LL SEE ANY?
WHO KNOWS? ONCE THEY WERE PLENTIFUL, AND NOW THEY'RE IN DANGER OF EXTINCTION.
CAPT. BOB'S WHALE WATCH CRUISE
TWO, PLEASE.
CAPT. ED'S COD WATCH CRUISE
P. WALLACE '03

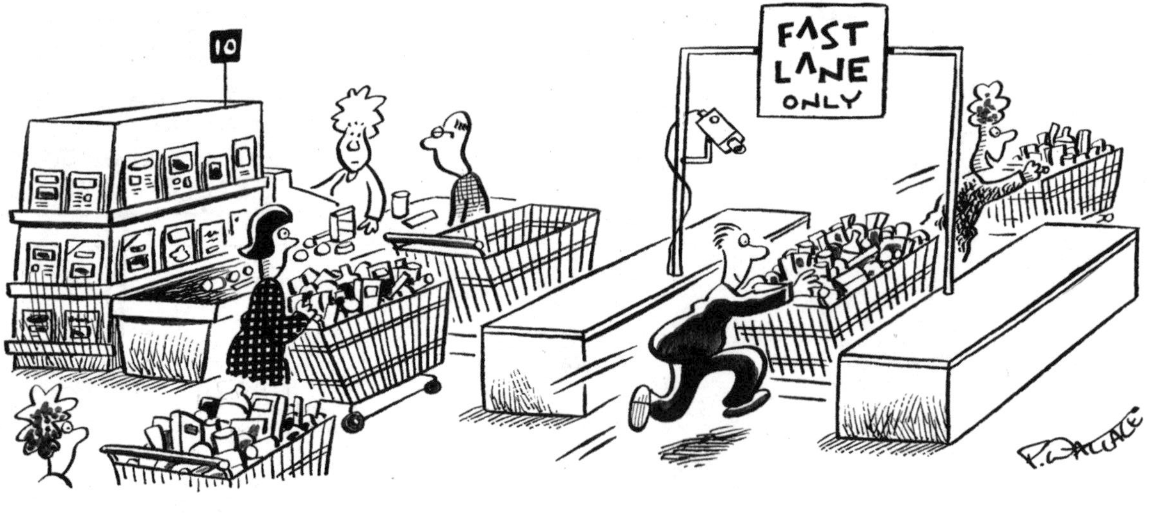
10
FAST LANE ONLY
P. WALLACE

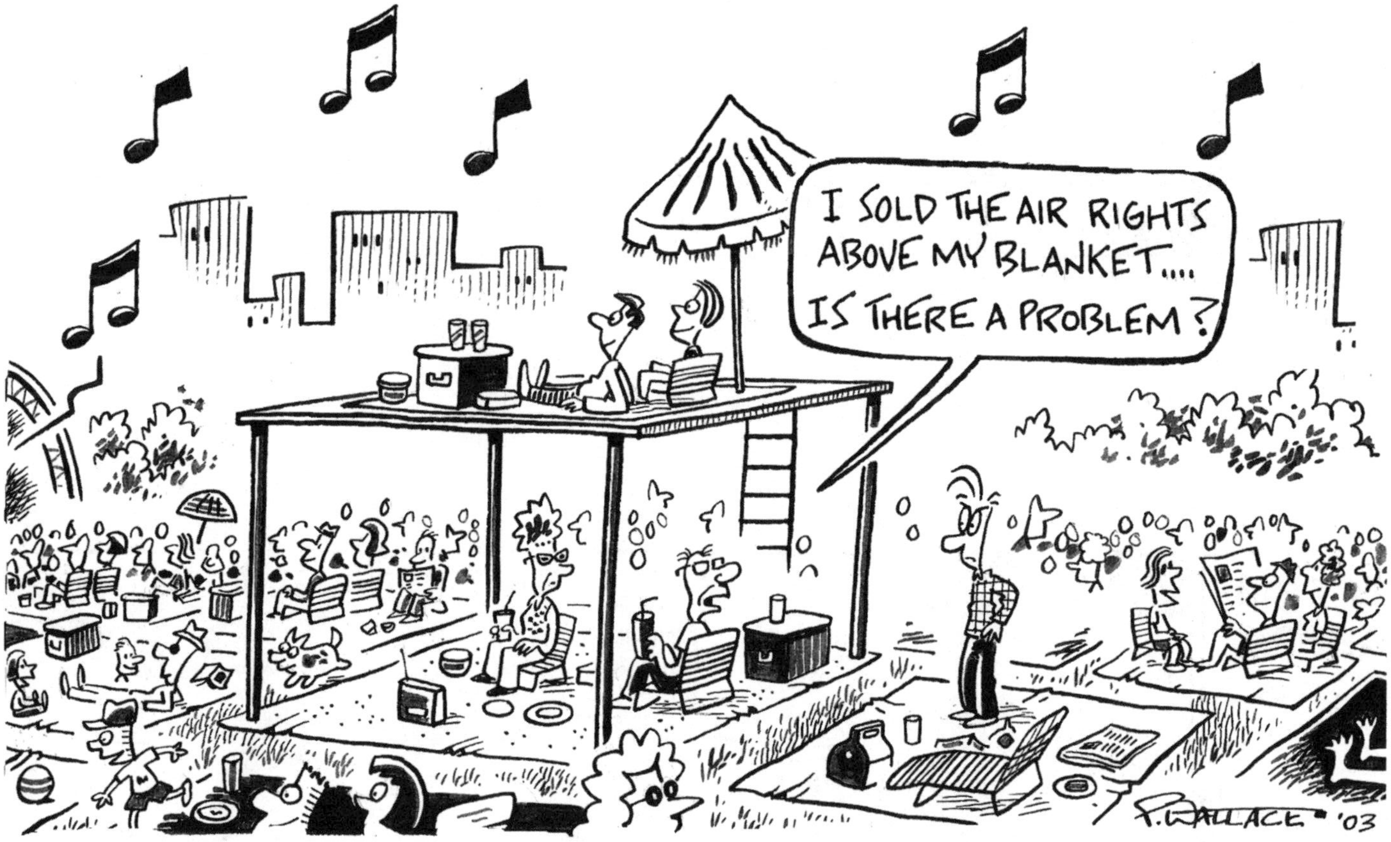
I SOLD THE AIR RIGHTS ABOVE MY BLANKET.... IS THERE A PROBLEM?
P. WALLACE '03

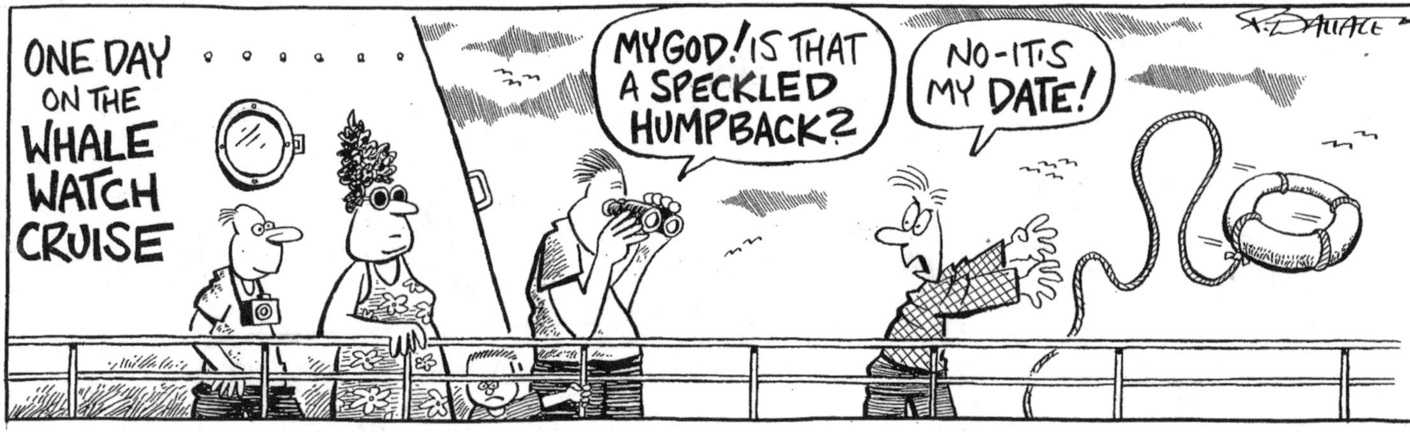
ONE DAY ON THE WHALE WATCH CRUISE
MYGOD! IS THAT A SPECKLED HUMPBACK?
NO-IT'S MY DATE!
R. WALLACE

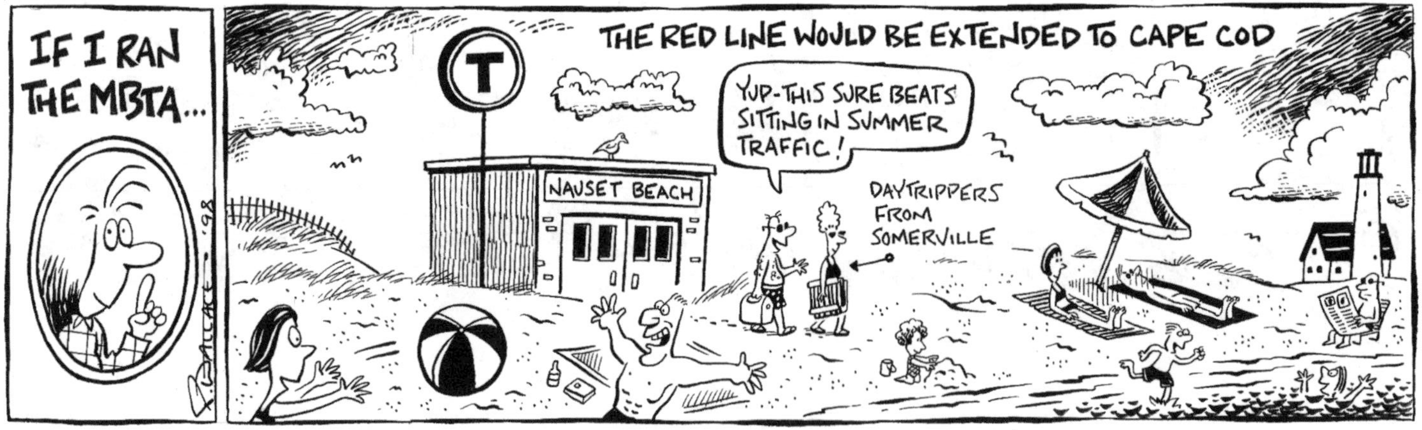
IF I RAN THE MBTA...
R. WALLACE '98
THE RED LINE WOULD BE EXTENDED TO CAPE COD
T
NAUSET BEACH
YUP-THIS SURE BEATS SITTING IN SUMMER TRAFFIC!
DAYTRIPPERS FROM SOMERVILLE

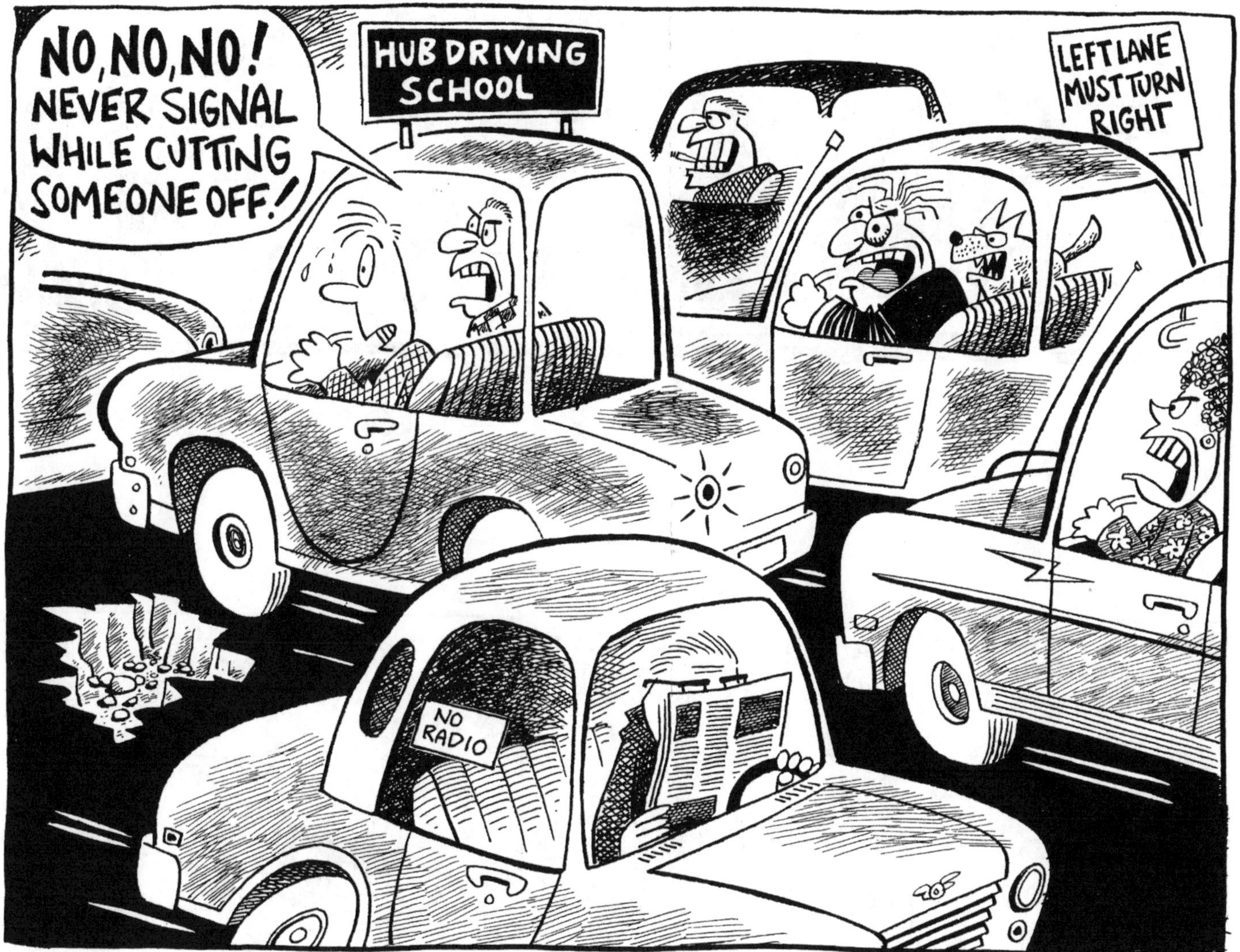
NO, NO, NO! NEVER SIGNAL WHILE CUTTING SOMEONE OFF!
HUB DRIVING SCHOOL
LEFT LANE MUST TURN RIGHT
NO RADIO

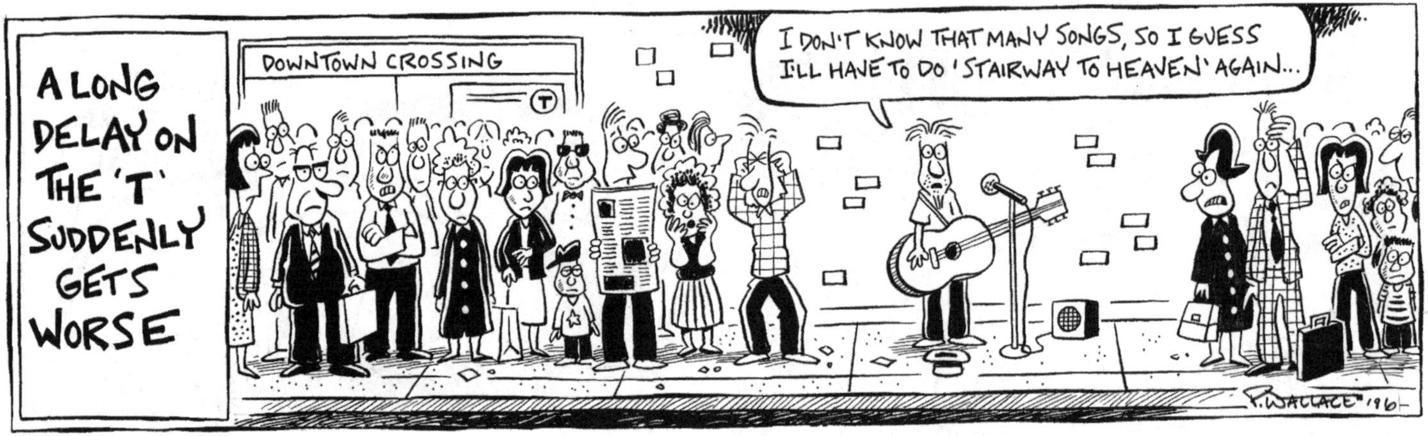
A LONG DELAY ON THE 'T' SUDDENLY GETS WORSE
DOWNTOWN CROSSING
T
I DON'T KNOW THAT MANY SONGS, SO I GUESS I'LL HAVE TO DO 'STAIRWAY TO HEAVEN' AGAIN...
P. WALLACE '96

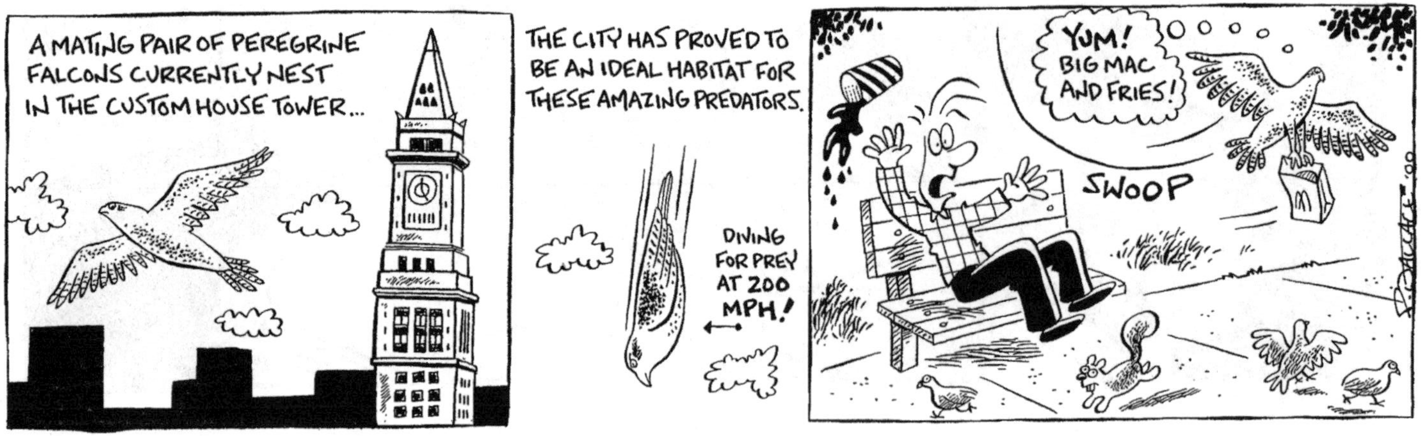
A MATING PAIR OF PEREGRINE FALCONS CURRENTLY NEST IN THE CUSTOM HOUSE TOWER...
THE CITY HAS PROVED TO BE AN IDEAL HABITAT FOR THESE AMAZING PREDATORS.
DIVING FOR PREY AT 200 MPH!
YUM! BIG MAC AND FRIES!
SWOOP

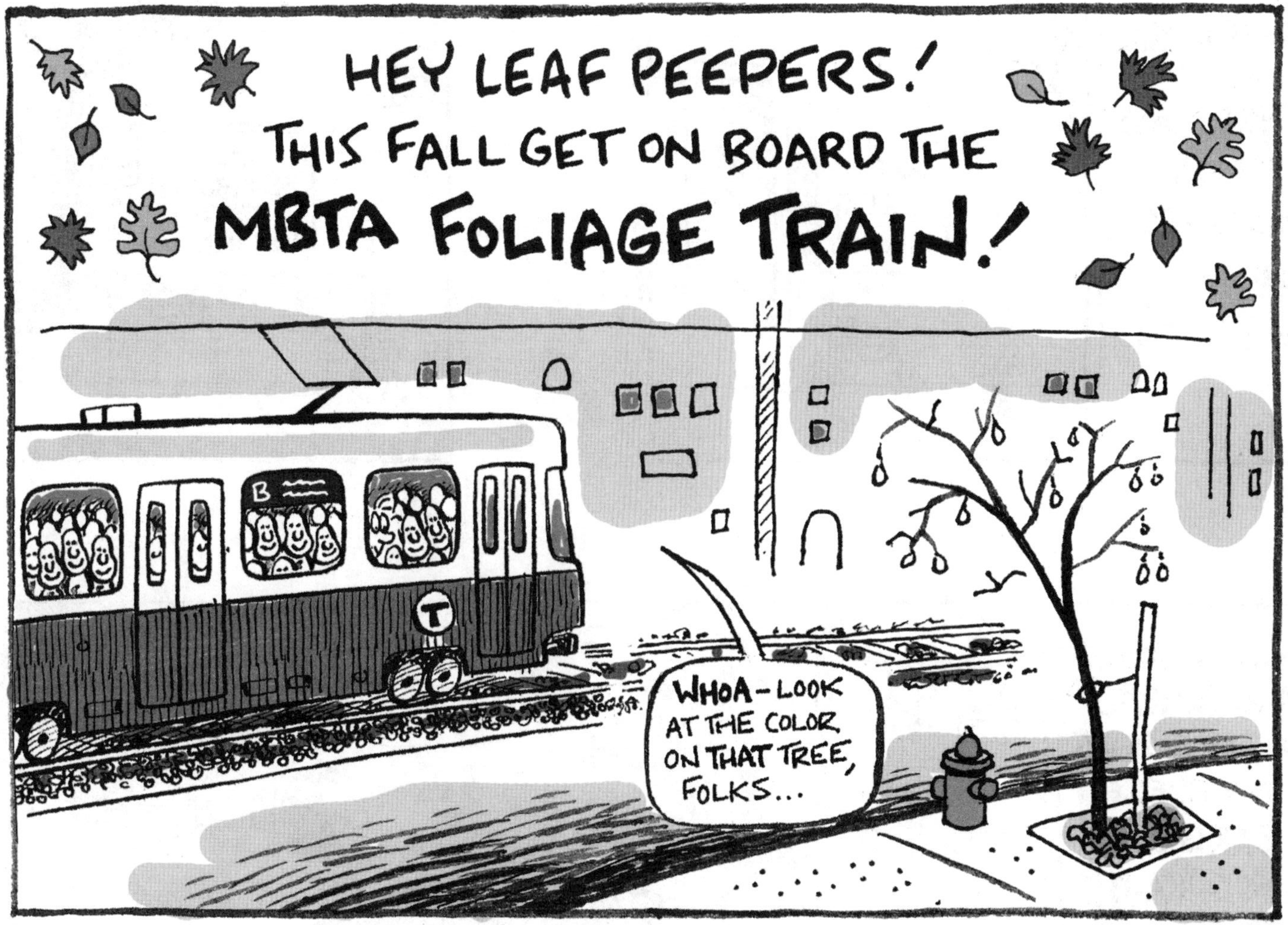
HEY LEAF PEEPERS! THIS FALL GET ON BOARD THE MBTA FOLIAGE TRAIN!
B
T
WHOA-LOOK AT THE COLOR ON THAT TREE, FOLKS...

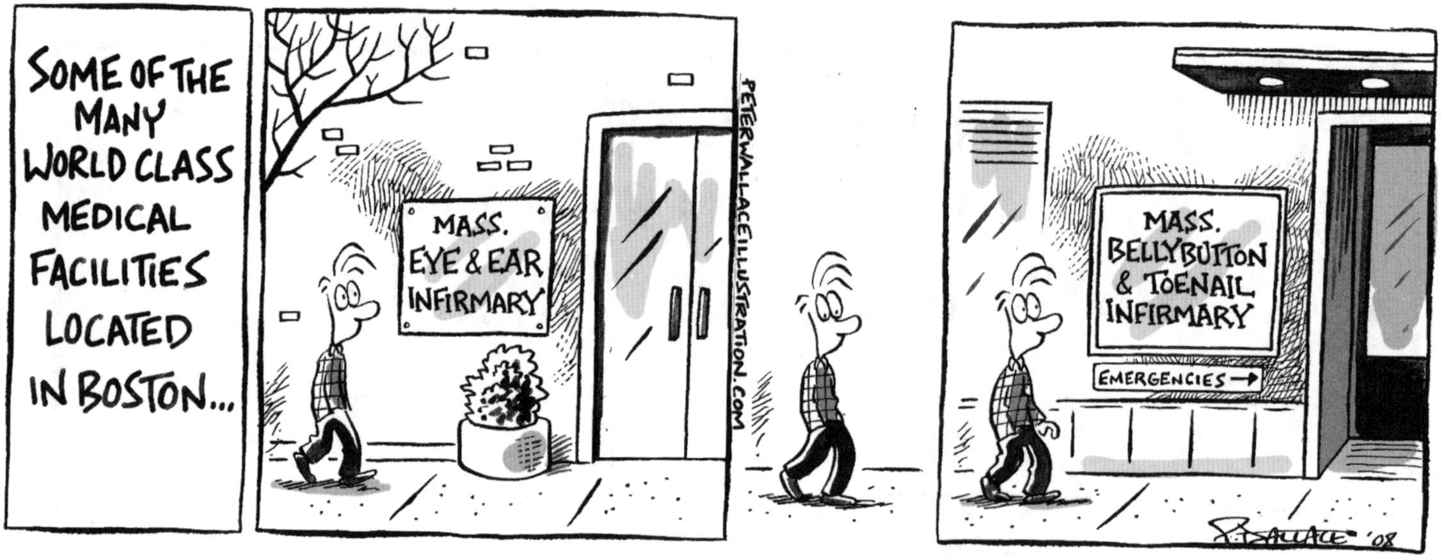
SOME OF THE MANY WORLD CLASS MEDICAL FACILITIES LOCATED IN BOSTON...
MASS. EYE & EAR INFIRMARY
PETERWALLACEILLUSTRATION.COM
MASS. BELLYBUTTON & TOENAIL INFIRMARY
EMERGENCIES →
P. WALLACE '08

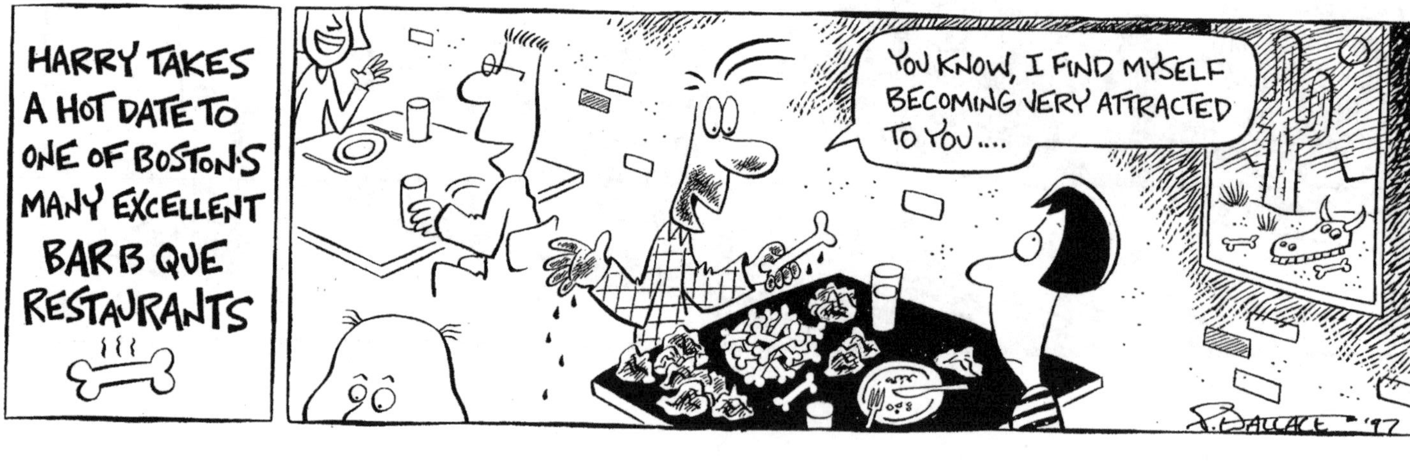
HARRY TAKES A HOT DATE TO ONE OF BOSTON'S MANY EXCELLENT BAR B QUE RESTAURANTS
YOU KNOW, I FIND MYSELF BECOMING VERY ATTRACTED TO YOU....
P. WALLACE '97

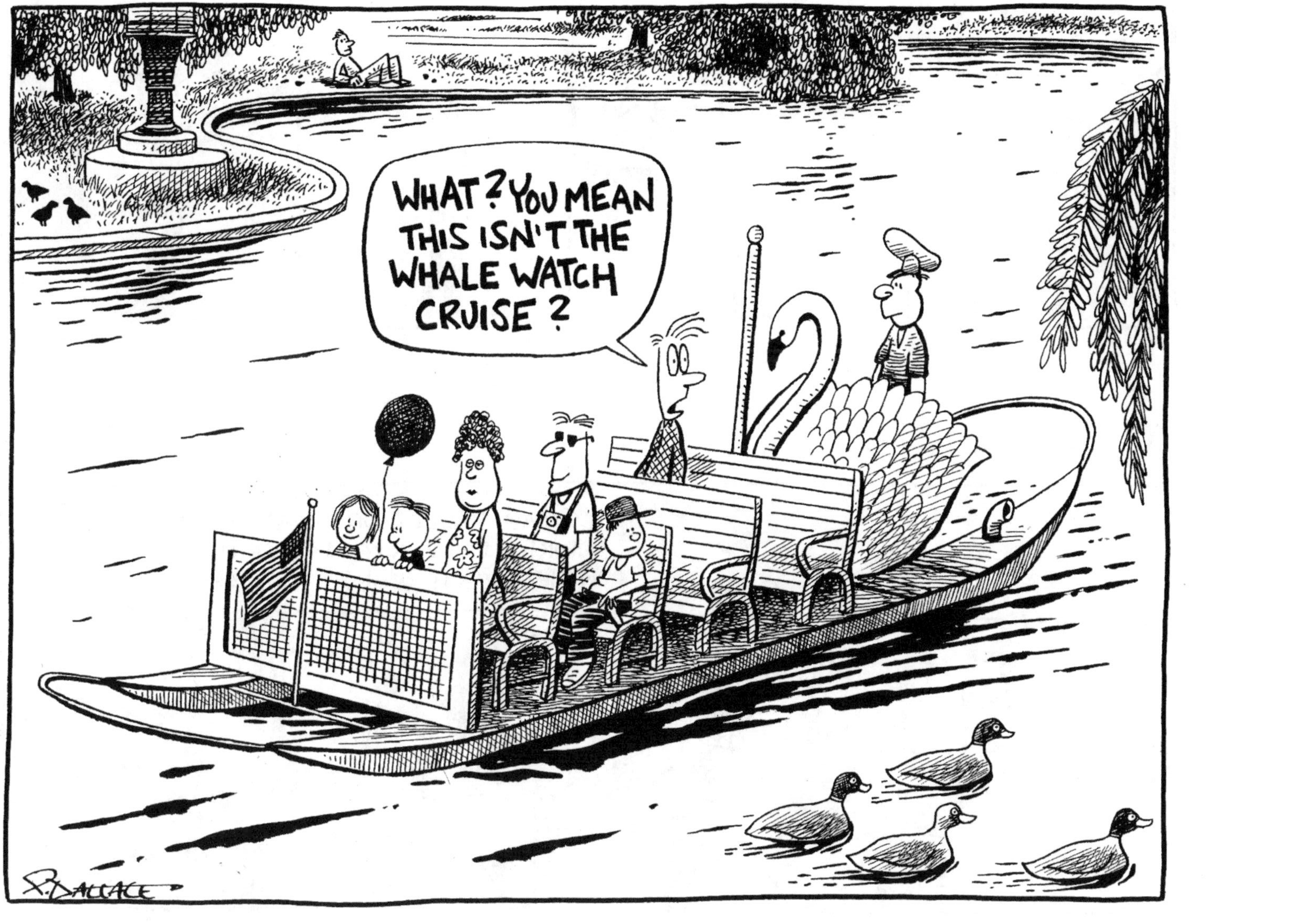
WHAT? YOU MEAN THIS ISN'T THE WHALE WATCH CRUISE?
P. WALLACE

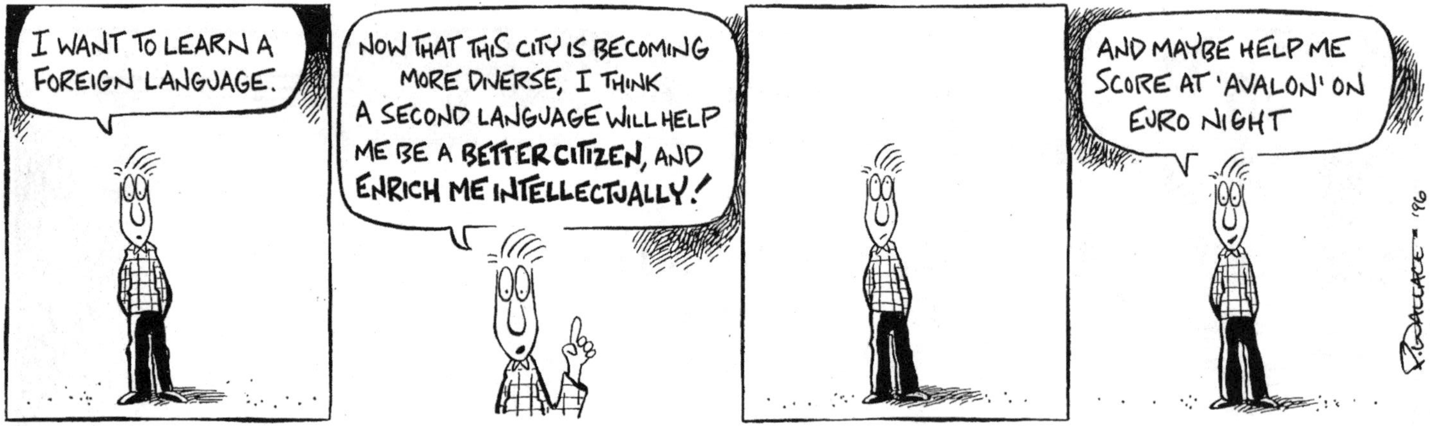
I WANT TO LEARN A FOREIGN LANGUAGE.
NOW THAT THIS CITY IS BECOMING MORE DIVERSE, I THINK A SECOND LANGUAGE WILL HELP ME BE A **BETTER CITIZEN**, AND **ENRICH ME INTELLECTUALLY**!
AND MAYBE HELP ME SCORE AT 'AVALON' ON EURO NIGHT
P. WALLACE '96

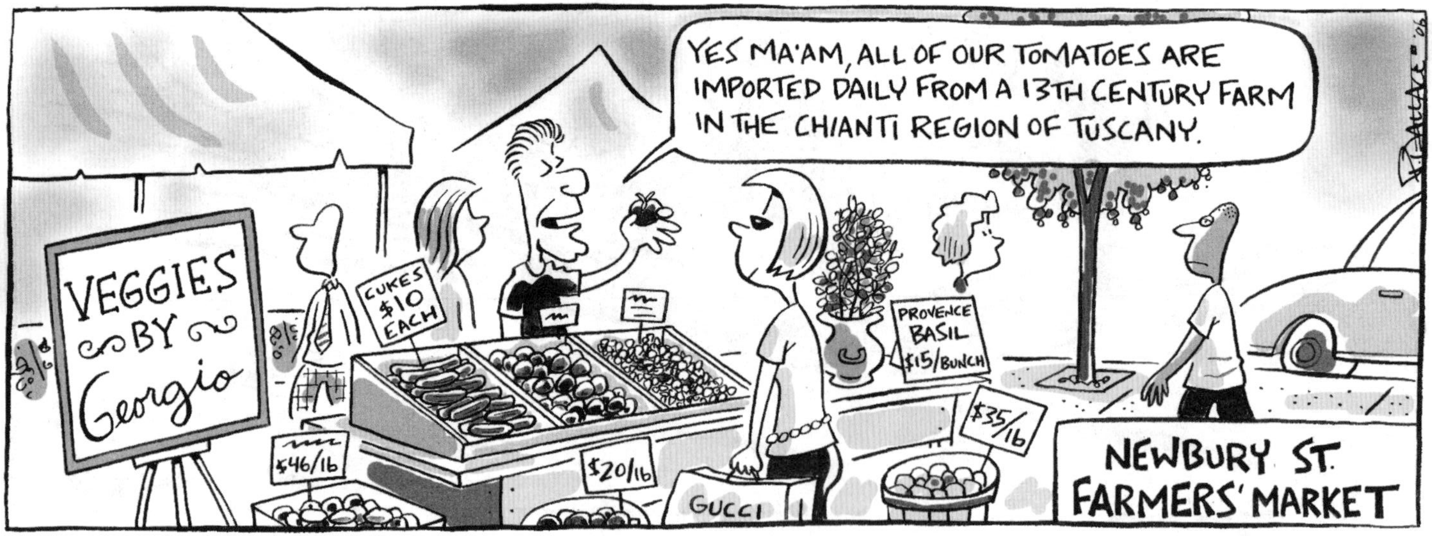
YES MA'AM, ALL OF OUR TOMATOES ARE IMPORTED DAILY FROM A 13TH CENTURY FARM IN THE CHIANTI REGION OF TUSCANY.
VEGGIES BY Georgio
CUKES $10 EACH
$46/lb
$20/lb
PROVENCE BASIL $15/BUNCH
$35/lb
GUCCI
NEWBURY ST. FARMERS' MARKET

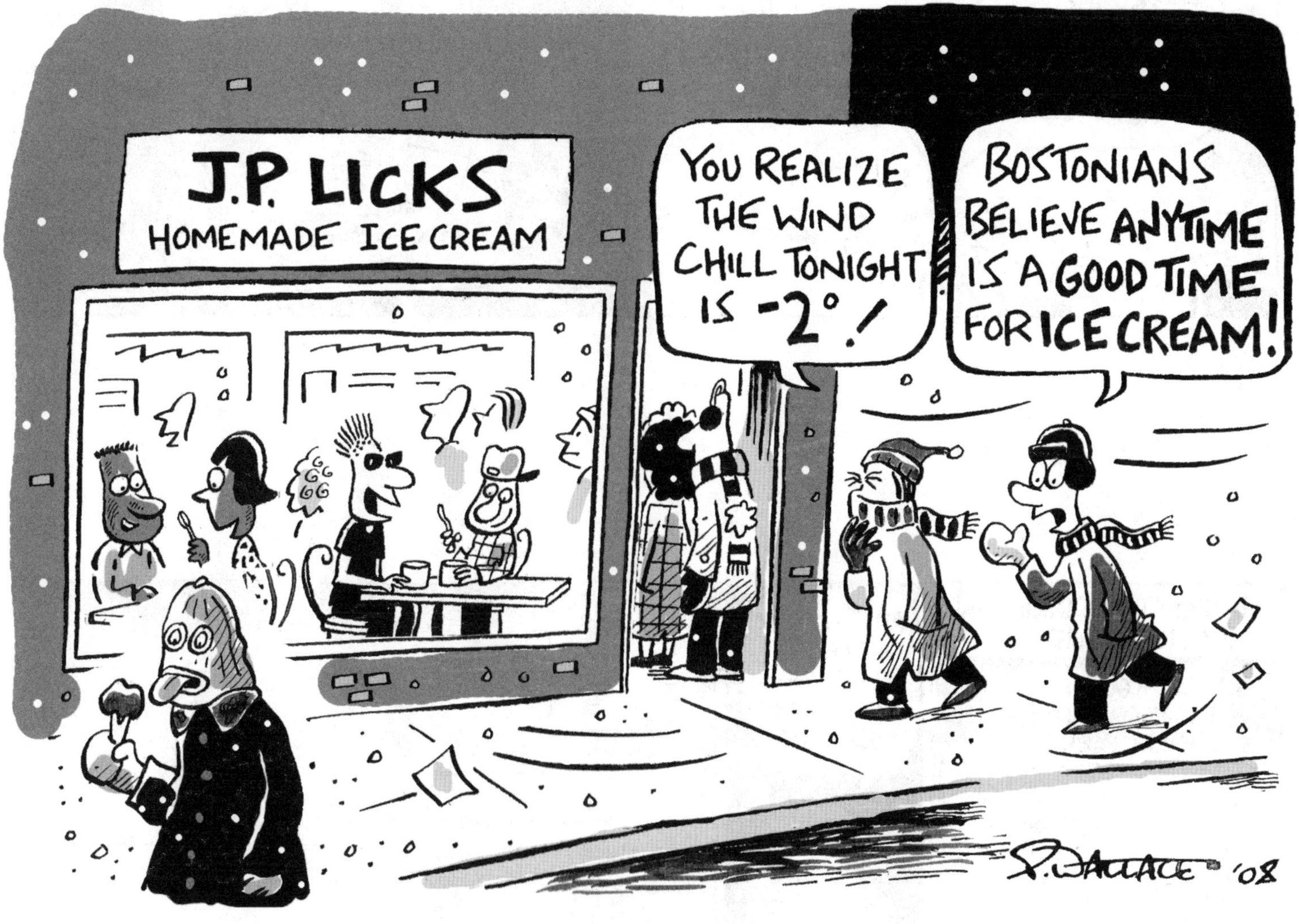
J.P. LICKS
HOMEMADE ICE CREAM
YOU REALIZE THE WIND CHILL TONIGHT IS -2°!
BOSTONIANS BELIEVE ANYTIME IS A GOOD TIME FOR ICE CREAM!
P. WALLACE '08

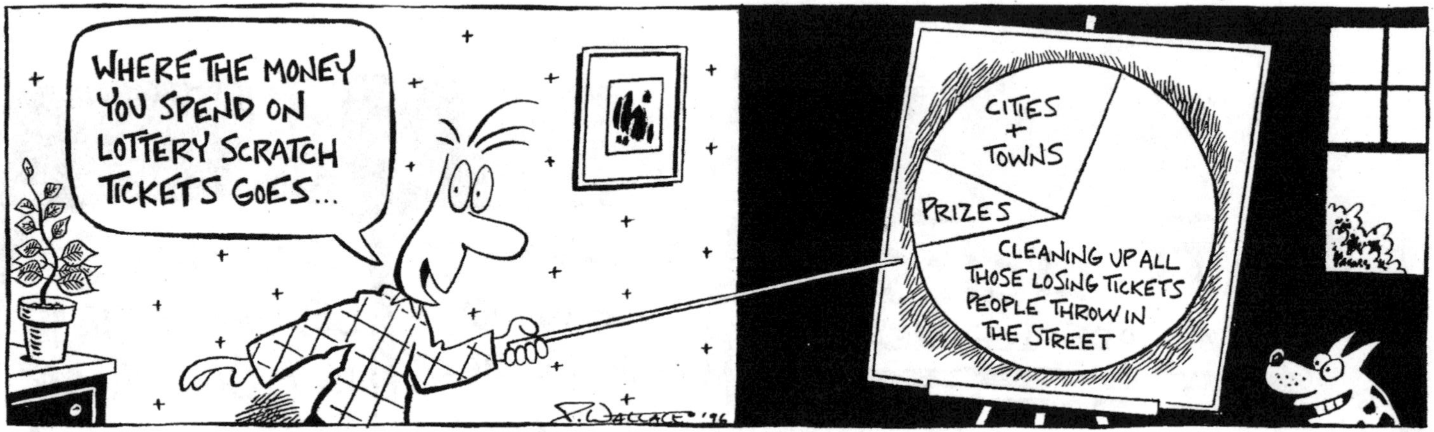
WHERE THE MONEY YOU SPEND ON LOTTERY SCRATCH TICKETS GOES...
CITIES + TOWNS
PRIZES
CLEANING UP ALL THOSE LOSING TICKETS PEOPLE THROW IN THE STREET
P. WALLACE '96

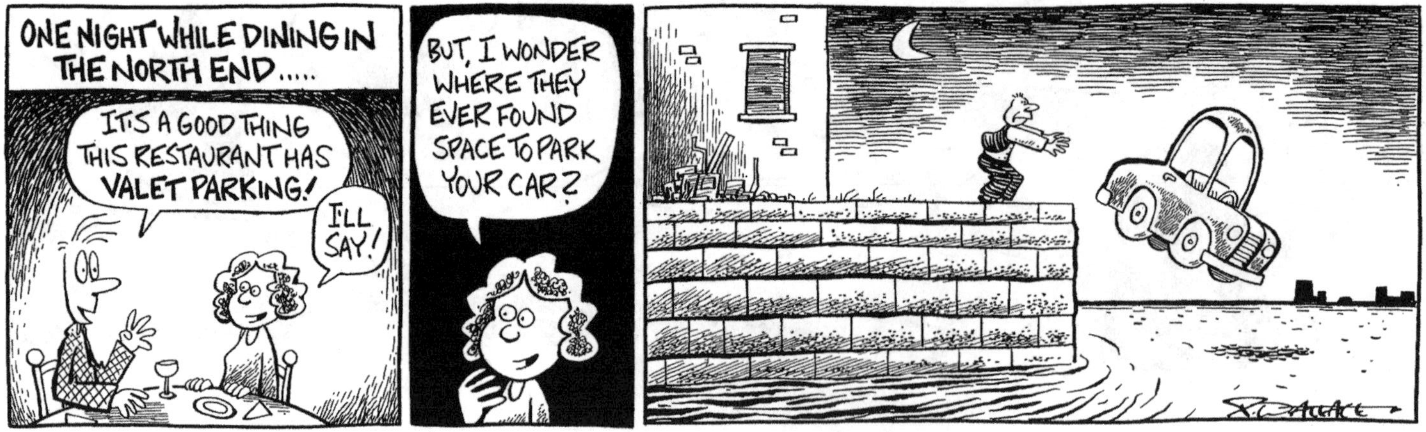
ONE NIGHT WHILE DINING IN THE NORTH END.....
IT'S A GOOD THING THIS RESTAURANT HAS VALET PARKING!
I'LL SAY!
BUT, I WONDER WHERE THEY EVER FOUND SPACE TO PARK YOUR CAR?
P. WALLACE

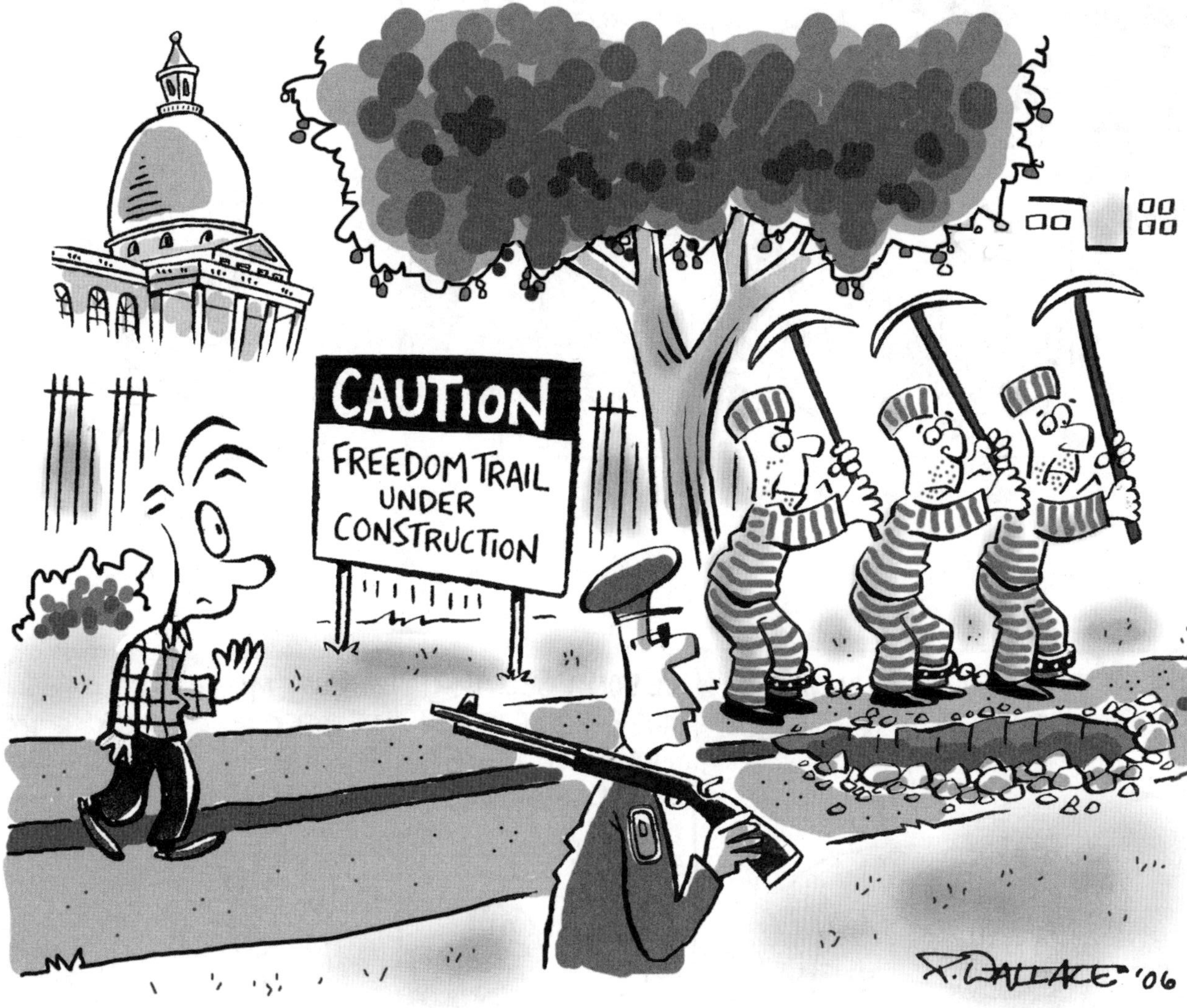
CAUTION
FREEDOM TRAIL
UNDER
CONSTRUCTION
P. WALLACE '06

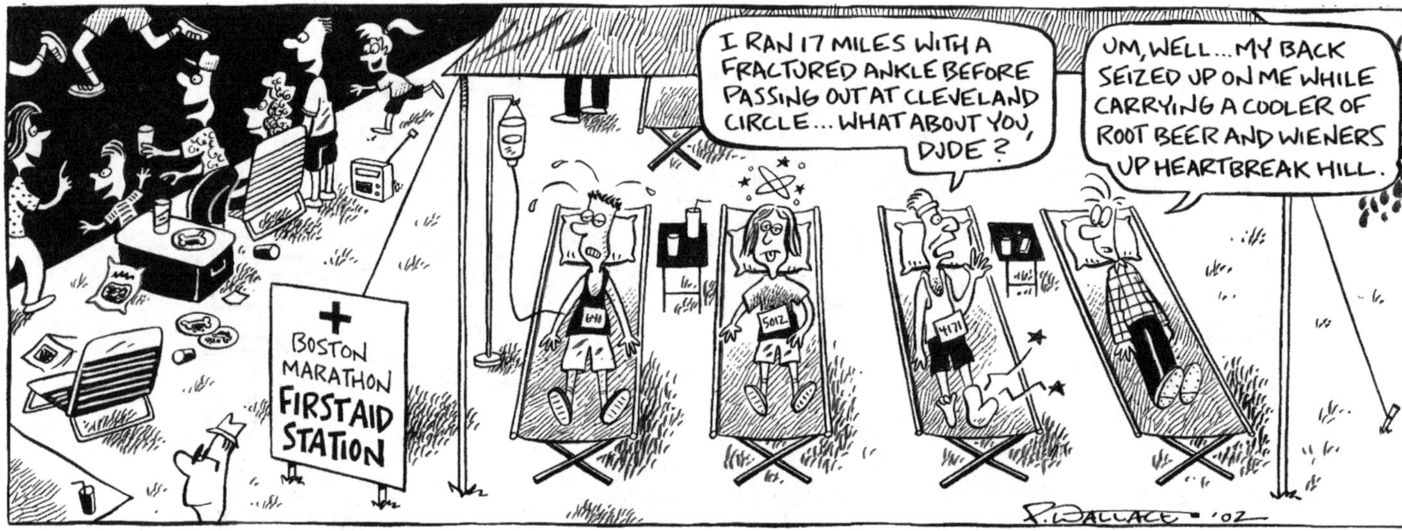
BOSTON MARATHON FIRSTAID STATION
I RAN 17 MILES WITH A FRACTURED ANKLE BEFORE PASSING OUT AT CLEVELAND CIRCLE... WHAT ABOUT YOU, DUDE?
UM, WELL... MY BACK SEIZED UP ON ME WHILE CARRYING A COOLER OF ROOT BEER AND WIENERS UP HEARTBREAK HILL.
P. WALLACE '02

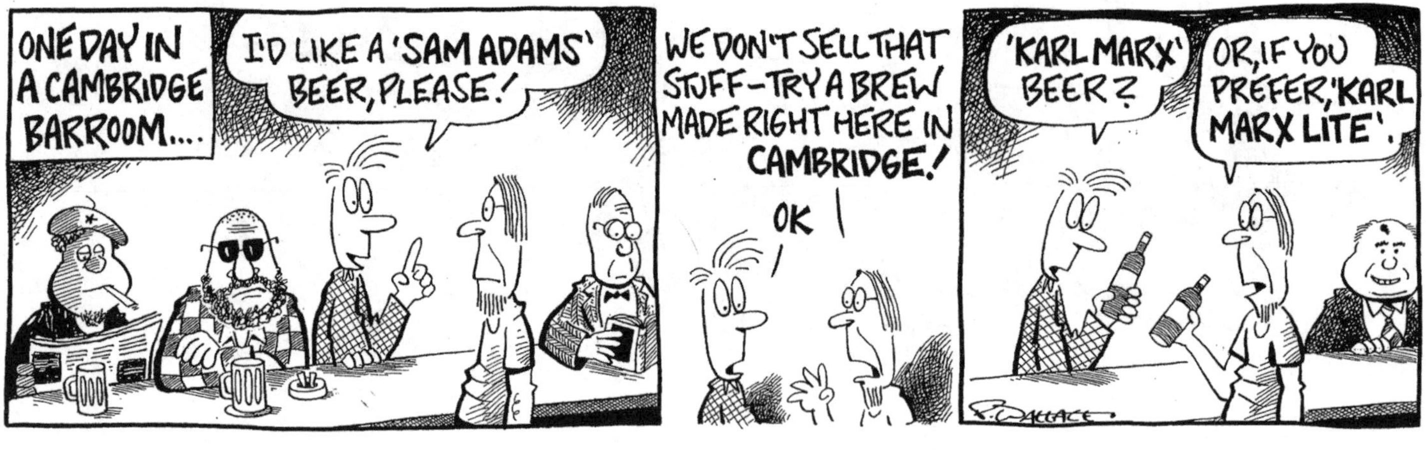
ONE DAY IN A CAMBRIDGE BARROOM....
I'D LIKE A 'SAM ADAMS' BEER, PLEASE!
WE DON'T SELL THAT STUFF–TRY A BREW MADE RIGHT HERE IN CAMBRIDGE!
OK
'KARL MARX' BEER?
OR, IF YOU PREFER, 'KARL MARX LITE'.
P. WALLACE

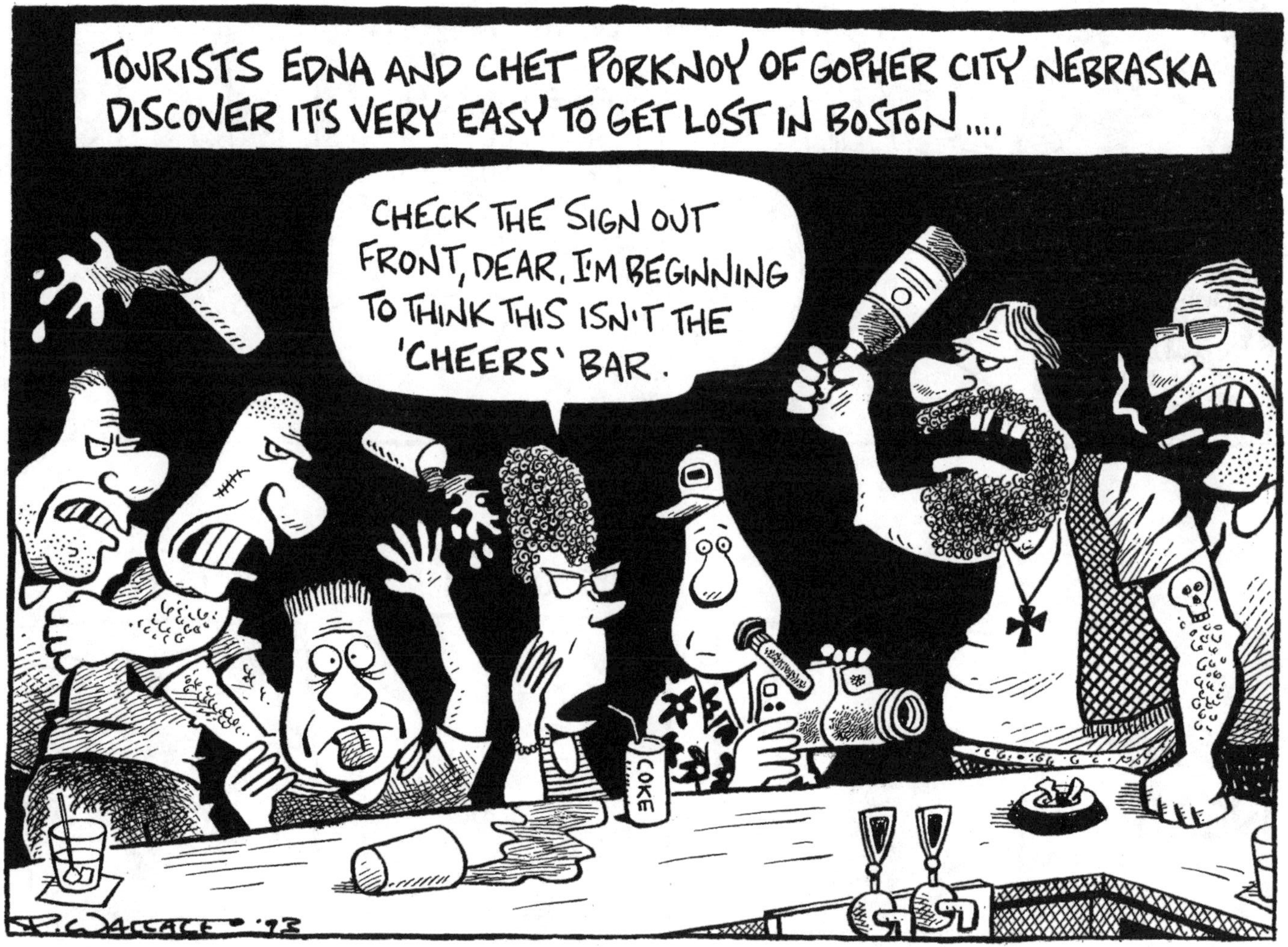
TOURISTS EDNA AND CHET PORKNOY OF GOPHER CITY NEBRASKA DISCOVER IT'S VERY EASY TO GET LOST IN BOSTON....
CHECK THE SIGN OUT FRONT, DEAR. I'M BEGINNING TO THINK THIS ISN'T THE 'CHEERS' BAR.
COKE
R. WALLACE '93

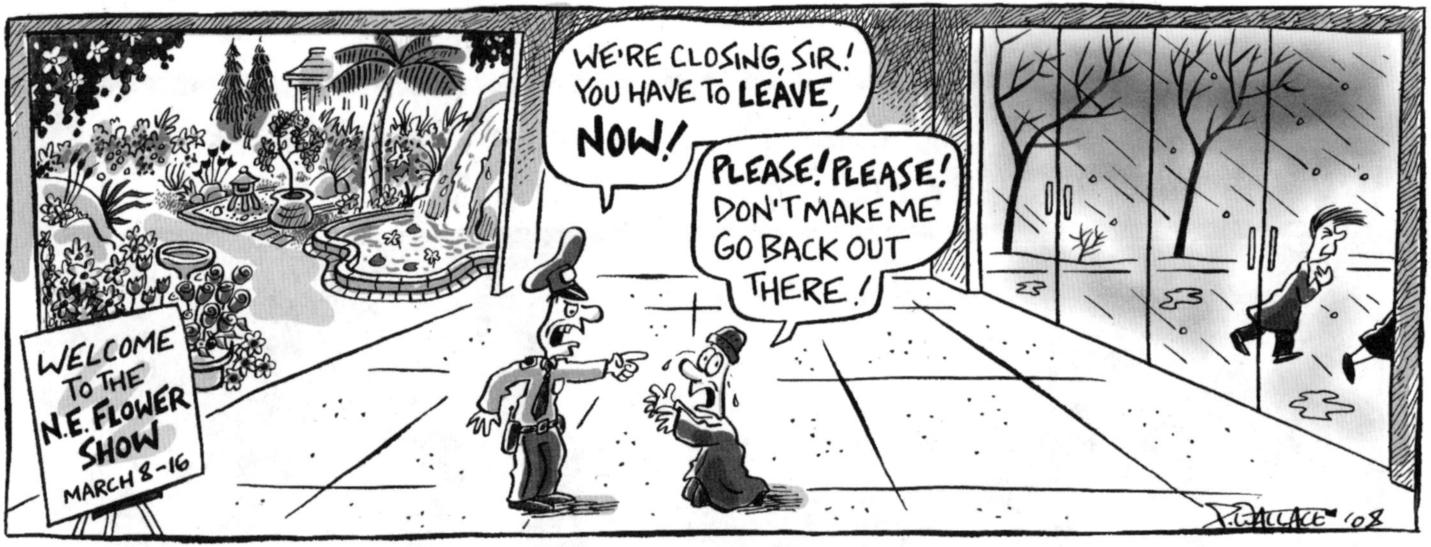
WELCOME TO THE N.E. FLOWER SHOW MARCH 8-16
WE'RE CLOSING, SIR! YOU HAVE TO LEAVE, NOW!
PLEASE! PLEASE! DON'T MAKE ME GO BACK OUT THERE!
P. WALLACE '08

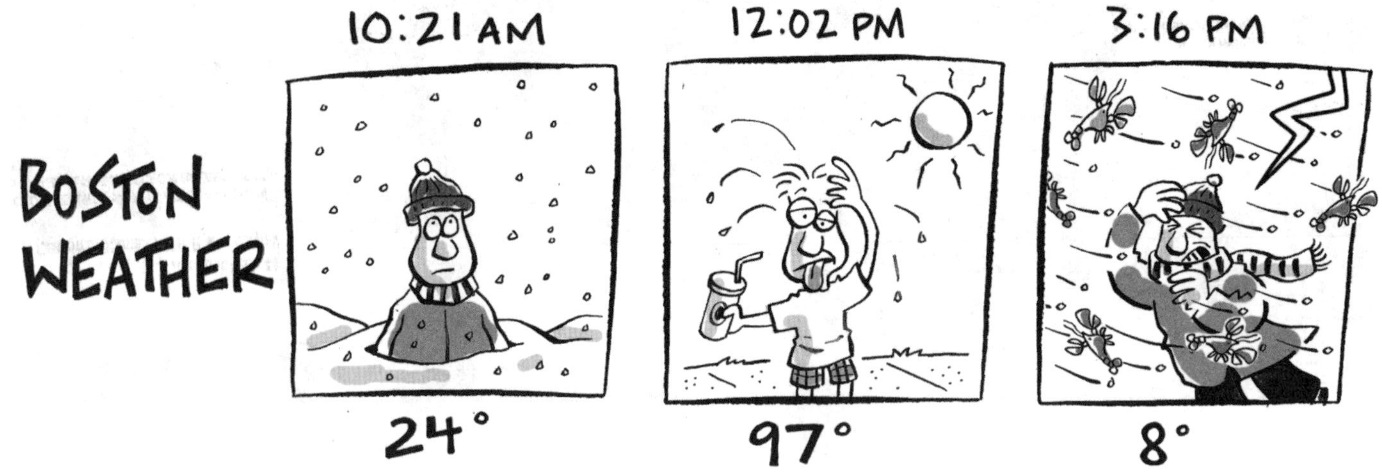
BOSTON WEATHER
10:21 AM
24°
12:02 PM
97°
3:16 PM
8°

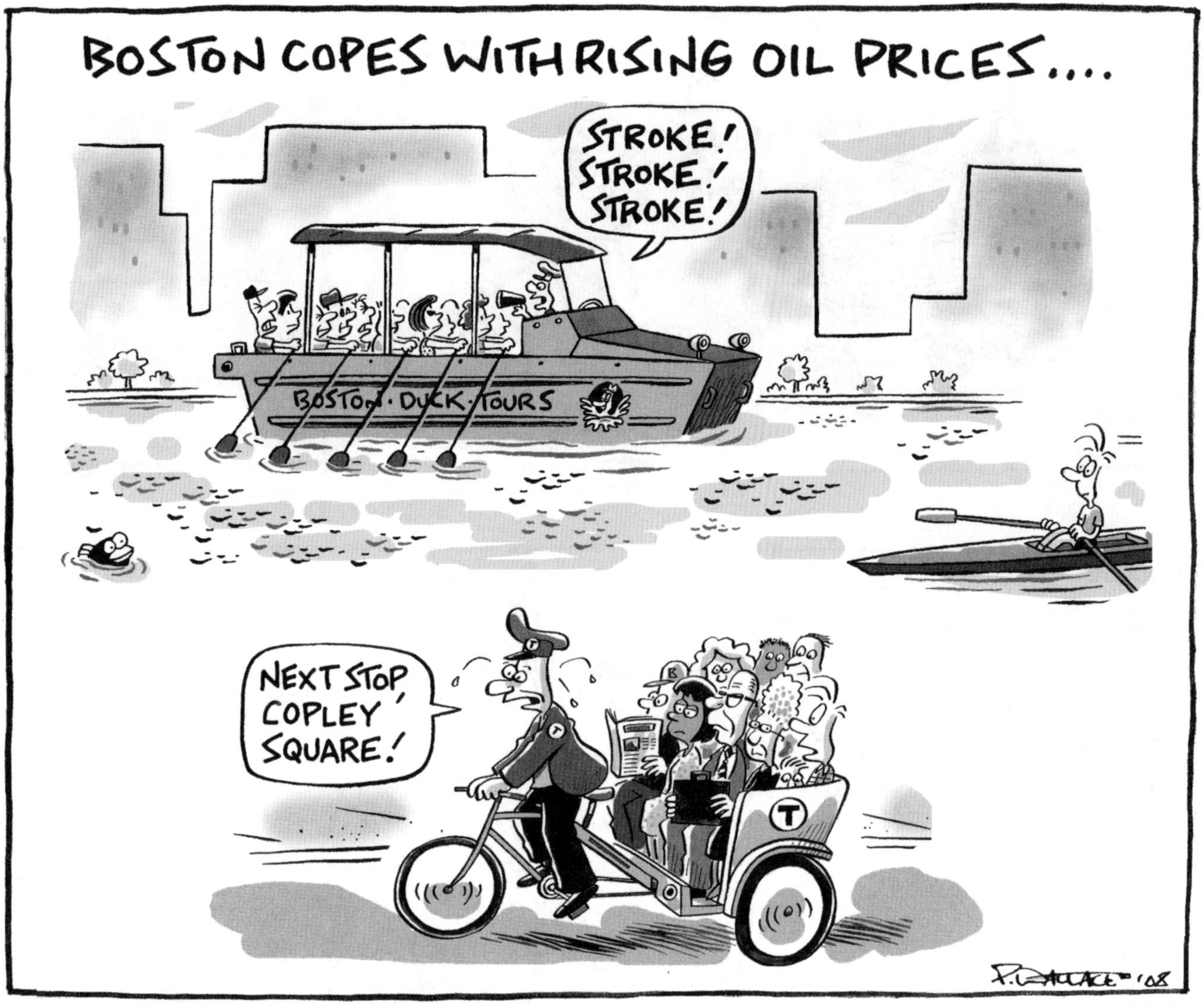
BOSTON COPES WITH RISING OIL PRICES....
STROKE! STROKE! STROKE!
BOSTON · DUCK · TOURS
NEXT STOP, COPLEY SQUARE!
P. WALLACE '08

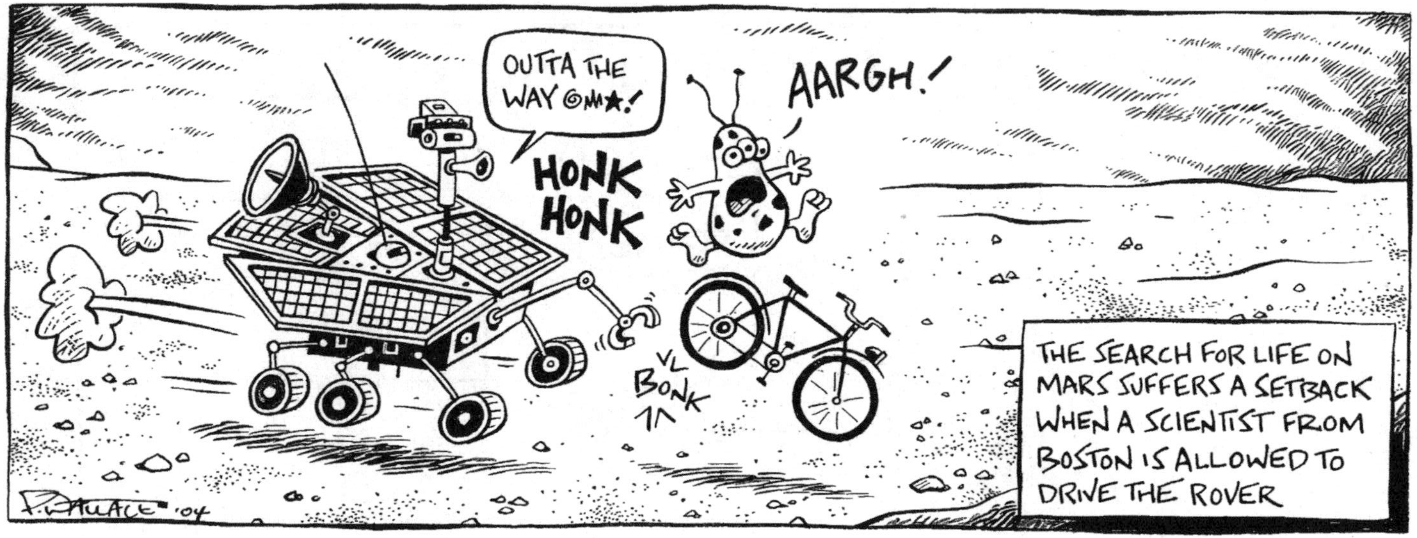
OUTTA THE WAY @##★!
HONK HONK
AARGH!
BONK
THE SEARCH FOR LIFE ON MARS SUFFERS A SETBACK WHEN A SCIENTIST FROM BOSTON IS ALLOWED TO DRIVE THE ROVER
P. WALLACE '04

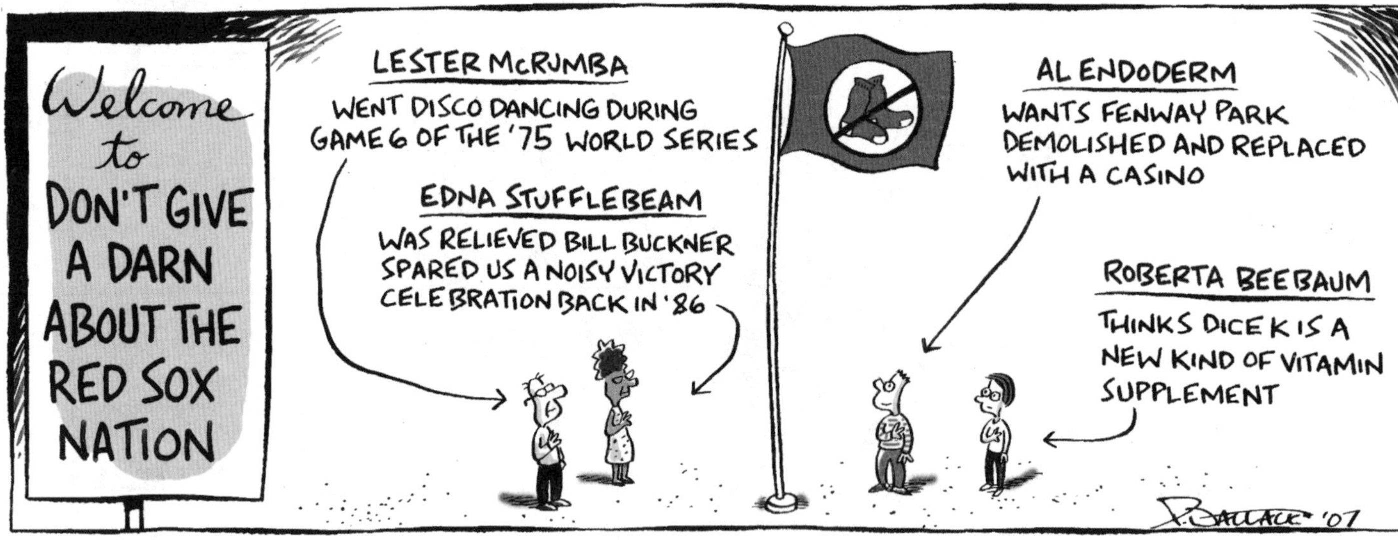
Welcome to DON'T GIVE A DARN ABOUT THE RED SOX NATION
LESTER McRUMBA
WENT DISCO DANCING DURING GAME 6 OF THE '75 WORLD SERIES
EDNA STUFFLEBEAM
WAS RELIEVED BILL BUCKNER SPARED US A NOISY VICTORY CELEBRATION BACK IN '86
AL ENDODERM
WANTS FENWAY PARK DEMOLISHED AND REPLACED WITH A CASINO
ROBERTA BEEBAUM
THINKS DICE K IS A NEW KIND OF VITAMIN SUPPLEMENT
P. WALLACE '07

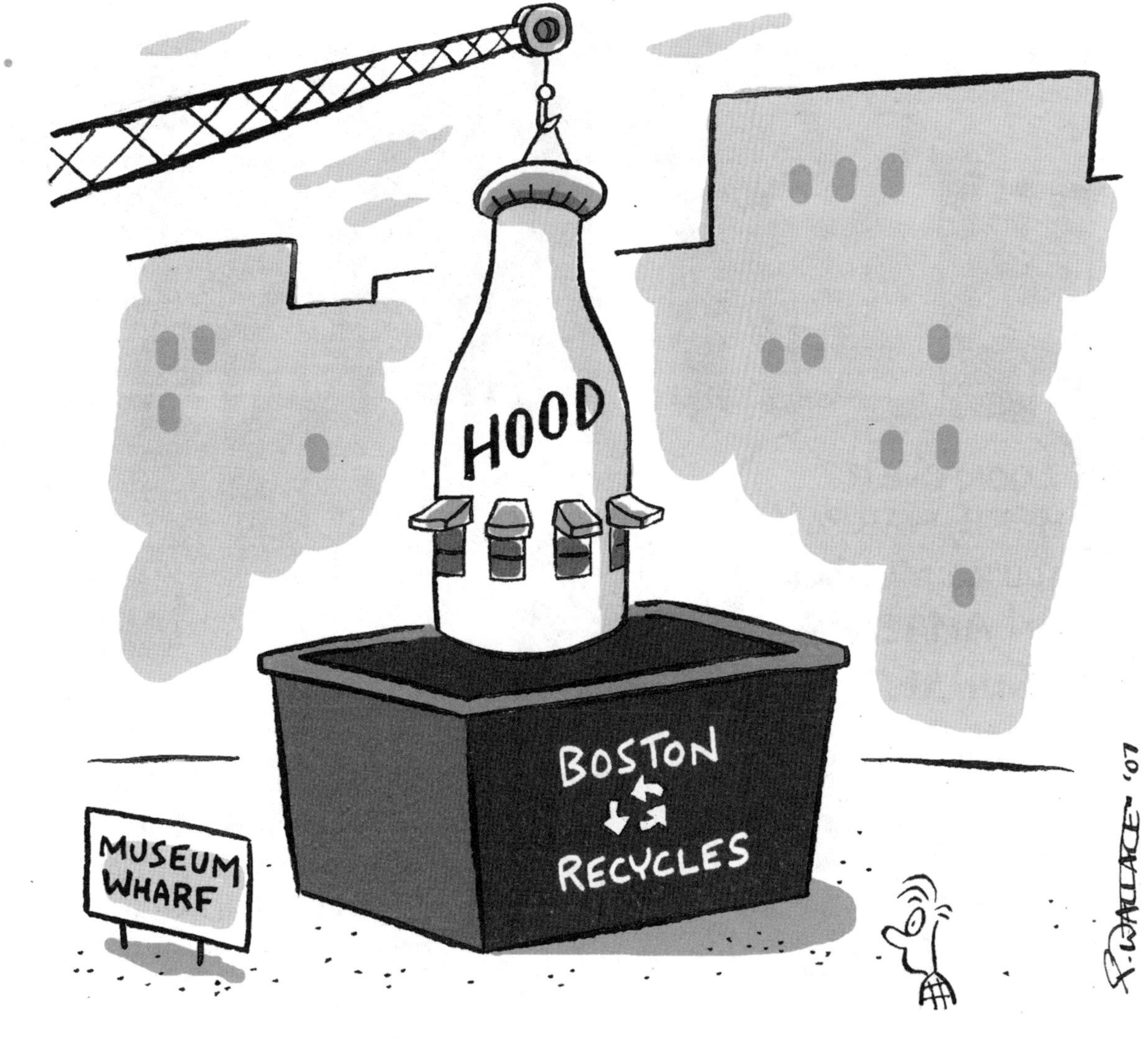
HOOD
BOSTON
RECYCLES
MUSEUM
WHARF
R. WALLACE '07

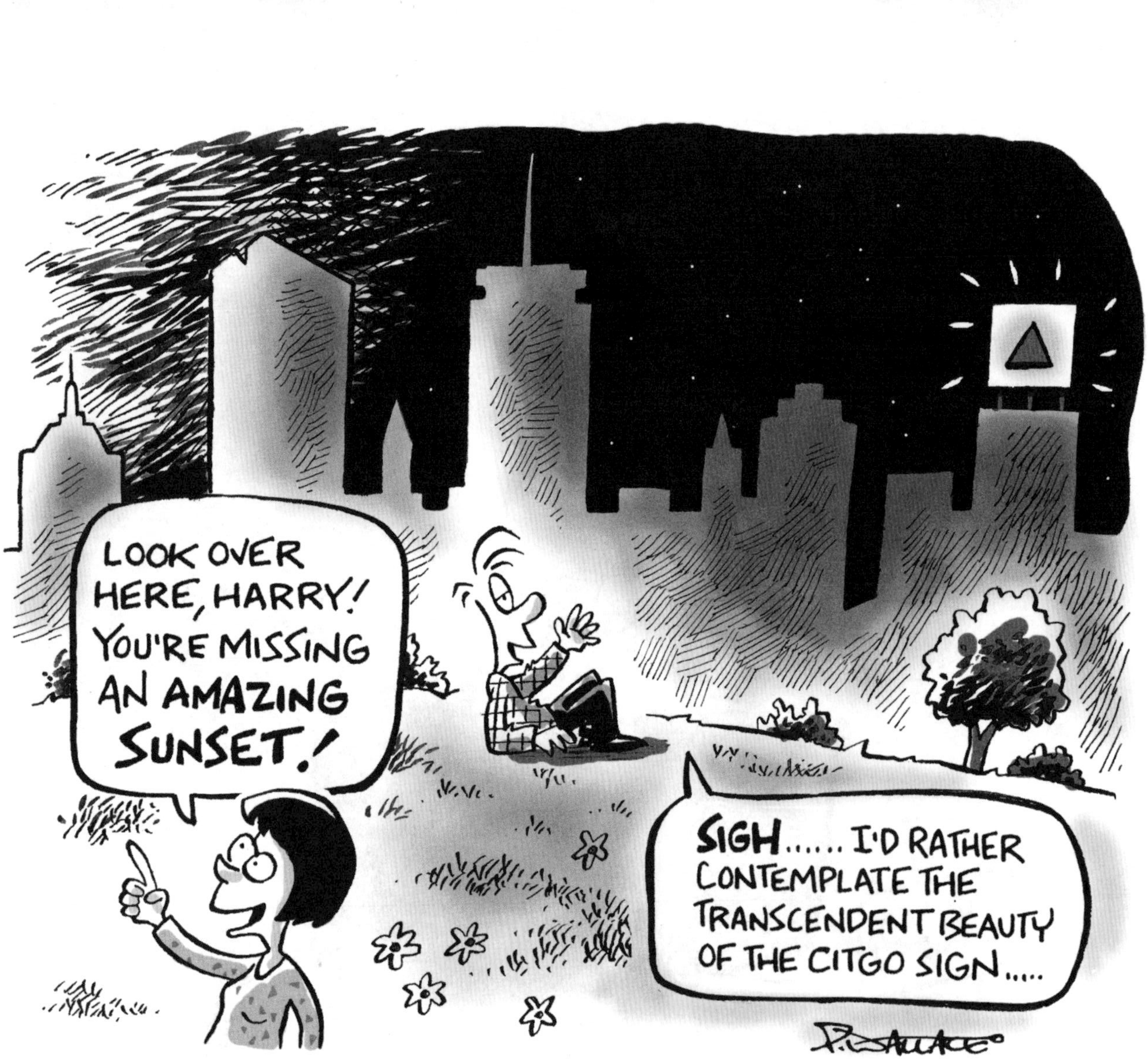
LOOK OVER HERE, HARRY! YOU'RE MISSING AN AMAZING SUNSET!
SIGH...... I'D RATHER CONTEMPLATE THE TRANSCENDENT BEAUTY OF THE CITGO SIGN.....